MY WILLOW

My Willow

Bud Lang

Copyright © 2012 by Bud Lang.

Library of Congress Control Number:		2012914969
ISBN:	Softcover	978-1-4797-0141-4
	Ebook	978-1-4797-0142-1

All rights reserved. No part of this book may be reproduced or transmitted in any form or by any means, electronic or mechanical, including photocopying, recording, or by any information storage and retrieval system, without permission in writing from the copyright owner.

This book was printed in the United States of America.

To order additional copies of this book, contact:
Xlibris Corporation
1-888-795-4274
www.Xlibris.com
Orders@Xlibris.com
120404

Contents

Chapter

One	The House with the Magic Lights	11
Two	I Have Seen Enemies	21
Three	What I Can't Have	33
Four	Some Right Answers and a '53 Studebaker	41
Five	Who are the Burtons?	59
Six	Encounter of the Other Kind	73
Seven	Private Lessons, Yesterday and Today So Far.	85
Eight	Not Long Enough to be Ashamed of It	95
Nine	Way to One Side	103
Ten	There Were Things I Never Did Get Around to	113
Eleven	Getting Some Requirements Out of the Way	125
Twelve	Some Heroic, Some Villainous	133
Thirteen	Five Pounds of Self-Rising and Some Black Pepper	143
Fourteen	Doing This for Each Other	163
Fifteen	Feel It in My Mind	175

INTRODUCTION

MY FATHER, JOHN C., had worked a job and his brother had used the kids like plow horses on the farm. The time of the brothers' partnership had long been used up. Mama said so. When Mama said so, it was so. She said so when I refused to work and took the fifteen cents that I had saved, walked to a train station, and caught a ride to Huntsville when I was nine years old. The boys all knew why Hugo wore the belt around his overalls and that was for beating us kids to make us work.

The brothers, John and Hugo, cut a rather good deal with the government when they were hauled into the interrogation camps at the beginning of World War II. Both Daddy and Hugo had to work the farm for the war since Daddy lost his job with the railroad when he was incarcerated and couldn't show up for work. They made good money until the end of WWII, growing wheat and soybeans and other edible crops in Alabama when just about nobody else was willing to do so, or had the knowledge. Well the government had no excuse with which to force them, certainly not like the one they held over my father, his brother and my grandfather. There were not any birth certificates on file for them so they were assumed to be German born.

My family also grew some sugar cane and dabbled in grapes – Papa seemed to have some knowledge – until the war was over. Papa, that's what we called my grandfather, would talk about Weisbaden and his youth and taught us all how to prune the grapes and to make them produce huge amounts of fruit. It was said that I even knew how to use a machete in the cane patches like a man by age eight and to prune the grape vines as well as anyone.

After the war was over, my father went back to work, this time fixing Ford tractors. The brothers bought two farms and went their separate ways. Mama said so. Hugo took the one at Rockhouse Landing and John took the one across the river. Mama complained a lot about giving everything to Hugo but it was her orders, her plan, she paid the price to get rid of him.

Maybe the people where my family came to looked okay, and maybe we didn't look okay to them. Germans across the ocean had just lost a war, the one we thought we had won. "We were Americans on this side of the ocean. Some used to be Germans on that side when they were there. The other part of us was Cherokee and that part of us had always been American, even before anybody else was American," I remember that I assessed.

When my father bought the farm, he likely didn't check to see who else might have wanted the farm. Was that the problem? Maybe it didn't matter to him. He bought it, and the family moved onto it. Could that be wrong? Maybe he didn't do a lot of things that some in the community wanted him to. Did he care what others wanted? Whatever he did or didn't do, the family didn't measure up with the initial evaluation by some locals in power. What was the source of their power?

It could be the family learned and the lesson began the first day. Lessons were issued throughout the years and some were learned by some of the family, yet it seems none were learned or heeded by the second son, and I was the second son. My defiance of the local application of the rules of society as it was handed down by the self-empowered was sufficient to stimulate a challenge of my willingness to feel the freedom as my personal perception of what I believed was my right to decision. I had learned that I had rights. Those rights were challenged. Did there have to be issues with that?

I met the challenges. Then again, maybe I was merely there to greet the challenges, even the first day when I was shot in the leg. Again six years later when the bullet caught my right cheek as I sat outside the Negro Baptist Church listening to the choir. We never learned why it was not alright to listen to the choir, and I never learned who pulled the trigger that time, but I knew who all seven of them were who ambushed me and beat me unmercifully at the edge of the high school campus three weeks before high school graduation.

At what time did I become an angry young man? At no time! I became a young man dedicated to being what I could be, and that is one who is to be capable of changing the force in my society that would disallow me to be what I could be. As I look back, I am almost certain that I was already what I was very certain that I was not, a very angry young man.

At no time was I defeated in the times of which I speak. No, I kept coming back for more, even from those who left me hopelessly incapable of an immediate response. Willow picked me up after an ambush beating. Ah, my Willow! I found a partner in life. I found so much more than that. I found a life.

The love that I had carried for Willow Preston since the first day I saw her three years earlier had built up inside me and had grown like a mountain. I found out when she took me off the ground, when she joined me to become a part of all of me, just how much love she had been holding back for me. Together, we were one team, a formidable dedicated answer for any challenge. We met challenges. We met them together

The names of all of just about everything herein have been changed, including the names of so many of the places. There is a place in the Tennessee River Valley of Alabama that is Newton's Bluff, it just has another name. So the place is fictional. The times are real as I grew to play the hands of fate that were dealt to me and Willow was in a hand dealt to me. The things that happened here are the real things that happened in real places but the entire story is fictional, inasmuch as the story is merely based on what happened to two people who became one toward the end, one force, then one heart with one body.

My Willow lived in this time and in this place. Her name is fictional along with all the rest of her story that is based on fact. Lots and lots of details are made up.

No excuses are offered for the morality that Willow and I experienced. No excuses are offered for the choices that we made. This is a story of what we did and how we handled the conditions of the two lives that we had together at the time and in the place.

BUD LANG

CHAPTER ONE

The House with the Magic Lights

The place was recognized as the house where I lived but there were no strong feelings for home. Hearing a knock at the door would startle the kids and Mama too. The chance of a friend knocking was a lot less . . .

THE YOUNG MAN'S father told him, "son, 'fore you start to go diving into a creek, you better be sure there is some water in it, then you better know how much." The boy understood what it meant but he wished his daddy had taken his own advice when he bought that land over in Newton's Bluff, Alabama. The young man was close to ten years old at the time, but he could have told his father, "Daddy, 'fore you go out and start to making us dive into Newton's Bluff, then you better know if it's got decent people in it, then you better know how many.'"

I was told we were moving a mile away, but it would take 26 miles to get there. That was a bit confusing, but we were told also that there was magic lights. No longer would we have to have somebody move the coal-oil lamp from room to room, and there was not but a couple of kids in the house old enough to move that lamp on their own. They told us kids that every room in the house had a light already in it, like at the school house, and all you had to do was to flip a switch to turn it on.

That had been better than eight years earlier and on this particular day, my busted-up body had been returned or delivered in a rather severely damaged condition to the place where we had found those magic lights. It was the first place that we had ever lived that had electric lights. I was supposedly home. When I couldn't make it on my own, I had been brought there. The thought was to bring me to a haven of safety, to a place dear to my heart, to a place where I could feel the comfort of home while my body healed a bunch of wounds.

I had recognized the place as the house where we lived, but there were no strong feelings for the warmth and comfort of home. Words like residence, address, location were more definitive, but my mother was there and the other members of the family, except for Daddy and he would be coming there soon. My thoughts were that I might as well refer to it as home since that was the word used to refer to the place where the family lived. Simply, the thought was that there was not the exuberance that a person was thought to feel about coming home.

By going a little ways down by the Tennessee River, it could be seen where the family had lived before, across the river over near Rockhouse Landing. It was almost like an island over there and electrical wires had never been run across to the houses. It was like we never saw many people there but it was great to see them when we did. Oh, we saw traffic as folks went down to the landing, but that was like traffic instead of people. "People," Mama would say, "were more like the ones who came to see you and you went to see them." Kids always got excited when somebody knocked on the door. They knew company had come.

It was altogether different by the bluff. Hearing a knock or a car door slam out front, startled Mama, the kids would find a place to hide and peek to see who was knocking. They knew the chances of a friend knocking were a lot less than of the others. There had to be some rules, "you let one of the grown-ups answer that door when they knock."

In previous years, there had been a lot more days of fear and times not so pleasant that the family had not learned how to endure in their early years, but this day was turning out to one of the better ones, for me anyway.

I had cast a loving eye at Willow Preston for about three years because in my opinion this was undoubtedly the most fabulous human being on earth. Close to 18, I was at the time, running the farm, trying my damnedest to get an education so I could get off the farm or so I could get away from Alabama, the part that I was in anyway, maybe it was the farm but I hungered like crazy to be rid of it.

I had practically no experience with girls. Oh, I had notice some physical attributes of Carrie Terrell that I liked but she lived next door and was almost like a sister. Also, I had looked at Willow Preston for close to three years, but that was love with no experience at all to justify it or whatever needed to be done in order that the feelings that I had for her could be placed into the love category.

Willow was with me and Willow was touching me and I could find no reason to consider that there was anything else that could possibly matter in life. Newton's Bluff was not so bad, the house was near to feeling like home and I was not thinking about the people who lived around there being of the deplorable sort. About the best way to describe how things were at the time is that not a lot was mattering to

MY WILLOW   13

me except the fact that Willow was with me and touching me. The touching was a bonus, a wonderful bonus.

I knew there was previously a wide line between us, her being rich and me being so gosh awfully poor, at least according to the socially established grading system, and nobody crossed the line in 1956, not in rural, or shall we say, not in backwoods Alabama, and Newton's Bluff was about as backwoods as you could get. Well, maybe not so backwoods as where we were before, but backwoods anyway. Willow crossed the line. She charged her rich and her beautifully shaped little hind end right on over the line and made it clear that she knew where she was and was not moving, no way, no how.

"What a wonderful day" my mind told me that I was having! The physical part of my body might be having something else to say about it, cuts and abrasions some with bandages, bruises about everywhere, but that's another story. Willow was with me and that was the part that was setting the tone for the quality of the day at the time. My thoughts considered, "this is so good, I am almost certain I would have paid those boys to beat my ass just to get the time with Willow."

I had no idea what I was up against and how I was going to have to act or what I was to do that was the correct thing to do to make sure I didn't do anything to mess up what was happening with Willow and me. Certainly I didn't know what was the reason why I had Willow or why Willow had me at that moment. After all, I wasn't dead. At least I didn't think I was even though there was an angel with me. I recognized my surroundings alright. I had seen friends today. I had seen some enemies, too. The important thing was Willow. Whatever else was up there in the head was just occupying some of the extra space.

We hadn't had much time to talk. Willow was driving and I was afraid to say anything for fear that I might learn that it was all a dream and I would wake myself.

"Do you even know," Willow broke the silence, "how the thing got started with those people?"

"Not a clue, really," I assured her. "This thing has been going on since the day we came here and nobody has any idea why. I can tell you, however, about my first day here and that should give you some sort of a hint, maybe. Maybe not."

"Daddy had bought this farm around the first of the year. Ben was home from the University in Tuscaloosa, and he was mother's brother who my parents had raised like an older brother to me. He got school expenses on the GI Bill and Daddy took care of the rest. Junior was home, like me he never went anywhere, and he was my first cousin who my parents also raised like an older brother to me.

"Hugo, my Uncle Hubert and his boys, maybe three of them, and Lloyd Marshall, Daddy's best friend, and his son, had all come over with Lloyd's daddy's ton-and-a-half truck, a 1946 Chevrolet flatbed.

"Everybody loaded and boxed and loaded, and I was one of the lucky ones who got to ride up in the cab of the big truck to the new farm, they told me it was

26 miles away, 13 to Decatur and 13 more beyond, but it was a whole mile away. I was confused but I was young then. We were moving just across the river that was a mile wide.

"It was the first time I had ever ridden in a big truck. To me it was the biggest truck I had ever seen. We lived like on an island with one way in and one way out, across an old bridge. I didn't like to go out because the bridge scared me out of my wits with the boards clacking. The noise was devastating. I had crossed it once when I was about four and the war planes of World War II scrambled out of Redstone Arsenal at about the same time by a coincidence that a young mind could not realize, and I would not go out again by my own choice. I couldn't stand loud noises, not that loud.

"The farm that we were leaving at the time was surrounded by the Wheeler Wildlife Preserve that was created by the flooding of the Tennessee River by the TVA in the thirties, 1938 I believe.

"The house for the home across the river was not exactly on the farm but was in a small settlement not so very far away from the farm. It was a great experience for me, or so it appeared at the time, living where you could walk outside and see another house. We were living in a town, if you could call it a town.

"To get light at the new home, all you had to do was turn a switch. The lights were electric lights. I had never seen them in a house before but I knew people who lived in town had them, kids that I had gone to school with. Daddy said we were kind of like up-town folks, since we had electric lights. Where we were moving from over in Limestone County, there was no power, and you knew little about what was outside the area where we lived, never going out you know, having to go over that bridge.

We had to go out when I started to school. My brother told me that I would have to cross that old bridge so I tried to avoid school. Family wouldn't let me. I got lucky though. The bus driver found another way out and a new bridge that went toward Huntsville and came back to the school. I decided that the bus driver was the smartest man in the world and I wanted to be smart. I studied really hard in school so I could be smart like the bus driver, then maybe some day I could grow up and be a school bus driver.

"There was a name for it like it was a town but there was no town. At least I had not seen a town. I assumed a town had stores and streets. Newton's Bluff had a gravel road. Daddy showed us where there had been plans for a sidewalk that went past our house and on down to a curve, but it was no more than a path with gravel on it. There was a school up around the big curve there somewhere, I had been told, but I had not gone so far as to see it. I needed to explore.

"Mama let us quit putting stuff away at noon, at which time I decided to go see where I would be going to school the next day. I grabbed my bike and took off up the road toward the school. Ah, that bike! I have to tell you about that bike. World

MY WILLOW | 15

War II had just ended. During the war, you could not buy a bicycle, no way, no how! Daddy got me that one the year before. I may know someday how he did it.

"While exploring, as I passed the house next to mine, I realized that there was a second house that sat further back from the road that I couldn't see until I got past the first house. There was a bunch of kids and adults standing outside.

"An adult sounding male voice called, "Hey, Kid!" I stopped. It is what a young person does in respect for an adult, though it may be a stranger. Eight or 10 adults and kids walked out to the road, I was assuming at the time to greet me and welcome me to town or the neighborhood, or whatever it was.

"I watched as they all gathered around me, looking at my bike. It was a nice one, the best that Western Auto had to offer. Unusual, too, inasmuch as there was a war that had been going on and the bike was reasonably new. My thoughts did allow a bit of apprehension to creep in, like maybe these people want to steal my bike. To tell the truth, I was scared.

"Comments were made about the bike and how new and nice it was. One guy asked if I was the kid who moved in next to his grandfather there as he pointed to the house next to ours. I answered him affirmatively. The guy responded, 'you know you don't just move in around here and start running around like you own the place. Instead you have to earn your right to pass up and down these roads and go past these houses.'

"With everybody laughing and smiling, and horsing around, I knew they had to be joking. I had my foot on a bike peddle already so I kicked the foot down and it didn't go anywhere. I turned around to find that one of the guys had lifted up my back wheel. He told me that I had to fight the little kid first, then I could go.

"I did all I could to leave and to avoid fighting, telling all kinds of excuses that I had to be home for lunch and to help to unpack and put away stuff, but none of it did any good. The kid was about my age and size. We were both close to 10 years old. The other kid had no heart for a fight so I put him down quite easily. He started to cry and to threaten me, 'If you don't let me up I'm going to . . .'"

"Knowing he couldn't do it without me letting him up, I let him up. I just wanted to get out of it and get away. Go home. I had no idea or cared nothing for what his threat was, merely that I needed to allow him to get up and did. I tried to get on my bike and leave. One of the adults decided, 'whenever he beats you up then you can leave.'

"'Oh,' I decided, 'these are not the right kinds of rules,' but I couldn't leave, so I beat the kid up again. I kept beating the kid up, putting him down at least, until I learned what his threat was, 'If you don't let me up I'm going to go to my house and get my gun and kill you.'

"Suddenly the adults began to disperse. I saw my uncle Ben coming down the road walking toward us. With this cue, I hopped on my bike and rode to meet him. Ben saw that I was messed up, rather dirty for a ride up to the school. I told him what had happened. He assured me that he would take care of it.

"The place was a wreck. Mama had us out after lunch picking up trash along the road and in front of the house, when, lo and behold to everyone's surprise, the kid had gone home to get his gun and had come back to make his threat good. Honestly, I still didn't believe him, I ran toward him, scared a bit if I remember but never believing that the kid wouldn't do anything more than throw down the gun and run home. Instead, he fired. The bullet went through my right leg.

"Nobody realized that I had been hit. I took the gun from the kid and beat it against a telephone pole breaking it in half. I took the half of the gun that I had in my hand and destroyed his bike with it. Someone saw the blood running down my leg. That was when we realized that I had been shot.

"Uncle Ben had brought a German Luger, or an automatic pistol, home from the war. He loaded it, put it in hip pocket and went looking for the adults who had started the ruckus. I don't know how many he got but he took on one who was brave enough to come in our yard and gave him a horrible beating. While the man attempted to escape, he tore down a hog-wire fence. Mostly Ben was hitting him with the open hand to keep from causing major damage, 'unless humiliation is major damage,' Ben said.

"Before it was over, the entire town was in on the affair. Uncle Ben showed the people that the gun was not used and he noted that he knew none of the people who he had beat up. 'We don't even know the kid who shot my nephew here,' he said, 'but I will promise you that if one of these kids comes to any harm from any of you, and I will come for you, take me out and others will come for you.' His speech went on to tell the people that all we had done was to buy a farm and move onto it. He went on to tell them that all of us were sorry that it was not to their liking that we were there and we were sorry that we were not welcome in Newton's Bluff, Alabama but we were there and we were staying. Adding a small note out of context, in all the years that I lived there, I don't believe there was anything to go missing that one of us was not accused of stealing, while I know of none of us who ever took anything that didn't belong to us.

"The ladies viewing what had happened to me took me inside and took off my clothes and washed the leg. They said swelling was starting but it was only a flesh wound. 'Yeah, only,' I thought to myself, 'because it wasn't on their leg,' but I kept my mouth shut. Ben gave the gun to my father and drove me to the hospital. He told the story that we were moving and some idiot had left the gun loaded and standing by a door. A baby crawling through the door knocked the gun over and it discharged. He sold the story.

"There was a while I couldn't walk but the others would help me out to the porch and I would sit and watch as the people walked by and Uncle Ben quizzed them about who was there at the Terrell house that Sunday afternoon, and when he got a name Uncle Ben and Cousin Junior Turner left for awhile to go kick some butt.

"The kid who shot me came to see me every day while the leg healed. The adults pushed him into it, made him do it, we all assumed and it didn't matter. He was just a kid. We became the best of friends."

Willow knew him, I knew that for a fact, and he had already moved away, South Georgia maybe, so I never gave her his name. She never asked for the name.

Here I was so very comfortable with a person, when just a few hours earlier in the day, Willow was no more than a dream that I could see across the room. I thought about all the bad times but this time was a good time and it outweighed them all, so I didn't mind thinking of the bad and relating. I went on telling Willow about the things that had mattered to me in the past, telling Willow about myself. I hoped I was holding her interest.

"We figured it out, I was nine at the time," I went on the relate, "and I was in the third grade. The most beautiful teacher that I ever had, Dorothy Terrell, Carrie and Sara's older sister, was my teacher and took care of me in school, even allowed me to stay in the classroom with her during recess. Not knowing that being shot in the leg was something more than just the usual for a nine-year-old, we went on with life.

-0-

My father had a fun statement that he threw out often as a philosophy of life, "a first time here and there ain't never hurt nobody." I missed my first day in school because of the bullet going through the leg. I couldn't help missing that day but I have always felt some guilt because of it and I can relate that story to you.

"Mama walked little Frank to his first day. I guess she should have walked him home, as well. One of the kids beat him up. This time it wasn't one of the same family so I guess it was the regular routine for the area where we were living, the new kids simply got pounded. The only teacher in the entire school who drove to work, picked up my brother and brought him home. She learned that I had been shot, so she volunteered to pick me up and bring me home every day until I could walk.

"Mama didn't like the routine of the new kids getting pounded, so she went looking for the mama of a fat kid named Jack. Jack's mama must have been working. Jack came to the door, and Mama said, 'send your mother down to my house when she comes home boy or I am coming back down here, and tell your mama that she don't want me having to come down here.'

Ms. Goodall was not a bad lady but she didn't understand that Jack would have to be hurt and why Junior, who was in high school, would have to hurt her other son. 'The town we moved to made these rules,' Mama assured the lady, 'and anybody who don't like them can just go see the ones at the Baptist Church, and see if ya'll can work out a different set of rules.'

"Mama didn't appear to be mad because she was talking rather straight and to the point but what she was saying was scaring the daylights out of me. I had no idea what to expect in my future. This was all new.

"In a way, I kind of felt a little bit sorry for the Ms. Goodall lady. Her husband had run off and she was having to raise a couple of 'really worthless kids.' I didn't feel sorry for Jack. He was one nasty kid, worthless and nasty too, I guess. Not only did I have to beat him up after my leg heeled but I made him run all the way home, and he was fat.

I continued to relate how growing up in the area was a strain, how it seemed that fighting was all the kids knew, and the adults as well, and how those coward-assed adults had the kids at each other constantly fighting. It was a game to the adults. They thought it was funny, laughed about it all the time down at the little store.

"We adjusted," I said. "We got a few busted lips, some bruises here and there and an occasional victory to hear others brag about or whine about. Time went on by and 'somehow in between we must have grown,' according to the lyrics of one of Grandma's songs. Yeah, we grew but we had not yet grown above or otherwise out of the filth of a society that we had moved into."

In my condition of course, I couldn't do much more than talk and Willow was a good listener. I told her about growing up in a place that I believed strained the good out of all of the people who ever had any, a place I thoroughly hated. "maybe this next tale will help you to know more of how the mess began.

'This was about exactly three years ago. At the time I was 14. I remember because I made an issue of it, just a short while before my fifteenth birthday. I had learned by then that Shorty Terrell was the most trouble of any of the Terrells, and he considered himself the ring leader of the group, like the "boss hog" or whatever kind of label he put on himself. He was top dog at the Baptist Church and the oldest of lots of brothers and a sister or two. My grandfather said that Shorty was "a legend in his own mind." If that was the same as unadulterated ass, then I could agree.

"Shorty came by one day and told me that he had gotten permission to borrow a disc harrow from my father. 'He said you would help me load it,' Shorty told me.

"I asked, 'Load it on what?'

"'Your daddy's cotton trailer,' he assured me.

"I was a kid. Kids didn't question adults so I helped as best I could but I had no idea how to load a disc harrow 10 feet wide into a trailer eight feet wide, so Shorty showed me that we had to take the sides off the trailer then tow the disc up onto the trailer. I found the wrenches, unbolted the front and side boards and the rear gate came off with the side boards. The trailer was ready. Shorty sat on his tractor and watched.

MY WILLOW | 19

"We connected the disc to our John Deere tractor and towed it across the road and left it on the edge of a ditch embankment. I then hooked to the trailer and backed it up to the disc. Again, I was doing the work and Shorty was directing.

The trouble started when I attempted to tow the disc onto the trailer with a long chain and the front section of harrows caught onto the edge of the trailer and pushed the trailer rather than going atop it. Shorty yelled for me to stop, I stopped. It was most apparent what had to be done. I explained it to Shorty.

"'Then do it,' he ordered, 'and don't just stand there, because I don't have all day to wait while you stand and talk to yourself about what is obvious that you have to do.'

"Being fully fed up with his smart-assed attitude and mouth, I was wondering in my own mind if I could get away with it if I just left him to do it alone, then I considered what he might tell my father and I didn't care to get into something with him. Oh well, I sucked it up, went to the shed and got some more chain. I hooked it around the rear axle of the trailer, then snaked the other end under the disc. 'You can hook to the chain on the trailer and pull it back to the disc,' I suggest to Shorty.

"'For one,' he barked, 'I am not as stupid as you want to make me seem, and for another I can't move the trailer back until you move your damned tractor back and put some slack in the chain.'

"At this point, Willow," I stated, "I feel I must stop and ask for your forgiveness for the disrespect that some of the words may imply, because I have complete respect for you but the words are what the story is about."

Willow squeezed the hand that she was holding and nodded approval with a big brilliant smile. I felt I must continue relating the story of the disc harrow, when all that was important for the moment was the smile, the squeeze and the love I had for the girl next of me.

"There was a bit of hesitation on my part because I was deciding if I had heard enough and was going to take my daddy's equipment and put it back where it belonged. Shorty barked again, 'do it, you little son-of-a-bitch,' to which I turned and looked at him. He said, 'the reason I don't climb down off this tractor and beat you to death is because they have stupid laws protecting you ignorant teenagers.'

"I walked to his tractor, looked him in the eye and told him, 'Shorty, the reason you don't climb down off that tractor and try is because you know I will kick your teeth down your throat, then have you arrested for an attack on a teenager.' I added, 'furthermore, the thing that is slowing me down is your mouth and if you open it one more time, I will put my father's equipment away and take my chances with him.'

"I walked to the John Deere, started it and backed up about three feet. I watched as Shorty took care of his assignments. The disc pulled up onto the trailer nicely.

"Shorty had to disconnect his tractor and drive around to connect to the trailer, so I wanted my tractor to be out of the way, but I thought about it, changed my mind and left it where it sat. Shorty couldn't get to the trailer to connect it. I picked up chains and blocks to put away, then I just waited, purposely wasting time.

"I saw that Shorty was enduring a bit of strong question in his mind into whether or not I was going to be an ass, he was being cautious about even speaking. I saved him from a long suffering and went directly to my intended routine. I walked to his tractor again. I said, 'I'll move my tractor in a couple of minutes so you can hook up and go away, but you know, Shorty, that stupid law protecting ignorant teenagers won't stop protecting me until better that six years from now, but I won't forget, and you can bet your fat ass that I will come for you, then you can climb down off the tractor with no excuses.'

"As I went to move the John Deere, I stood the trailer tongue straight up for the purpose of causing Shorty to have to get off his tractor to lower it. While moving the John Deere just a few feet out of the way, I had second thoughts. I jumped off and ran back to the trailer and held the tongue for Shorty to back into. Together we made the perfect connection and I put the pin in to secure it, then suddenly jerked it back out and held it in his face.

"The stupid man was fuming, doing everything in his power to keep from exploding into the rage that his attitude was leading him to. Continuing to hold the pin up so he could see that he couldn't drive away, I said, 'Shorty, don't come back to borrow any more of Daddy's equipment and expect me to assist you.' I dropped the pin in, turned the clip to secure it and said, "I'll see you in just a bit over six years."

I went on to declare to my Willow that this particular incident was just one of so many and that I knew that the animosities between the two of us was growing. "I felt," I added, "that the man was aware of the martial arts training and that he could get lots of intimidation in before I ever arrived at birthday 21."

"Papa, as we called my paternal grandfather," I told my Willow, "had a philosophy about everything. He recommended that you borrow stuff before you steal it, that you know you are stealing good stuff."

"Now Papa sounds like a very interesting man," Willow said.

"Yeah, Papa was very interesting. He said he was smarter than other people because he was able to judge what was good before he would steal it, like the little points of wisdom, clichés, all the expressions that he came up with all the time. Papa, was a shade whittler. My grandmother said that Papa was smarter than anybody else at what was important to him because he knew how to pick a shady place so that when one shade moved out another one moved in. That way Papa didn't have to get up off his lazy butt and find a new shade."

CHAPTER TWO

I Have Seen Enemies

As a young man I was able to relate to what had happened to me, the cause the injuries and being left unconscious, the hero and her aides who found and assisted me, and the doctor who appeared with his heart and the professional aid.

WHEN I BECAME fully conscious, though I had been going in and out on occasion and had some fuzzy realizations, I knew that I was in good hands and there were lots of people doing what they could to take care of me. I knew I was at the home of my friend Dan. I knew there was a doctor, a nurse and others there.

The doctor told me that I had suffered a serious concussion that was causing the loss of consciousness so often. "The right ear will have to be surgically reconstructed," the doctor told me, "but we can wait and get you to a surgeon in Birmingham some time later, when we get you to the point where you can take care of yourself."

"I will take care of him," the beautiful voice said. It was the voice of Willow Preston.

There were other voices, lots of them. I knew people were there.

I saw enemies alright that day and counted seven of them, including the one holding me from the back while that big guy in front pounded my body unmercifully. I saw him, too, the big Terrell kid, Phillip. I blocked punches as best I could, but found myself being incapable of a defense other than covering my face, and somehow in an attempt to stop the continuous barrage of blows to the stomach I found the strength to turn my body, or maybe the grip around my neck from the back was relaxed or loosened. My eyes opened to see Clint Thompson, then I felt myself fall to the ground. Going down I remember yelling, "You two are my meat," meaning the kid holding me and Phillip Terrell.

Hearing voices, lots of voices, I saw at least four young men, two my age and two maybe a year younger, the sons of the twin Terrell brothers, Fats and Jim, as they were ripping and tearing at me, and ripping at my clothes. I also heard the one voice of Phillip Terrell, yelling "pick him up, pick him up, pick the motherfucker up!" I felt as if my left arm was pulled from the socket as Terrell used it to sling-shot my body into the side of the bus. I remember seeing the yellow coming toward me. I registered in my mind the extreme fear of my face colliding with the yellow mass. I must have turned my head.

"It's Dan Bradley's voice I was hearing," my almost conscious mind told me, "my very good friend Dan Bradley." There were other voices and a female giving strong directions as I felt I remembered being lifted and covered. Maybe I was dreaming that the female voice was Willow. I was so in love with her and had never been able to do anything about it. So I just dreamed. "I dream about her in my conscious state of being so why not in the unconscious," I thought.

Dan had suffered polio at a younger age, and had limited use of the left leg, but he and the wonderful girl had brought enough people out to lift their injured friend and put a blanket under me, then another over the top. There was another female voice coming toward us I could hear yelling, "don't pick him up." It was Dan's mother, Nan. I could only feel relief at realizing she was there. Miss Nan was a nurse, who worked the third shift and had apparently just arrived home from work. Willow was Dan's cousin which made Nurse Nan, as we all affectionately addressed her most of the time, Willow's aunt.

The memory can play tricks but I felt relieved or secure or something. I knew that the next time I was conscious enough to realize my surroundings, I was at Dan's house. Dan lived across the road from the school. There was a doctor there. I recognized him because he was the husband of a seventh grade teacher who was so very dear to me, Ms. Haggerty.

Dr. Haggerty was directing Nurse Nan and a couple of fellow students on how to care for some of the cuts and abrasions. The focus seemed to be on Willow Preston, the one I was convinced could keep a heart beating days after death, especially my own heart. At that time in my painful life I had no desire to hide my love for the little girl, none at all. She kept telling the doctor that she could do it and how she would take care of everything that he requested just as he recommended. I had known how wonderful she was and now everybody else would get to know it.

My attending entourage noticed that I was awake and announced it. There was a big cheer from throughout the house and several stuck their heads around the corner and again cheered me on. Dan joked about not bleeding on his pajamas and told me that the entire class would be happy to know that I was able to smile.

Dr. Haggerty looked down and said, "Son, you took quite a beating, but there are no broken bones that I can find without X-rays, and as best I can tell it doesn't appear that there are major internal injuries, yet I want you to come to the clinic . . . , don't worry, you can't make it on your own but arrangements have been made to get you there at 2:00 PM so I can check a couple of potential problems just to be sure. If I may be crude, you have suffered quite an ass kicking and I want to be sure that you are as tough as I think you are."

He turned, picked up a pad and pen and said, "I have to file a report to the police over this."

"Yeah, sure, whatever you have to do," I agreed.

"Okay!" There was a pause. "Okay, you have to tell me who did this." There was demand in his voice but a courteous one that could be interpreted as an "if you don't mind" type of demand.

"What I can tell you, Dr. Haggerty, is that my memory is failing me right now and about all I can be certain of is that somebody grabbed me from the back and somebody else hit me in the stomach so hard that I was about to lose consciousness. There were several of them and the loss of consciousness was rather immediate."

That part was the truth anyway. I knew that it was not all he needed to tell him but it was all I intended to tell him. I was of the mental attitude that I didn't want anybody taking care of my business and there was no doubt in my mind, a fuzzy but functional mind, that the business would be taken care of one or two at a time. I was certain of that. It was a silly conflict and I knew it. "I tried to stop it my way," I told myself, "now we do it their way."

The doctor looked at me as if he understood that in my condition I couldn't be expected to remember. He wrote a quick something on the pad, turned and said, "Ms. Bradley here is a good nurse and she and these two girls here, who are your classmates I understand, can help you to get to moving on your own. I want to see if you can get to your feet, just to see how much trouble you are going to have doing so."

No questions about it I had noticed that Willow was touching me somewhere at every moment so I didn't need to wait for her but Nancy Bradley and Nurse Nan came over to assist.

Nurse Nan said, "You get to put your arms around these two lovelies," and she showed the girls how to lift my arms and head then showed me how to work with them to slide my bottom to the edge of the table and to lower my feet to the floor. The pain was awful but Nancy Bradley on the right was also Dan's cousin and as lovely as they make young ladies, while Willow, undoubtedly the most perfectly beautiful human female ever, was on the left. I could tell I was alive alright with the heart beating just like Willow made it beat. I knew that there was nothing that could keep me from loving the girl but I also knew that there were millions of reasons that she couldn't know about it and most of those reasons were the numbers of dollars that separated us on the social ladder.

As I stepped to the floor, I realized that the legs worked surprisingly well. When the doctor saw that I was instantly rehabilitated, he said, "I am going on back to my office now and I have made arrangements to have you there at 2:00 PM today." I imagined that I could tell the doctor that I couldn't take a step without Willow but I knew better than to say it, yet I really didn't have to. "When I told you that I made arrangements to see you in my office, that included transportation to the office and transportation home after I am through with you there."

The doctor turned toward the door and stopped and looked back with a huge smile of satisfaction, or whatever the smile was for, it looked as if he just had to say one little last something. "I didn't make any arrangements at all," Dr. Haggerty admitted. "This little girl refused to move to 'where I can't touch him,' as she put it, and she has told us that she will drive you to the clinic and she will drive you home. None of us argued with her because her decisions were presented to us in a manner that was not open to discussion. See the two of you at two." He pointed to Willow and me and this time he did leave.

I looked at my friend Dan and said, "I wish I could tell that girl how much I love her and for how long it has been."

"There are no words big enough for the 'how much' part," Dan assured me, his friend, 'but you are being told in so many actions without the words that she feels the same and I have known, so you need to know now, and you need to prepare yourself because those two will force it out of you, make you express it."

I didn't know what to say. I didn't say a word.

"Nancy and I are going for lunch for us all," Dan told me.

Nurse Nan had the girls seat me in a chair with arms. Her theory was that, "he would be more comfortable with the arms to rest his arms upon." The right arm was bruised severely but the left seemed like there was little injury except in the shoulder and it just would not move on its own. A sling had been prepared for it to rest within.

It was nearing noon, somebody said, and several of the students were going back to the school or to their lockers, it was assumed for lunch. One dropped a little padded stool for me to rest my feet on. I had Willow sit on it, "so I can see your face," I surprised her that I got so near a declaration.

Nurse Nan sent Nancy and Dan to the cafeteria. It was only a half a block away. She wanted to change and that left Willow and me alone for a short while. I had seen that Willow had taken charge of making certain that I was well cared for. I had observed too, that she couldn't seem to get more than an arm's length from me and that was merely for the instant that it took to reach back for me. The doctor had told me that Willow had taken command in my being cared for. He even knew that when Dr. Haggerty told Nurse Nan, "if we can't get rid of her, we take advantage of her."

As Willow sat on the hassock in front of me, she touched me with both hands, one on each knee. Her seat being a little lower caused her to have to look up at me. I felt I could see all the way into the bottom of her heart and there was love for me and nothing more. I wanted to tell her what I felt in comparison but no declarations had been made. No word was passed between us. There had been nothing to close that wide gap between us that we had both seen for three years, plus we were reminded often enough, at least I was. The way she was acting, it was like there was no gap, no barrier, nothing to keep us from declaring what our hearts had felt for each other for all of the time.

Except for passing each other in an aisle behind stage for a second or two at school one night, I had never been alone with Willow. Now, we did grab a kiss that night and neither of us could take the blame for causing it or doing it, or the credit should that be the case, because we just did it when neither would yield passage to the other. I had no idea what to do the second time that we got a chance to be alone, and it certainly didn't appear that Willow was a lot more willing to throw caution to the wind than I was. I thought there was a slim chance of getting rejected and knew I wanted to wait for a better time. Furthermore, a poor backwoods hick of a farmer's boy just did not wear enough confidence around on his back such that he would believe he could just hop right on over those millions of dollars and start to believe the most precious of all girls, perfection to the nth degree regardless of the money, was going to jump right up and hop on him like old Rover on a hot bitch dog. Uh, uh! No way! Call me cautious if you will, but I was not jumping in although I knew that she was all that I could ever want and they could keep their money.

The fact was clear in my own mind, I wanted to talk about love but didn't know how, so I just talked. "What do I see in your eyes?"

"Nothing! I don't have anything in my eyes," she assured me. It was almost like, "I'm clean officer, I didn't steal anything."

"No, I didn't mean something like that, Willow, but you are expressing some awfully strong feelings in those two beautiful eyes of yours," I assured her, "and you took command of the care for me and you can't go far enough from me that you can't touch me. Then, you tell me you have nothing in your eyes, while I see it there and it is a lot like a gleam or something?"

"I don't know what to say," she admitted. I thought somehow in the way she said it she confessed that her problem was about the same as mine. I knew how I felt about her and I knew I couldn't be the first to say it, because I had not been authorized to cross the line. Of course, I knew she couldn't. Furthermore, I even was able to realize that I wanted her to say that she felt love for me and I knew she wouldn't do it for fear that the love would not be returned. It was my fear, so I knew it could be hers. I understood, but I just couldn't bring myself to accept that understanding was enough. It wasn't what I wanted. I wanted Willow to express her feelings. She had to do it first, about like the rich offering to the poor but it was not acceptable for the poor to beg from the rich.

"Hey, just tell me what happened today, I mean relative to you," I suggested, hoping maybe in the discussion we could come up with an opening to address what it was that we both wanted to address but couldn't. We wouldn't, at any rate.

"The taking over?"

"Your involvement from the beginning."

"I guess I'll just go ahead and tell you all about my foolishness, over reacting and my screaming."

"Yeah, and everything that went on while I was out," I requested, while I was actually trying to ask her to tell me that she was hopelessly in love with me, and what she did was to have completely lost all control over that love, with it being so powerful it caused her to react the way she did.

"I understand now," she agreed," and I don't want you be critical of me, but I feel I need to tell you how silly I reacted rather than have you have to endure somebody else's version of it."

"From what I understand and how I feel about it, Willow," I was firm and emphatic about it, "nobody is going to be critical of you. You are today's hero. You are my hero today. I have been conscious long enough to learn that much, so I want to hear about my hero."

"I know you know," she began, "that Clint Thompson was in on it at first. He came into the room yelling that you were hurt. I lost control, began screaming and knocked over desks and peoples' books and paper went flying. Honestly, all I can say is that I went crazy when I heard about it and I lost all control. Dan and the Anderson kid that you two run with helped Nancy and Ms. Aldrich tried to restrain me and they could only do that by walking me in my panic to where Clint had said you were lying unconscious. They will tell you that I drug them there with Clint leading the way, so I tell you now I did do that so they won't get to have all the fun exaggerating by telling you that I did.

"You did drag them there, then, to where I was unconscious," I attempted to clarify for her.

"Yes," Willow stated the word carefully in a practiced manner to ensure that it was not to be misunderstood as a declaration of any kind. "I got to you and you were bleeding all over, practically naked where they had ripped your clothing to shreds. I checked your pulse. I screamed at Dan to get you some blankets and he and the Anderson kid . . . , Larry . . . , yeah that's his name, ran into the gym at school and Dan went to his house.

"I had six kids lift you, three from each side, and put a blanket under you and another one over you. Aunt Nan came and she told us exactly how to do it in case you had some broken bones, but I had already done it the way she said. As she ran to you she screamed at us, "don't lift him, don't lift him" and we lowered you down

MY WILLOW   27

and waited for her to direct us in the proper method to use. Aunt Nan took over because she is a nurse. She called Dr. Haggerty.

"Aunt Nan had us lift you by gripping the sides of the blanket, three on each side. A boy took my corner of the blanket so I could keep my finger on your pulse, and I was crying so much, and we took you to Dan's house. Aunt Nan had this rolling bed there that we put you on."

"Now don't forget the part where you yelled 'where's the doctor' every minute or so," I suggested, "and the part where there was something warm and soft touching my hand and you were holding my hand with both of your hands."

"You were awake? I was kissing your hand," she admitted with a show of guilt in her expression. There were even tears welling up in those beautiful blue eyes and starting to spill down the cheeks but Willow wiped them so quickly that they never got the chance to fall and splatter, but they were tears of joy. She was very pleased that I was happy with her. She still wouldn't open up to her apparent feelings, leaving the door closed for me so that I couldn't begin to believe that I could pass through.

"I know you were kissing my hand, but I didn't want to interrupt you," I admitted, "and I didn't want to accuse you of showing any affection or anything of the sort." I hesitated long enough so that she could realize that I was pleased with what I had discovered, hence the guilt feeling was not necessary. "It was like I would wake for a little while then go back to sleep, then the doctor was here," I related, "and I went back out as soon as he put that needle into me and I didn't wake again."

"He gave you a sedative," Willow informed me.

"Why were you kissing my hand Willow?" She didn't say a word, just looked at me. "Are you having the same problem as I am that you are realizing that we are over the line that has been drawn between us?"

"I know I have gone far over the line," Willow admitted, "and the world knows about it now, at least the world that you and I live in, the school here, but they were not surprised, much like they knew what we didn't know or did know and lied to ourselves about it."

I wanted to say "I love you, Willow," but it seems that I didn't know how to do it. With what she said and how she said it, I felt that I had to figure out a way to take the pressure off her mind in possibly feeling that the affection was in one direction. I said, "I promise you, Willow, that I don't think I can go one minute without having you with me. I am glad this happened today, and I know you think I am lying, so I will repeat it; I am glad this happened to me today because of the time that I am spending with you and what is happening with us."

"I have sworn to everybody here that I am not going to leave you, so I guess we're both over the line and can't talk any more about it because Nancy and Dan are here with the lunch."

Nurse Nan didn't change her clothes. She crashed in the chair in her room and is sound asleep. I couldn't feed myself so Willow had to do it. Dan and Nancy laughed at us. "Look at the two love birds, Dan," Nancy teased, "they are eating out of the same plate, off the same fork."

"Comments like that, Nancy," I threatened her, "justify payback, which means that I am going to have to get physical with you. When I am able, you get a monster hug, and one for Dan, a bunch for Nurse Nan, and about everybody. You have all been wonderful and I know I can never repay you, so all I can do is promise to try."

"Lots of hugs," they both agreed, "lots of hugs."

Dr. Haggerty gave me a good once over at the clinic and found that there were three small breaks in the right arm that the X-rays showed that he couldn't locate without them. He assured Willow and me that there was no need to consider wearing a cast because the breaks were along the bone rather than across. We all knew it was from being slammed against the bus. Another find involved the right ear. Everybody already knew that it would require reconstructive surgery a little later but there was damage deeper into the ear than we had originally assumed. "It may not ever cause us a problem," Dr. Haggerty was hopeful in his comment.

Willow drove me home. I had her park nearest to the house to avoid as many bird droppings as possible, assuming that they were a big problem for the convertible top. Mama came out to assist Willow in helping me out of the car. Mama thanked her but Willow assured her that she was merely doing what was her duty. She added, "and I will be staying for awhile because I promised the doctor that I would call the clinic every hour until 9:00 this evening to allow them to determine if I have to bring him back to the hospital. Then I will give him his killer-of-all-pains knockout pill and wait awhile." I had been told about that awesome sleeping pill.

They plopped me in a chair, much like in a holding pattern so they could get me set up properly, or to satisfy themselves. When my mother was far enough away not to be able to hear, I asked, "were you lying about having to call the doctor every hour to decide if I went back to the hospital?"

"Yes."

"Why would you do that?"

"To be with you." Willow was not joking. She was not ashamed.

"We were talking before Dan and Nancy returned with lunch, so back to that line of discussion, we have crossed the big line. With close to three years that we have known each other and there has been nothing. Nothing! No indication of any interest at all! All we have done is see each other in school, except for the kiss behind the stage that got you into so much trouble that I didn't count, and now it is indescribable, unbelievable, unreal. Questions are whirling around in my woozy head 'can this be real'?"

"When we first met, we were 15 and our society had a rule for us that under no circumstances were we allowed anything but to like each other. By the time we turned 16 and your birthday is three days before mine . . ."

"Good! I have a thing against older women," I joked.

Okay," she laughed and continued, "when I turned 16, the magical age when dating and involvement with the other sex is permissible, my parents decided that my involvement would be with a guy from our church named Jacob. That relationship, that was not a relationship, was discussed and gave your brother reason to tell your parents that I was trash, going away those weekends on those religious retreats with my parents and it was like I was going away with a guy."

"You never put up an argument, never did anything," I said, "to refute any part of it."

"There is no way to try to defeat any of that kind of stuff, and I didn't see any damage that was being done to me. I had no feelings for anybody but you and that was not allowed anyway, so what was the harm, and what good would it have done to fight? My family, including Nancy and Dan, knew better. I know what I am, who I am . . . , so I let it go," she explained.

"It is strange Dan didn't know," I commented.

"Dan knew of my feelings for you and he knew just as well the line that was drawn," Willow said, "and so did Nancy. They were not allowed to tell. Since my father's death, this thing has really been bothering me and I have tried to break over, cross over, however I had to get over, but you know we have three weeks before we graduate and I have been concerned about what I am going to do, but I was scared to try to tell you, afraid that it wasn't just the line but maybe you didn't care for me as I do you."

"If it bothers you to talk now, we can do it later, but Mama keeps peeking through from the kitchen."

They put me in a reclining chair and it seemed comfortable and about the best thing to get out of when the time came for that. It certainly was a lot easier to get into than a bed would be. There was a wood-fired heater there, normally so Mama could warm the kitchen. The room was supposed to be a dining room but too many bedrooms were needed for the number of kids around.

The ladies, Willow and Mama, decided that the girls would be happy to take my big room and I could have theirs. It was much more convenient for the bathroom and the kitchen was just trough the door. "I think we can handle it," I told Willow.

Mama got Willow a soft chair to put close to mine. Willow reversed it, "so I can look at your face," she smiled. Mama gave her a pillow from the pile that was originally in Willow's chair. She named it her Willow pillow and placed it on my stomach, laid her head on it and said, "if you can stand it I can sleep here." It was okay. She rested her eyes for a moment. My thoughts were that if the pain was so great that I could only survive maybe 10 or 15 minutes of Willow sleeping on her Willow pillow laying on my stomach, then I would want that 10 or 15 minutes."

"Go to sleep little baby," I began to sing, "go to sleep little baby, come rest your bones on the alabaster stones and be my ever loving baby." That's all of the song I knew, so I stopped and said, "It's an old mountain lullaby that my grandmother used to sing to the babies as she would rock them to sleep."

"Don't stop, now," she smiled, "I didn't know you could sing."

"You probably still don't but that is the only part I remember, I think maybe because I didn't know what an alabaster stone is."

"We used alabaster stone in our church rituals. The white columnar pedestals were referred to as eastern alabaster and the shining plates of stone that corpses were laid on for funerals was alabaster," Willow educated me. "My father was laid on the stone and given the grand ritual that is afforded the highest ranking members of the church. Actually, he was the highest ranking member of the cult and I believe the lower ranked people killed him to take over the position at the top for redistribution of the money, so some investigative types have said, but proof in those secret societies is impossible."

"His body was found just outside the compound. I know they killed him when he defended me. You see, I refused to attend the Christmas retreat last year. I just couldn't take it any more, not believing in what they were doing, not knowing where my life was going and certainly not wanting to pray night and day, day after day, over some soul to brain wash them and get them inside the church group, maybe take everything they owned, or so some investigative people and outside the group said they were doing."

"When I didn't attend the retreat, it is theorized that my father defended me and they killed him." Willow was crying and I was having a tough time accepting tears in those beautiful blue eyes.

"Hey, absolutely most wonderful woman," I spoke to her, "I cannot stand to see tears in your eyes, and I am feeling your pain for your loss but Mama is going to be coming through that door just about 5:00 O'clock or any minute now and I don't want to learn what her reaction would be toward seeing our feelings for each other displayed." I added, "she may like it, and she may blow sky high, I just don't know."

"I think I would like the blow-sky-high," Willow giggled as she wiped away the last of the tears. "yeah, the crazier the better, then maybe I can come up with the strength to tell her that I will stay with you all night and nurse you to health." She closed her eyes, held my left hand against her cheek, smiled and pretended to doze.

The door to the kitchen had apparently been ajar as I saw it ease open and the smile and nod that my mother gave me was full approval of Willow, then the door closed with a thunk. Willow's eyes sprang open and she couldn't help but see the look of satisfaction that I had on my face, and her bit of fright from the startling thunk went away and was replaced with a smile. I told her, "Mama just opened the door and gave you 100% approval."

"Should I go give her a hug?"

"Absolutely not, and be away from me for 30 seconds or more!"

Willow was too smart to be conned by a large pile of animated raw meat, so she hopped up, ran into the kitchen and was heard saying, "you approve of me" and a bunch of girl chatter that nobody could understand, really.

CHAPTER THREE

What I Can't Have

Life became difficult when the farm and the school demand all that is left in a body after the minimum of sleep, maybe not that much. Conflicts were to arise, and people were to choose to take the actions to settle them.

THERE WAS STRESS for Willow. I knew she was tired. She rested on her Willow pillow so she could rest a hand on my chest and I could put my right hand on her shoulder and neck and stroke her cheek with little thumb strokes. She wanted me to tell her about some of the primary things that bothered her and that was those that were leading up to the event today. It was almost like, "I want a list of the people messing with you so I can go beat them up." She was wonderful okay, but nobody, and certainly not I, could imagine this tiny little sweetheart of a person roughing up anybody.

I worked out a private routine. I allowed Willow to rest then when she would talk to me and allow me to know that she wanted me to tell her more then I would do so. Otherwise, I ran some thoughts through my mind. Some were just to help to get around a sharp corner in my life that was coming up, the one where the kid is no longer the kid but an adult, fully responsible, without ties, the kind that come from topside, umbilical like.

Life has milestones, I thought. It is not strange but people think too deeply about things sometimes, at least I was guilty of that sort of thing, and the thoughts would start to get to be a bit weird on occasion. I had plowed and plowed like crazy since back in January, doing my dead level best to get it all ready to plant. It had gotten all tilled and the disc harrow has to be brought out, looking for that milestone that is the one a person has got to get to and has got to get to it at just the right time. On the farm, one has to reach that all-ready-to-plant milestone and rest a bit and be proud. Next, there is the all-planted milestone that one has to seek at just the right time. Lots more milestones!

Oh, it was not all just plowing and thinking. I had to go to school some. Graduation comes in less than a month. This particular milestone had to be worked in. There was little to do academically, merely to attend classes, the minimum of thinking there.

The farm was ready to plant. Graduation? There was a few days to wait but I was ready for that. All considered, there seemed to be a bit of a cause for celebration, however, that would have to wait.

There's not much a person can do while plowing but think. Think too much? Yeah, maybe. A month ago all I could think about was Willow and that one kiss. I wasted too much think time on the tractor on those thoughts. I knew Willow then as this absolutely fabulous rich girl and I was the dirt farmer who couldn't get near her. I bumped into her one night behind the stage when I was rehearsing a play. We grabbed a kiss, just eased right into each others arms. For sure it was no big deal to her, fun maybe, but to me it was a kiss of a lifetime. There would be no way that I could ever forget that kiss, and that might be considered one of life's understatements.

Obviously, there was no need to spend time on that. Maybe there is no need but, dammit, the idea just came around and made a mess of itself that I was so hooked on that little rich girl that it kept me from having a relationship with anybody else. I felt like I would get over it after graduation when I didn't see her across the room all the time. Of course, the rich and the dirt poor don't mix, and it is not difficult to understand that. Life is what it is and people just deal with it. Yet, I will get over it. She gave me so many wonderful daydreams and a few night dreams, too. I understood, what I could have, what I couldn't have.

Most of the people who know me saw me as a pretty good guy. I know for a fact that the people who spent time around me thought of me as something unusual, taking over the farm at the age of 15 and making it work well to keep the family going. Well, not everybody. There are a few who have been on our case since we bought the little farm and moved from across the river. I didn't understand why we were not wanted at Newton's Bluff, but I had wrapped myself into what I was doing, mainly maturing, and just didn't pay a lot of attention to it. I did on the occasions where there was a conflict and it bothered me quite badly at those time. Otherwise, I was too busy. I was very serious about my work. I had heard stories about how forefathers had made great strides and created the better farms in the area. I knew I could do the same.

Though I say it does not bother me so much when I am busy, and maybe that is true, but the fact is it bothers me severely at times when it can. I don't see what I have done to people to cause them to dislike me. Certainly, I don't fit anybody's mould but I don't see what that matters. Certainly, I am an individual and I do my own thinking. After all, having to spend the time alone on those tractors, there is plenty of opportunity to do that and few competing opinions to influence those thoughts. Really, a person learns in all the books that Americans are free to do their own thinking. That's the great part of being American. So why so the church people interfere? Why do they beat me to death for not thinking like they do? It is a major quandary for the thinker.

Some say that I assumed the role of an adult in some respects, yet I am still a kid when the age numbers are laid out on the table, and the numbers just are not adequate to afford a position among adults. If somebody says something and I disagree, then I believe it to be respectable to state my position in a respectable manner and age is of no consequence, certainly not when the right to the opinion has been earned.

Willow looked up at me. Those beautiful eyes sparkled as she asked, "you want to tell me what you are thinking and I can close my eyes and rest while I hear your voice."

"Be careful Willow, or you will express strong feelings for me," I advised her.

"The feelings for you are stronger today but otherwise the same as before," Willow said with the huge smile of a winner. Now tell the one that you, yeah you, feel stronger about today all the things you are thinking."

I wanted to talk to her. I showed no hesitation. "I'm thinking how wonderful you are and another thing or two. We were talking earlier about how this thing started and I think it can be tracked back to my attitude and how it fits here, actually how it does not fit. Sunday mornings people go to church here. No big deal. Most of the time I do too. With too much farm work and too much school work sometimes I just don't have time for going to church. This little story was one that was talked about a lot around here but it was one that really shouldn't have had to happen had I chosen not to challenge the people here. Knowing fully well that there would be an attack on me if I defied the rules of command over me, I prepared for my defiance, attempted to execute a defiant plan."

I couldn't bear the screeching and screaming and all the commitments for praying for me on my way down to hell that the Baptist people were going to do for me, just for me. Mama had always told us to go to the Baptist Church, she never went once but we had to go, but I started to go to the Methodist Church when that bunch screamed at me for saying I didn't have time to go to church. 'You don't have to have time to go to hell either, but you will,' I was told. Honestly, I couldn't understand what was meant by that, so I started going to the Methodist Church. I still had to plow on some Sundays. The Methodists never said anything but the Baptist didn't quite leave me to the discretion of the Methodists."

"Nope, they continued to pound on me rather heavily. Carrie Terrell told me that she had heard a lot of the adults talking about me stopping going to that church and bellyached about me being idolized by so many people, with me doing the adult thing of taking the farm over and how well I was doing it, and how well I did at baseball and basketball."

As I saw Willow was attentive and comfortable as she listened and held my hand, and occasionally touched it with her lips, I went on with my story.

"Carrie told me that she actually thought that some of the people in her church were afraid that I would take some of their people with me when I went and they were upset about it. I told Carrie to go back and tell them that I only wanted her and her little sister Sara to go with me and your mother wouldn't let you. We laughed, knowing that would be a fun reply but we knew that there was a lot more to the problem than that. The fact is I didn't give a rat's hind end who went where. I couldn't imagine anybody thinking I could care. After all, to me church was something a person did to get together with friends, and to keep up with what is right and wrong. No big deal to me."

"What about Carrie Terrell? I have asked myself a few times. Well, had it not been for all the reasons why not, then Carrie might have been the girl of my dreams instead of my Willow here, and you know that I am merely trying to establish a point. One, Carrie and Sara lived next door and were looked upon about like a part of the family. Two, Carrie was a year older. Third and final strike, she had a thing for my older brother that the community wouldn't allow to go any further than a handshake. Three strikes against me. Hey, it never was a bother but most of the same world and some in Newton's Bluff knew I loved the girl but I loved my friends JB and Bob, too."

"The preacher that the Baptists have now, they have had for about three years. He has decided that we can't go fishing on Sunday. Nope, it ain't that it is a sin to go fishing on Sunday, but the preacher and the congregation are outlawing fishing on Sunday and enforcing it. It's about the only time that I had to get together with my friends on a routine basis, so I did not yield to them.

"Oops, major altercation! If I went to church on Sunday morning, what is the big deal about going fishing on Sunday afternoon? I felt that I was as right as they were in overextending their right to rule, so I stood firm. They didn't see it that way, and I heard somewhere that I had declared war against the Baptist Church."

"I would ask myself, 'what are the rules here? If the Baptist Church over there says it, then it is the truth when it is a lie?' I had in my mind that it might be the preacher and personal vengeance. Our little battle started over Sunday fishing, actually. Yeah, the preacher had the idea that he wanted to 'feel the pulse of the community,' as he stated it, so he was to do things that everybody else did. He joined Bob, JB and me for routine Sunday afternoon fishing trip when he first got here.

Nobody invited him and didn't want him, so when he got to jabbering about the 'pulse of the community,' I simply told him that the pulse was that 'the fucking Baptist hate the fucking Methodists and the fucking Methodist hate the fucking Baptist.' The three friends were laughing so hard that the preacher got madder and madder. The more he raged, the more we laughed and he got so mad he turned to run and hooked his pole on a tree limb. He kept running and flattened his fat bottom right in the middle of the path. He just left his fishing pole and ran home."

I had to stop the story here and I had to say, "I apologize for the language that is disrespectful to you and I fully respect you, but I used the words as I used then in disgust or anger and I felt I had to use the words that were the story."

"I know," Willow acknowledged, "and you ask for my forgiveness and I forgive you." The only bad part here is that she closed those beautiful eyes that were so great to look at.

"My friends and I disliked the man strongly. We disliked Shorty Terrell immensely. My father had told me once that those two were about as tight as a "couple of copulating copperheads" and they wanted you to fear them just as much. Though I didn't fear them, I felt that the fight between us was a bit childish, and I was the child."

"I knew, when we came here four or five years prior to the preacher, that we had trouble, including me getting shot in the leg and the disc harrow incident, but we had seemed to be okay with the community since that time and before the preacher came.

"Along about the time the preacher came to the Baptist Church was also about the time of the 1954 U. S. Supreme Court Decision, the time when it became an issue that the negro people were not allowed to walk down certain roads or to live in certain places and they could not play with white kids. That preacher and his brigade made the rules and enforced them, deciding that if the Supreme Court could make decisions for the country then the people here had to make decisions for the community. I stayed in trouble all the time over breaking those rules, fishing on Sunday afternoon and plowing all day, even starting before daylight."

I went on the tell Willow that if it had not been for the negro people, 'my Mama and Daddy could not have raised us all. At least it seemed that Dave and Lulu Swoopes spent as much time raising the kids as did Mama and Daddy.' I went on to tell her, 'Lulu sang more of the songs that I sing than did my grandmother.'

"I fought back at the church people, or at least I didn't yield to them and that was supposedly the same as fighting back. There was a bunch of them in that church but there just a certain few that didn't even try to understand others. The preacher, about as bad as Judge Roy Bean, and Shorty Terrell, worse than Judge Roy Bean, and the wives of three of the Terrells pranced around the countryside enforcing rules, their rules. That was where I tripped up so madly and made my mistakes, I think. So many people advised me, ignoring the rights of those people to make rules, was a big mistake on my part. They also reminded me that those people mean well. Of course, the preacher's son, Jack, our age, nasty minded, arrogant, never meant well unless he meant to throw some unsuspecting soul into a well.

"My personal problems that I experienced with the preacher's son, was that I took care of protecting Carrie and Sara. My theory was that he thought of them as his personal meat because they were members of his daddy's church. They were nobody's meat to me and I disallowed Foster to abuse them without coming through me first. My thoughts were that even if he could come through me, there would be others, but he tried me twice and failed miserably, so he left them alone. I was told that he raped others but I couldn't protect everybody, just those close to me and I had a good image with them.

"We are getting to where we are now," I continued. "I know you are in my same classes, precious Willow, but I relate this in the manner that I do to ensure that I include personal impact as I feel it." Following a short smile and an extreme thrill that it provided me, I continued.

"On my short break between plowing and planting, I seemed to be running into more trouble than I thought was normal. My first-period class got me in trouble because my assignment was to assist the principal who taught the class. The assignment subject was announced for the next week, the United States Supreme Court. Foster decided that he would take a hint from his father and rant and rave. He accused the principal of saying that he was going to put a 'nigger' in the seat where Foster was sitting, when all Mr. Abbott said was that he wanted to discuss whether the state should apply their resources toward preparation for integration or should those resources continue to be applied to fight it."

"Foster took the class into a name-calling rage. He actually called the principal a son-of-a-bitch and both of us 'nigger lovers.' I hadn't done anything relative to the class discussion but Jack Foster knew me and turned the entire class onto me, at least the ones that he could and they were rampaging with insane rhetoric. I had to listen in respect for Mr. Abbott as my teacher and my principal. Furthermore, all day long, I had to face questions from people throughout the school regarding what I said that I didn't say. I was angry, upset, hurt, humiliated, confused and all the rest."

I looked to ensure that my mother wasn't listening at the door and said, "my attitude had become at home that Daddy would agree with me and Mama would tell me how well we had done before we changed and how there was no need to change. My thoughts were that we had murdered the Native population and brought another one here and enslaved it, therefore, 'how well we had done before' was not so well."

"I had found an old Cherokee recluse, I told Willow," out on one of the islands in the Tennessee River to whom I had become attached and had begun to depend upon him to pound the heck out of me when I was wrong and direct me in how to react within society when I am right. He insisted that we call him Ol' Charlie, so Ol'

Charlie Wolf he became, Wolf Island, we named it, was a retreat, haven, hideout. Yeah, all of them."

"I spent my Saturday there after the Friday class blowup," I told my Willow. "Charlie said he was doing his best to wind me down. He said also that I had a mean streak, but he agreed when I told him, 'I call it my alter ego, and I use it to give me something to blame or some place to put the blame' when things go wrong. Ol' Charlie Wolf knew somehow that what I wanted to do would give me plenty to put into that place."

"I knew, too," I said. "It is just that I had to face my enemies and I had to expose them as personal enemies and I had to open my heart to the rest of the people so they could see that I had no problem with them and their religion, or even the Baptist denomination, and certainly not the Newton's Bluff Baptist Church. What I am attempting to make certain that is understood is that I have no problem with the religion and the church, but I do have problems with the fact that some people are using it to pound me unmercifully.

"I was coming to a time in my life where I could go away from the farm, quit fighting the elements, quit fighting, quit . . . , make a change in my life that could be different. I had to tell the people that I had never had a fight with them but with Shorty Terrell and the Reverend Robert L. Foster and those who took directions from them. I had to tell that to the people in that church. I had no vision of convincing them, but I had to tell them."

"Maybe that is why I woke up Sunday morning with the desire to go to church if it was not just to start a fight. Telling them would start a fight. Ol' Charlie had told me that the day before and I knew he was right. I still had to do it.

I had bought the old Studebaker, if you call three years old, back in January and had a load of plans to make it road worthy. I had just busted most of those plans by staying out on the island too long and not getting home until after dark. I could hardly wait to ask Daddy if he got it running but was worried he would fuss at me for dropping the entire job on him. I sat at the breakfast to a grand greeting and the word that it was running great.

"I apologize," I told my father, "for dumping the whole thing on you but I had missed my ride home from the island" After eating we went out back to see it, and it was nice and clean. He told me that he had run it through a car wash. We took it for a bit of a spin.

"When we parked after the ride and walked toward the house, I told my father about plans to go to the church. My father told me that everybody butts into my business so he needs to make it unanimous and inform me that he thought I might be going to that church to start a fight.

I told him 'No, emphatically, No! I swear I am not going to the friggin' Baptist Church to start a fight but I am going to the friggin' Baptist Church to participate in the one already started. I am going in and sit down in the back of the church and the first time that lame-brained fat-assed preacher says the word 'nigger,' I am bouncing my hind end right out tripping over a pew or two if I am able to pull it off."

"Daddy said, 'and you have to do this alone?'

"Daddy, I don't see anybody on anybody else's case but mine."

"You be sure to come right back and give me a full report." What he wanted to know, however, was whether of not I got tarred and feathered. We both got a bit of a laugh in and Willow gave me another of her routine smiles with the huge thrill attached to it. "I went to that church that morning," I told my attentive listener, "brave and defiant but I went and this is my story."

"I parked my Studebaker over the normal parking line so it would be seen that I was there. I sat in the back pew and laid a hymnal on the floor in front of me. My plan was to trip over the hymnal as I left the church at the word 'nigger.'

"Maybe 15 minutes of ritual and business and the preacher came on. His subject was 'The Supreme Court Declares War,' the sign out front had said that. I mean right out of the tube he stated his subject and told that his son's principal had stated that he was going to put a nigger in the seat where his son sat. I stood, tripped over the book and bent over to pick it and put it in the rack in the back of a pew.

The preacher yelled at me and accused me of stopping his sermon. I told him that all I was doing was trying to leave to keep from hearing his profanity. Amid lots of yelling at me, I had to define profanity for him and 'his congregation,' and define for them how it is that the words 'nigger' and 'nigger lover' were profane words. 'Just like sonofabitch like Shorty Terrell called me," I told them. I went on to tell them that the preacher was a liar because the principal at my school never said what he said. 'I was there,' I told them and I also stated that his son was a liar and had knocked up a little girl who had a speech impediment over in Hartselle.

I apologized to the congregation and admitted to all who had referred to me as a 'nigger lover' that maybe all 10 or so of them were right and that I loved my fellow man and never check his skin color or nation of origin, however, I was sorry for them that they chose to follow the likes of their preacher and, while I was there I would note while not making direct reference to Shorty and the preacher for what they stood for, and I never defined what that was, but I did mention that I was hoping that the people who followed the leadership of the church would understand that they should not 'tread upon me because I was tired of being tread upon' by those who chose to follow the directions of their church leadership to do so.

I had trouble leaving the church because so many left with me, as if there was no sermon that day. They smiled and waved.

Seven people from that church did what you found was done to me this morning.

CHAPTER FOUR

Some Right Answers and a '53 Studebaker

"The life of the yesteryears builds the basis for the life of today but today is when we can deal with whatever the frustrations may be for the life we have to experience tomorrow." John Clinton Lang.

WILLOW TOLD ME that they had sold their big house to the Bradleys, Nancy's parents, and her mother had put the money away in a home account in New Jersey and they were living in the little house down by the curve. "My mother plans for us to live there until I graduate from high school, then maybe we move back to the reservation in Old Town, Maine as she plans it or to the village on Spectacle Pond as she plans it, maybe even to Vineland, New Jersey as she plans it," Willow outlined. "My grandmother, the one who changed her mind about you, has already returned to Vineland.

"You know I was born on Spectacle Pond, that's a lake 30 miles east of Bangor," Willow told me. "I don't know how much you know about my early history, but I can tell you some of it."

"Oh, I would really love that, because all I know is that you came from New Jersey three years ago, and I have heard you refer to yourself as a bastard Penobscot, which I believe is one of the five Algonquin people."

Willow laughed. "I don't know a lot about my people, but I am a moon baby and realist who believes in being what you are and letting the rest of the world deal with looking for a problem with it." She looked at me with a triumphant smile and

41

said, "in response to your silent question, July 19, three days after yours, which is likely why we are so much the same in that respect, you know, both of us being moon babies."

"Perfect answer," I stated in surprise," and you are an amazing woman to be able to read my mind so perfectly."

"I cheated knowing your birthday," she confessed. "I got as much information about you as I could because you made my heart start to pound and keep pounding ever since."

"Hey, now you are stealing my line," I challenged. "I have always described you as one so fabulous that you can keep a man's heart beating long after death."

"Oh, how wonderful of you," Willow cheered me, "you have said that about me? It's such a beautiful thought, and I could kiss you."

"You promised!" I didn't get my promised kiss just then. It was almost strange to me that she would suggest then not respond, but then I realized there was likely some discomfort in the environment and with the newer group of people.

"The doctor wants me to take you for a walk. He says about a mile and if you think you can make it. I can tell you all I know about Willow Preston while we walk. What do you think?"

"Can you drive a stick shift?"

"I learned on a stick."

"Let's try my Studebaker and go to the bluff so I can show you how beautiful the trail is along the river."

"Are you sure now?"

"Right now, Willow," I told her as honestly as I knew how to do at the moment," and you may think I am the silliest person in the world, but all I want to do now is to steal an idea from you and never have you be where I can't touch you. I know you will have to leave me at any given moment, so I will make the most of what I have now."

"Do you start to say the silly part when we get to the bluff?"

"I already said the silly part, pretty girl," I assured her.

She laughed at me as she raised the chair, then she called Mama in just in case Mama could see if I was suffering too much pain. "They didn't get to my legs," I told them, "and my back is okay once I get straightened up, so don't baby me any more than completely," and I chuckled and was not capable of hiding the fact that it hurt terribly. I was making sure they understood that it only hurt when I laughed, as I told them, "I need pain to stop me from laughing and causing pain."

When they got me erect and the Studebaker keys for Willow, I had help but put my arm around Willow and told her that I couldn't walk if I couldn't touch her. She offered to hold my hand. I accepted.

The biggest part of our ordeal was "getting my busted-up butt into that Raymond Loewy designed, almost-below-ground Studebaker Starliner coupe without waking up all the neighbors," as Willow says, "the ones of those people thirty miles east of Bangor."

With luck and some pain, along with a bunch of profanity uttered under the breath, we did it! Actually, Willow did it! As she sat in the driver's seat, she looked around and said, "I love this car and I see why you do."

"We have had a world of fun working on it, even neighbors have helped out and we have made friends with the little car already. Daddy has done so much of the work but because it was fun to him, while our friend and neighbor David Landry is teaching me to do the bodywork."

"Speaking of your Daddy," she said, "what is he going to say or do when he comes home?"

"It could get weird," I assured her, "if we don't handle it right, he could start knocking off people."

"I was afraid of that and the others were at school," Willow said, "so we fixed it so when he returned our call that they would tell him that you got hurt somehow but one of your classmates took you to the doctor so we didn't need him to check out from work."

"Do us a favor," I suggested, "and tell that to Mama before we go, because Daddy will likely come home before we get back."

Willow ran in and told Mama. When she came back, she asked, "did you miss me?"

I told her, "sure, you didn't have to hang out, stay gone for close to a minute or what seemed like all afternoon, talking about the weather, planting flowers, you know."

"That's the right answer, of course, but she did say that you were probably milking the attention for the injuries because of me," she said. "Would you take advantage of me like that?"

"Yes."

"That's the right answer again."

It was a lot easier getting out of the car than it was getting in. I could use my legs more and lean forward and lift myself up. There were not any parking places at the bluff but we could always park in the trees at the eastern side and even hide in the trees if we needed to, but Willow, the perfect nurse that she was, felt the need to be sure that her patient had the room clear to get in and out.

As we started to walk I felt I could fully understand the doctor's request for walking. Just the couple of hours in the chair at home and I had begun to feel soreness but it felt as if I could work it out. The rest of my body hurt so very badly that I was not certain that I could do the two miles there and back but I felt I could have done 200 laps just to do them with Willow. She was just about the most fabulous person in the land and I was becoming more and more aware of the reality of the fact that she was with me and we were living out my dreams, lots of my dreams all at one time.

We started the walk as agreed, holding hands. The pain was just too great. I had tried so many times to block the punches that the arms were mutilated. I suggested to Willow that she carry me but that was not the suggestion that she liked. She liked the one about going half way this time and we could try the full trip on one of their trips tomorrow.

Willow looked at her list that the doctor had made for her and stopped, "the doctor says one mile the first two or three times then if you feel like it try for two miles," she said "and that means today at 6:00 one mile, and 6:00 and 10:00 tomorrow one mile and try for two at 4:00 in the afternoon." She held the paper and read awhile longer. "The trip today is just for trial so we don't have to do it, but you are doing so well, let's keep it up," she challenged.

"Hold on girl," I begged, "I know we are kidding around with each other about how suddenly in our lives we can't bear to be apart but you know you have to go home here rather soon, don't you? I mean, you are talking like you are planning to stick with your assertion that you are not going to ever leave me."

Folding her paper and putting it back into the pocket of her jeans, Willow said, "while you were dozing soon after I got you home, I called Nancy to bring out my clothes for tomorrow and her Aunt Nan is taking care of excusing you and me from class for three days and more if she needs to. Your mother is expecting me to stay tonight and I am expecting her to expect me to stay another night, and you are not in any condition to put up anything but a verbal defense and we can put cotton in our ears, or just not listen."

From the reaction, I was totally at the mercy of that smile of triumph and Willow's teasing maneuver where she moved in front of me to ensure that I got the full view of her expression of personal victory. "Where are you going to sleep?"

"On my Willow pillow," she grinned.

"But my little sister's bed is in the room," I reminded.

"What about me, where am I sleeping?"

"Where you were today, but if I sleep in your little sister's bed I have to move yours next to mine so I can touch you."

"And you sleep on your willow pillow, where I can see your eyes and touch your cheek?"

"I like my Willow pillow."

"I like my Willow." As soon as I said it, I realized just how much I wanted to say 'I love my Willow,' just had been the case for the past few years, I was scared to say it. I felt so adolescent. As the timing seemed right I asked, "was there something else that you wanted to tell me about my Willow?"

"How about just about everything that I know about Willow Preston?"

"My favorite subject, you know," I told her in a lighthearted but serious manner.

"Likely I would have been called a bastard half-breed Penobscot had I not been adopted by the husband that my mother took from the many religious compounds that would sprout up in the wildernesses of Maine every Summer. Just so you know about as much as I know since I was maybe four or five years old when we left Maine, the Penobscot Nation resides on a large island in the middle of the Penobscot River and the reservation office is considered to be in Old Town, Maine, the place where they make the Old Town Canoes. The Penobscots are one of the five American Indian nations that formerly made up the Wabanake Confederation, the same five tribal groups who are formerly the Eastern Algonquins. That is my knowledge of the history of the Penobscot portion of my family," she smiled, softly and confidently.

It was a way of showing pride for what was her small bit of knowledge, hence her apology for knowing so little.

"As I am told, the frat brats from the university close by were locally famous for grabbing the pretty young Penobscot maidens from the bridge to Old Town or on the streets or roads. The maidens were gang raped, then dropped somewhere near the reservation so they could make their way back home. My mother was one of those maidens.

"When it was determined that she was pregnant, with me of course, she was exiled by the tribal elders, which was the normal routine inasmuch as nothing could be done with the rapists, they were white, to a place east of the reservation. I am told that they took her to Bangor, then drove her 30 miles east to a place near a mountain lake where there was a small village. The Penobscot women took care of my mother and delivered her baby, me.

"As our history has told us about all American Indians, the religious groups or churches came to the villages to preach to the heathens every Sunday morning. They even came to my mother's village. They even came to my mother's village on the lake called Spectacle Pond. My mother described one of the men as a tall charismatic preacher from Beddington whose name was Preston.

"They fell in love and married when I was three and gave me the Preston name. They never had any more children. I don't know if they could or couldn't. We moved to Vineland, New Jersey, which is where I began school and continued for my first nine years. Daddy had purchased a huge vineyard in Vineland, or maybe he inherited it, I never knew. I never was given information as to how my father became so very wealthy. The Preston family in Maine was rich anyway so nobody asked questions so that we young people could learn by the traditional way young people learn about what goes on in a family.

"Daddy was into transportation and other things while we were in the Vineland area. I remember that he was very influential in the community and the area around there. I realized quite early in my school years that my mother held back from the attention that the family was receiving as a result of my father's wealth and influence, but it didn't last long. It is said that my father forced her into the attention, into the fancy dresses and gowns, shopping trips into New York, Philadelphia and other cities with the socially elite in the community.

"I loved my father. He was a good father when I was a child but we began to travel different paths as I questioned his exertion of absolute power over me as I entered my teens and grew so far away from him, his doctrines and his leadership or guidance or whatever it was desirable to call it. He exercised absolute power over my mother and me, at least attempted. It was stifling. Mother accepted it as her duty, 'her calling' as she stated. I rebelled at home but never really completely until last Summer when I completely rejected my parent's religion. I came close to the rejection of my parents.

"Though I did not reject Christianity, I challenged the beliefs that my parents held dear. In my own mind, I questioned it but I was never brave enough to speak about it. My mother and I fought toe to toe and my father eventually defended me againt my mother's verbal attacks. At some point in the many extreme arguments, I felt him sway toward me philosophically. In those compounds and as they took themselves to so-called sinners off the premises, they took in teams to pray over them, to cleanse them of their sins. To implant mental controls into the heads of the people.

"The teams kept the people awake for days until they were under the complete and total control of the prayer teams. I know now that it is brainwashing. I knew then but couldn't fight alone what I didn't feel was honesty and fairness.

"The discussions and arguments at home came to this. My parents brought prayer teams in. They brought people from inside the compound where my father was supreme to our home, but I had lived it and knew how to defeat the controls. I think my defeating the control is what caused my father to sway toward me in allowing me to dwell in my own philosophy, and that is that I have my own choices to make and those must be made by me outside the influence of the church organization and its people.

"I played them like finely tuned instruments. I made them believe that I was in their control – I had been with them and knew their routine – then the following day I announced to my parents that I was in control of myself. I defeated the prayer teams twice. They left me alone, at least as far as the tortuous prayer marathons were concerned.

I heard my father say one time, 'she's got no money, no wealth that we can gain, so why waste what we have on my own daughter, and she knows nothing of how we operate our business.' He went on to add, 'she can do us no harm.'

It is my personal theory that my father failed to convince them that I could do no harm and he was killed, and I will always believe this, because he stood by me."

It had been less than four months since her father had been found just outside the compound with his neck broken. Willow's tears indicated to me that it was not long enough beyond her period of grief such that she was comfortable talking about it. I didn't want her to continue and told her so. "Hey, let's move on to something where I can see you smile," I suggested.

MY WILLOW 47

"I got through my first nine years of school," Willow smiled and continued her autobiography, "and was looking forward to moving up in status as something more than a fish or freshman for my second year in high school but my father came home suddenly one day in the Summer and said, "pack you stuff, girls, we are moving to Alabama.""

"The shock was almost unbearable, but he stopped me and told me that I would be with my cousin, Nancy Bradley. My panic subsided a bit and he went on to tell me that my grandmother was there also. That did little to excite me because I knew little of my grandmother Bradley but it helped to know that I was not being dragged to the South just to be dropped among strangers.

"Just as a side note, the Bradleys and the Prestons were two prominent families in the Bangor, Maine area and often intermarried as the social elite deemed was the right thing to do in order to ensure that the wealth was never spread too far from its source. My Father's mother was a Bradley, so when my grandfather passed, she followed her youngest brother and sister to Alabama.

Her youngest brother is Nancy Bradley's father, the Doctor Henry C. (Hank) Bradley, who chose the University of Alabama for his medical education. According to Doctor Bradley, Alabama offered him the most of what he desired and had one of the more highly recognized medical schools in the nation. He always adds that it is a long way from Bangor, choosing never to state if this is an expression of pleasure or displeasure. It is the joy of the mystery about him that we so endear.

Dr. Hank and Sara Jane Franks fell in love, married and ticked off all the Bradleys in the entire state of Maine by doing so. To them at the time Aunt Sara was a commoner but they have all come to love her and have fully embraced her into the family. The Bradleys chose to settle here on Aunt Sara's home turf.

I remember no time in my life when Nancy, their first born, was not my friend. She spent so much of each of her Summers in Maine, then chose to come stay with me in Vineland almost all the Summers and as many holidays as possible while we lived there. Even if she did spend time in Maine in the Summers, I was there with her. We were as inseparable then as we are now.

Dr. Hank's sister is Nurse Nan as we so affectionately refer to her, who followed him to the University of Alabama. It is told for the record that Nan married, became pregnant and had to drop medical school. She went back to Bangor and had the baby. Her husband divorced her for abandonment, so she reclaimed her maiden name, and gave it to her son as well. She will not talk about Dan's father, choosing to state that both of Dan's parents have agreed. She told us once that she had made the Bradleys in Maine set up a sustenance account for her in the event not having a husband caused a financial burden.

I think Aunt Nan intends to complete her education, to become a doctor, when Dan attends college this year.

We were arriving back at the car. I thanked her for relating to me her autobiography, but I privately concerned myself with the thought that her life had not been so free of bumps as those of us suspected of the families who lugged around the excesses of wealth.

I assumed she had either not heard my declaration so much earlier or had ignored it, but she opened the door for me and offered a suggestion. "How about if you try to sit just on the edge of the seat and once your weight is firmly down, scoot back into the seat, turn and pull your legs inside, all in one motion."

Nothing I could do would be painless in my condition but Willow's idea was workable. I could use my legs and spared the use of the arms and the torso, which made it a lot more comfortable to get into the car than it was on the first attempt.

As soon as she had me in my seat, Willow went around and got into the driver's seat, looked at me, smiled and asked, to my complete surprise, "now, now after all the walking and talking about your Willow, do you still like your Willow?"

"Yes, I really do like my Willow."

"Do you think it would be too painful to kiss your Willow?"

"Are you my Willow?"

"Yes."

"Then say it."

"I am your Willow," then she kissed me, long and sweet. I couldn't even get to hold her but there are no complaints coming from me. Not even a complaint about busted and painful lips.

"I think, Willow, other than the fact that you might have waited so long that I may not survive this one," I said as soon as I realized that I was alive in the real world down here on Earth and not flying around somewhere up there in a place called heaven with an angel, "we just pledged ourselves to each other and sealed it with a kiss."

"We did," she said with a bit of a giggle but that was okay. "We're acting like good nurse and good patient, pretending we are being mature about things. But, I don't know how to handle relationships," she said as she turned serious on me. "I have never really dated, I have never really had a boyfriend and I believe for a fact that I have one now and I don't know what to do."

"I'll find out for you when I get up and around."

"You can do that?"

"Of course I can. I just hitch a boat out to an island in the river East of here," as I pointed as best I could through the pain and Willow strained to look down river. "Oh, you can't see the island from here but my best friend, an old Cherokee recluse, about 86 years old, can tell us how to handle ourselves."

"You literally go out and consult with this old wise man?" Willow seemed to approve, or her manner indicated that, but I wasn't sure she believed anything but that I was pulling her leg.

MY WILLOW 49

"Yeah," I swore to her that I was telling the truth, "and he even predicted that if I would protect my lips in my next fight that I would be kissed by the most beautiful girl in the world."

She laughed, "maybe I can get another one before you get into that."

"Come on, let's drive," I told her, but that was after she got her other kiss, "and I will tell you about me just so we can be even; you've told me about you, why you have never had a boyfriend, so I will tell you about me and why I have never had a girlfriend. When I can get around better, I'll borrow the boat and motor rig that my father and his best friend have in partnership and take you out to see Ol' Charlie Wolf and the island."

Oh, that would be exciting and I can hardly wait to do that," she said.

Willow backed the little Studebaker out, went left on past the house back into the farmland behind, through hundreds of acres of plowed fields, some pastures and meadows with both beef and dairy cattle. We drove to a fence where there was a T in the road. "That is all mine that we drove through behind us, so we can turn around now and go back, Daddy's home and I saw Nancy's car was already there," I informed her.

"You are so very casual about this," Willow stated, "but it looks like all of this that you point to as being yours is a beautifully prepared farm ready to plant."

"It will be my third crop," I again informed her. "I took the farm when I was 15, because my brother went away, the white people here ran off the negro man and woman who had helped run the farm and raise us all, so I had no choice but to either run away like my brother and Dave and Lulu Swoopes or my father had to quit his job and run the farm. He has two guys to help me when they can. They are good to me but I run this farm. My father doesn't but he helps. I don't have time for girls. I have tried to develop relationships. No luck, really. There has been nobody to capture my interest. Nobody else and you can identify the exception."

Willow was listening. It seemed that my thoughts were that I was satisfied that there was another Willow trait that helped to bring her closer to perfection, she was a good listener, so I continued. "I found Ol' Charlie Wolf, the one you refer to as the old wise man, during my first year with the farm, on our short Summer break between cultivation and harvest. He took his family farm when he was 15 and turned into a model operation as his father had done before him.

Ol' Charlie had heard the fireside tales of Andrew Jackson's armies taking everything from his family and forcing them to migrate to Oklahoma, and how his father had his family and farm taken in the civil war. He knew how his father had started all over again, leaving him with the basis for what Ol'Charlie Wolf had taken from him when the TVA flooded the valley here. Ol' Charlie refused to leave his land; he is still there."

I continued as I saw the interest from Willow encouraged it. "I go there when I am troubled and come away knowing how to clear my troubles sometimes, but mostly we talk about them. I spent last Saturday there because of what happened in our class on Friday. He is really my great grandfather but my mother will not even admit that she is Cherokee."

"When I went out there this time,' I related the details of my report, "I hooked a ride with Mr. Milton, the man who has the farm at the T in the road behind our farm." I told her that the man didn't talk too much but he is a nice man. Being in the mood that I was that day, I picked the perfect hitch. I just didn't want to chat with anybody in the world except my mentor, Ol' Charlie.

Certainly to encourage me to continue, Willow spoke, "what do you think you would do if you didn't have Ol' Charlie Wolf?"

"I would lean on my father I guess," I answered, "keeping him at odds with my mother, but this life that I am living is forcing me to feel so alone up until you came into it with your heart and soul, your beautiful eyes, your everything to me so far. Look at what has happened. My paternal grandfather gets dragged back to Germany after the war, but I can live with that, I have Dave and Lulu Swoopes who get run out of town by the white folks when they are the only ones left that I have to hang with. Along comes Ol' Charlie and he don't give a rat's hind end if my mother ever agrees with my father and vice versa, so I lean on him rather securely."

I ask myself, 'did I start to need a partner and found one before I knew that I needed one, is that the case? Am I starting to need another partner and you are here to supplant Ol' Charlie? Somebody is always being taken from me, Willow, but I want to make it clear that for you I can give up anything and anybody, everything. Maybe I am severely afraid that I can't hang onto you, which is likely the reason why I say what I do."

Willow responded, "but we are in full agreement that we are together. The rest can fall apart and we are together. Together, we can have Ol' Charlie. How about that?"

"I like that," I agreed, "so I guess I had better tell you all about last Saturday."

"Ol' Charlie wasn't anywhere to be seen when I arrived at the island, probably he was back in the cave feeding the pups. Yeah, he called the mama and the daddy wolves both puppies in spite of their ages. I was thinking, 'I've been running that old farm for a couple of years and then some and doing pretty good at it while my daddy goes off and makes a living for the family fixing tractors and I get to graduate from high school. I have to finish that crop, then what? No more crops! I will repeat that over and over and over again and try to convince myself, no more crops!'

"I already have the Spring plowing done and I'm getting ready to put in my third crop, and I didn't even realize that I had started to speak my frustration aloud as I said, 'here I am getting to be one and I don't even know what the hell one is.'

"The voice from behind me asked, 'you're getting to be one what?' Ol' Charlie in his own inimitable fashion had arrived at his own parlay place and had successfully seated himself, and even in my condition of quiet solitude, he had not made sufficient noise that I was able to know that he was there.

"'Adult! I'm just frustrated, Charlie,' I responded.

"Ol' Charlie asked, 'then why did you come out here and mess up my day with your foul mood?'

"'I had made arrangements with Mr. Milton to ride out here in his boat and he came by the house to pick me up,' I assured him.

"'Milton didn't give a damn if you rode with him or not so you could have told him to go on and run his lines without you and he wouldn't have cared.'

"'What do you expect me to say,' I asked, 'that I came out here to screw up your day with my foul mood because I knew you would understand and appreciate my need just to have somebody to talk to?'

"'Yeah,' Ol' Charlie replied and laughed at me.

"'The truth is nobody will talk to me but you, not and be civil and not treat me like I'm some kind of a dumb kid. I want somebody to talk to me, to tell me why I am right or why I am wrong if I am wrong. I want somebody to tell me how I need to react and tell me a reason for whatever way I have to turn rather than tell me that we have done it this way for a lifetime or that 'them Yankees ain't coming down here and telling us what to do or something just as asinine.

"Following a good laugh Ol' Charlie said, 'the 1954 U. S. Supreme Court Decision is nipping at you every which way you turn, ain't it?'

"'It comes up in every class, it comes up in every discussion,' I said, 'and I can't seem to talk without every single person that I get involved with cussing me and starting in on some ridiculous rage.' I looked down wondering if I should say anything about it but decided that Ol' Charlie always understood and would this time. 'I can't get a date with any of the girls in my school because they call me a Nigger Lover.'

"'And you get pissed at them when they call you that?'

"'Yeah, I do!' I admitted confidently that I did with the feeling that I was doing the right thing, then asked, 'am I supposed to kiss their hind ends?'

"'No, not literally, but you should try sometimes to thank one of them. Tell them that you appreciate their maturity and respect their ability to recognize that loving your fellow man is the only way to approach this tough life and we all have to get through. Then walk away and see if somehow you don't feel a whole lot better about yourself. After all, when you choose to be something you need to know how to demonstrate pride in being that, whatever it is.'

"'Walk away and let that bunch of crazies shoot me in the back or at least cuss me from behind?'

"'Okay, so then don't walk away,' the old man raised his voice to trumpet his change of attitude, 'stand your ground and make them take the initiative to walk away or fight with you face to face, and I know there ain't two people in that school who will want to try you, and that might include the teachers.'

"'I don't want to fight anybody,' I barked, getting loud with him.

"'Then you let them continue to beat you to where you are now, every day from now on just like they have been and are doing every day now.' He hesitated momentarily, then gently stated, 'they have beaten you their way and you have believed that you have no fight for them because you are alone.' He hesitated again only long enough for a breath, then asked, 'when did you ever have anybody to fight your fights for you? You either need to suck up and get out of the fight if you don't have any fight in you and you are starting to smell like a coward to me.'

"I was starting to see his point but I couldn't make a plan as to how to approach my detractors. I didn't know what to say, so I think I mumbled something like, 'there is just too many of them.'

"'Likely half the people out there will agree with you immediately but you will have to speak out or there will be nothing out there for them to agree with.' Actually, I had not yet agreed to all that he was saying but I was being convinced to bring the fight to myself, to begin to stimulate dialog rather than to wait for it to come to me in stupid silly clichés and baseless irrational statements and insults.

"'I thought you were going to sit in that sand seat of yours and take it from a beat-up old 85-year-old, sorry-assed Cherokee recluse who sics his wolves on folks that come out here to his island and shoots them in the back with arrows and guns,' Ol' Charlie said with a grin, but it was a grin of success for the facetious approach to gloat about winning an argument, or a debate, or whatever this was.' Okay, come on and let's walk and talk about how I won you over to my way of thinking,' he laughed.

"'You have not wasted your time on me today,' I stated a bit argumentatively, of course, but this was the flavor of the talk we were having, so I stayed the course, 'but I am completely lost as to how I am to plot a strategy to stand against these people, yet I know, because of what you have imparted to this little brain of mine that I have no options. I have to do something or drop out of school or go somewhere and bury my head, like an ostrich. Run out like Dave and Lulu did, like Johnny did.

"'You have to make up your mind first that what you feel is right, then when you get yourself in a fracas measure your opponent and keep your composure.'

"'That's what Sonny, my martial arts instructor used to try to pound into my head.'

"Ol' Charlie continued. 'The consideration that I suggested earlier that you are a 'Nigger Lover,' is primary, and knowing that what you are is what you want to be is enough to face the taunting insults that these small-minded friends of yours throw at you.'

"'You are telling me that I have no reason to be pissed when they call me names, insult me?'

"'Yes!' His answer was short and direct for a reason. At least I thought it was for one reason or another.

"'I like that,' I said, 'I know what to do now so we can keep walking and you will not have to waste your time with some kid in a foul mood. But, we have been gone for more than two hours,' I clarified.

"'It took longer today because I had to drag you.'

"'No you didn't have to drag me, but I did have to stop a lot so you could look me directly in the eyes and impart wisdom.'

"'A man has to impart what he has.' We always got a good laugh out of Ol' Charlie's bits of wisdom and his fun comments. He went on to say, 'I always pat myself on the back verbally because I can't reach it otherwise, plus nobody else will do it for me.'"

-0-

"The class ignorant messed you up pretty badly, I knew that," Willow said.

"I'm glad you put it the way you did but there is more. You see my farm? It is what a mature, experienced person is capable of, yet I can't relate to society, to church, to people . . . to anything or anybody. I can't even have a relationship with another teenager, so I block everybody out, I fight with my mother, everybody but my father, and of course Ol' Charlie. That is why I went to see him on Saturday. I went to that church on Sunday to do exactly what I did, and you know the rest."

"I also know and I know that you need to know that Clint Thompson was the one who came to get help for you, stayed with you until the doctor sent him away, then promptly dragged all six of your attackers into the principal's office. That's why doctor Haggerty didn't need your list."

"He already had it then?"

"The list had already been turned over to the sheriff and all the boys taken to Decatur before you were conscious."

"I guess nobody knew that I came to when they were putting me on the blanket out by the bus and when Miss Nan came and took charge," I admitted to her, "and I heard that it was Clint who was so very aggressive at getting people to help me, and I heard him say that Phillip Terrell had told him that they were horsing around and were just going to play a trick on me."

"That is true," Willow assured me, "which is why he took the initiative to bring all the boys in to the principal's office. He said that he brought them each in instead of naming them because they lied to him and made him get involved."

"Did the Sheriff take him in, too?"

"No, not even for beating Phillip up," she said, "because Phillip couldn't get anybody to admit that they had seen Clint hit him, and I heard he beat up JD pretty bad, too, but he personally drug them all into Mr. Abbott's office."

I can only be sure that it was Phillip who was doing most of the harm to me. The others were holding me, merely involved. Phillip was the one who had the old score to settle.

"I want you to know how I feel and I am rather certain that Phillip Terrell will walk away from this thing free of guilt and free with stories of how badly he kicked my butt," I said. "I will even agree that he did just that. The difference in his story and mine will be that he did it with the help of six of his kin. I concern myself with the need for payback. But you remember the talk of Phillip "settling an old score?"

"All the other kids told the sheriff and the principal that he said that," Willow agreed. Phillip also told them that you ran his preacher out of town and came into his church during the preacher's sermon and tried to start a fight."

Basically true," I corrected, "but Phillip and his cousins should have tried to kick my butt me at the church, rather than to ambush me on school property, and I tried to leave when his preacher started using profanity and his preacher was the one who called me back for the fight that Phillip might be making reference to, then I guess he changed his mind when I removed my jacket and shoes. Furthermore, the preacher got scared and tried to leave town because he had a warrant for his arrest in Louisiana, I believe it was. One was being prepared for his son in Hartselle. Otherwise, the story is true.

"Yeah, the part where you went to church," Willow laughed.

"You were in class Friday," I offered, "when jack Foster, who is Phillip's preacher's son, disrupted the class, called the principal names and accused him of 'trying to put a nigger in the seat where I am sitting,' and calling me names as well, while all we were trying to do was to study a course chapter on the U. S. Supreme Court."

"I know both of them and also know about the old score," Willow agreed, "didn't you kick his butt in a ditch by the school bus or something?"

"Yeah! Foster is a bully; Phillip Terrell is a bully. Last year at the beginning of school, maybe the first or second day, I was wearing a new Detroit Tigers baseball cap. I have always been a huge fan, having lots of family in the Detroit area and we get to go see a couple of games in the Summer sometimes. On this day, I was sitting on the front row, Phillip saw the cap as he started to board the bus, grabbed it off my head and destroyed it as he was standing half way up the steps of the bus."

"Using the handbar for pivot, I swung my entire body from the seat to the chest of Phillip Terrell, leading with a knee that landed firmly in his stomach. He was knocked off the bud into a ditch, I then proceeded with almost nothing more than kicks to the chest and shoulders as I worked off the higher elevation of the top edges of the ditch, moving around him as much as possible, putting on a show to demonstrate what a smaller person can do with my skills to a larger person who is no more than a hulk of a bully."

"I didn't hurt him. I didn't intend to do so. I don't want to hurt anybody but I wanted to show that I had the skills to defend myself and the willingness to do so if I have to do it."

"Our bus driver took us both to the principal's office. The principal decided that Phillip's actions were on the school bus and that I maneuvered him to a position off the bus in the ditch whereby he had no jurisdiction over my actions. Yet, Phillip would go unpunished because he could not justify punishment for me. He did thank me for not inflicting injury.

"As I left the principal's office," I continued, "I took a shortcut outside the building to the place where my friends gathered to hang out and wait for the first bell. A Morris kid, Phillip's first cousin, was waiting for me at the corner of the building. As I rounded the corner, he attempted a sucker punch in taking a swing at me. I blocked it and began to back away. Though it was not my intention, my backing away lured Morris to a position where the fracas was visible to the principal's office. Morris threw punch after punch as I did nothing but block each punch and move to be in the position to avoid him landing punches. At an opportune moment, I did a half spin and kicked his legs from under him. Each time he tried to right himself, I kicked the back of his knees.

I turned myself in to the principal's office. He saw the entire thing and found no reason for punishment for me. I understand Morris got a good pounding.

They had a cousin going to another school. It is said that a girl left school to get him. As I went out for Fall baseball practice, I was passing an area where some kids had rigged a rope in a tree so kids could swing on the rope and drop themselves into a pile of sand as an after-school activity. It was off campus and not allowed during the school day but as I passed it a girl screamed. I turned to see a person swinging on the rope in my direction, so I dropped to avoid contact.

"Needless to say, it was a Terrell cousin, one they called Jay, the one who went to another school. He had apparently skipped out at lunch and came to our campus for the specific purpose of attacking me in retaliation for the roughing up the Morris kid and Phillip Terrell. With the coach's signaled approval, I roughed this one up rather severely. I maneuvered him off campus to a field and took several shots to his face bringing a lot more blood than I would have hoped."

There had been a couple of girls to come with Jay Terrell, the one who screamed and another, neither of whom I had seen before to my knowledge. They took him away but one told the coach as they were leaving, "his mother is really going to be pissed off about this but we will just have to tell her that Jay was trying to kill him."

"I didn't see who screamed," Coach Hawkins told the two girls, "but you could have save his life but we certainly know you saved him from serious injury."

"This thing has to stop and that is what my intent has been since I decided to confront them all at the church on Sunday," I told my Willow. "And, while everything is going so bad in my life, I discover you and enough happiness in one day to make it all worthwhile, but I have no confidence I can keep it up with you. I just told you, Willow, that I do not have the human capability to relate to anything or to anybody."

She had turned the car around as I was talking and started to drive back as she said, "we pledged ourselves to each other today, so we will work together to make everything happen for us and it will work for us." She turned slightly toward me, smiled and placed the back of her hand against my cheek. "If we could stop lying to ourselves long enough we would both know that the reason we never got involved with other people was because of how we felt about each other and the hope that we had that we could get over the line that we have now gotten over," she explained to me, then added, "we will both be just fine now."

I could not describe my feelings at that time. I would have believed it had she told me that I could feel no pain. Willow parked the car in the back near the tractors, pointed to the little Ford tractor and asked, "will you teach me to drive the little one?"

"You can drive the Ford and I can drive the John Deere and we can live happily ever after in the dust, the heat, the boll weevils, the draught . . ."

"Hmmm, sounds romantic."

"This is the most fascinating woman in all the world," my mind told him but I already knew that. I wouldn't even consider that she was bullshitting me just exactly like I would be doing to her if the chance was there. It didn't matter, I was crazy about her and wanted everything to be just like it was with her.

Nancy ran out to help me out of the car. As she opened the door, I told her, "the legs work okay but the rest of me is non-functional." Knowing I had to suffer the arm pain I put a hand out and gritted my teeth. I saw my father coming, so he quickly asked, "Nancy, how is he reacting?"

"Between your mother and me, we have convinced him that you are in love and the pain complaint is just your milking the routine for Willow, Miss Sympathy USA."

"Then you didn't have to lie to him at all, did you?"

Each of us laughed but I whined long and loud about the pain that it caused me, both the laughing and the getting out of the car, but Willow argued, "he needs some attention and somebody to care for him right now and that is not sympathy, and furthermore we have not used that other word between us yet."

"What other word, 'love' ?" Nancy said, teasing both of us, and announcing what was coming without actually saying it and we both were well aware of what she planned. "You two have been in love with each other for three years and every person in those classrooms have known it but the two of you, but we all see how you look at each other across the room and how you will never sit close to each other because both of you think it will allow the other one to find out about it, the love thing, I mean."

Nancy laughed and added a question for Willow, "Why did you start screaming and we had to restrain you when Clint Thompson came in and told us he needed help outside, that he was hurt?"

The truth had started the tears with Willow, of course, but the smiles and the laughter were there also.

"It looks like my Willow has had a bad day," I picked up on the teasing of her with the others.

"A great day, a wonderful day," Willow argued through her tears and laughter.

The kids and both parents had come outside, maybe to help me inside or maybe to see the Nancy Bradley show. "Okay," Nancy took her position at center stage again, "are we ready to make the big announcement that we all know about anyway just to make it official?" There was a big cheer, encouragement and laughter, and some of her audience didn't even know what they were cheering and encouraging. They must have been Nancy Bradley fans.

Willow walked over to where I was leaning against the car and quietly said almost in a whisper, "she won't give up until we say it," and I agreed.

"We want to do it anyway," I assured her and she nodded agreement." actually, Willow," I added before she could turn away, "that is what I have been trying to get out of you or to see if I could bring it out of me, all day long."

She whispered, "I know that and I was afraid if I said it, that you wouldn't have to."

"Now I have to?"

"You have to and I have to and neither of us can hardly wait so let's get it out in the open where we can see how beautiful it is," my Willow suggested.

I could only lift one hand but Willow, the ever-in-position-to-make-me-function-as-a-whole-person Willow, lifted the other one so she could hold both hands, Willow took them and without hesitation announced, "I love you, Bud."

I held eye contact and looked deeply into he beautiful blue eyes while the clapping and cheering routine went on and saw that the love she expressed was from all of her heart, so I expressed the same with honesty, "I love you, Willow." We sealed it with a kiss. We knew the passion was there but tried to hide it because the kids and parents were all cheering.

CHAPTER FIVE

Who are the Burtons?

This is a game the adults have played almost as long as there is a memory of this place, where they put their kids against others to do their dirty work, then they laugh about it in their Sunday yard parties.

ON OUR FIRST excursion of the day Willow worked my arm muscles more. They seemed to need it more. There was little play and more serious work because the first night of sleep seemed to invite swelling and pain. The pain could be worked out but playing was not the necessary therapy. The take-charge part of her character was invaluable.

After the session, Willow wanted to drive around to see what was beyond the farm and deeper into the Valley and I did not mind getting out of spending a lot of time in my hospital recliner. Not so deep into the exploration, she slowed at the sight of a compound surrounded by a huge iron fence.

"We're told not to get near the place. It's a lot like a prison," I offered, "but you could see the house in the compound in the winter time through a tall iron fence when the leaves are off the trees. It is made of red brick, a lot like some of the rich people live in over in Huntsville and Decatur."

"It's the Burton Mansion. People told stories about the Yankee General who came through the South burning everything in sight after the Civil War. It is said that he quit burning when he saw the place. It seems, according to the stories, that he delighted in torching the white antebellum mansions, very much like your parents' house but could not bring himself to the destruction of a house that looked so much like the ones where he grew up in Boston.

The legend goes that the General left soldiers here to care for the place and went back to DC for the purpose of gaining title to the place. The stories told never mention what happened to the previous owners but the house and grounds have been kept basically the same for almost another hundred years."

We couldn't see the place because the trees were already in full green so Willow drove past.

"There are three houses on the grounds behind the big iron fence, I explained. Mr. and Mrs. Burton live in the big house, my friend Sonny and his wife in one of the smaller houses and his mother in the third house. His father comes home but lives during the week in Birmingham, I believe. The two on the right side of the road are for the caretakers, you know, the lawn and garden, and I believe the second one is for the housekeeper. Those two gates are motorized now, but were formerly opened one at a time by the same man. He would open one and allow passage, then close it and mosey down to the other one for the repeat procedure. They open now by remote and supposedly one will not open until the other is closed. Down at that curve to the left, there are houses to the right back in there behind the trees that are occupied but were former slave quarters. You can get to them now only by the road that goes beside the school.

"Land as a part of that estate goes on forever, I told her. "I don't know how much it is, but the Burtons own the two big banks in Decatur and Huntsville, and I don't know what is in Birmingham and maybe other places, too. They are extremely private but never unfriendly. Sonny went into the Marines before I ever knew him or knew about him, because they were so private. Sonny was sent to school back East somewhere, it is assumed, and then he went to the Navel academy, and into the Marine Corps for active duty. When he got out of the Marines, we would see him as he would ride to the bank with his mother, to and from work."

I continued explaining as best I knew the Burton's and how they lived in their privacy. "My friend and I were working out back one day when this little 1952 Plymouth convertible drove up. Sonny Burton stepped out. My friend and I were keenly interested in cars so we talked about the little convertible. Though we didn't discuss it at the time, we wonder why a rich person drove such a cheap car like a Plymouth."

"At a lag in the car talk, Sonny Burton asked us about that huge number of Terrell boys who were in and around the town and how they were treating us. Sonny never waited for our response. Instead, he said, 'I have spent several years training and teaching Marine Corps self defense.' He continued, 'I have seen and heard of what goes on around here and I think I can help if you guys want to work with me.'

We both agreed in unison. It was like the offer of a dream to the two of us. We were both rather small and we were both badgered unmercifully at times when there were two or more of those people around.

"Pick two days and I will stop by and teach the two of you for two hours each day," he said, "and just so you don't ask, what I get out of it is the satisfaction of seeing you two be able to defend yourselves." He went on to add, "I know all the stories, even how you two became friends. This is a game the adults have played for as long as even my father can remember, they put their kids out to do their dirty work, they laugh about it in their Sunday yard parties. It needs to stop, and it has to stop at a level in our society where it is making the biggest mess right now, and that is with you guys, at least the young people."

Sonny went on to tell about the martial arts training that he had conducted at a Marine Corps base in North Carolina and how he had taken on the task of developing another training facility in Arizona. "There are no weapons involved," Sonny informed us, so either of your barns can suffice as a training facility. Later on into the training, if you like, we can go to staff training where you use a 6-foot pole, but we have to do that outside."

"My friend and I sat up facilities in both barns," I explained. "Tuesdays and Thursdays were in my barn. My friend's barn was for his practice and I used my own but sometimes we worked out together. After close to two years, Sonny arrived one day and said, 'when both of you can take me one on one, we are through with the classes.' He was moving back to Arizona because his wife hated it here so badly, and Sonny agreed, 'not everybody can live like they live in a prison.'

I told him that day, "I think I can take you now, Sonny," because I had speed and quickness that Sonny did not have, or so my coach had stated. Instead of a test-out on Sonny, he put the two of us against each other for the first time. I won the first bout, but Sonny wanted to take the test outside. I lost in the expanded space because the speed mattered less with more space to work in. For a couple of months, he worked us in spaces where we could work off of trees, parked cars and ditch banks, actually just about any thing that could be found."

Sonny came another day and told us it was time to test out. My friend took him the first time. I never tested out. "No need," Sonny assured me, "you are better and quicker than he is."

We both missed Sonny for a long time, still do, actually, and it has been close to a year.

"I know who the other one was," Willow admitted. "Didn't he move away to Georgia or somewhere?"

"Yep, that's him," I answered, "and the tests by the Terrell boys who didn't believe that there was much to the report of how skilled we both were, rather picked up after he moved away. I guess the Terrells and the Thompsons around here, maybe some other kin too, figured that we would work on them as a team, and they were right." I hesitated for just a moment. "The worst part of this entire thing is that I don't want to hurt anyone," I assured her, "and I don't even want to have to defend myself. I just don't want to fight."

"You don't have to defend yourself to me," Willow assured me, "because I have had to defend you already back before we learned what you were capable of doing to somebody who attacked you."

"You had to defend me?"

"I did, and two of the Terrell sisters did too, and their cousin Julie, and everybody teased us because they knew I was love struck and the Terrell sisters were like, well, sisters to you." She giggled, "and I am laughing at everybody else and not you or me or the Terrell girls, but, oh wow, did we get the last laugh at the rest of them when you kicked that kid and his buddy's butts at the basketball game that night."

I remembered that one. "That was the time that those two kids were unsnapping bras and I grabbed the hand of one when he tried to unsnap the bra of 'Big John' Terrell's sister. It was half time and the other one grabbed me by the collar and dragged me out onto the basketball court."

"Wow, that was beautiful," Willow giggled, "you let him drag you and you were sitting on the floor and those two goons were goading you to get up and you did a sitting spin and kicked the legs from under the one who pulled you out there and was atop that one by the time his backside hit the floor. You hit him in the chest, with a massive forearm shot, then almost like in the same motion stood straight up and kicked the other one in the chest and he fell half way across the gym." Willow was trying to hold her mouth it seemed, which was her way of holding back from laughing too hard. "It was so funny," she said, "and so beautiful after having to endure all the teases that we did over your being such a coward."

I pretended to ask, "me, a coward? Actually, I knew I acted like I was a coward because I didn't want to fight. We were trained to avoid fighting. I preferred to be called a coward then to have to hurt people, anyway."

"Yes, that's what the other girls said," she assured me. "I think the best part of all that night is when you helped up the second one and literally threw him back across to where the first one lay. You slid him face down on his stomach right up against his partner, then forced him to pick his buddy up and to 'take him outside and beat the hell out of him 'for getting your stupid ass hurt.'"

"All modesty aside as I bow like the star of the half-time show," I said, "I did get a thrill out of the way the crowd protected me and the way they cheered. Really, I was eating up the attention and feeling somewhat comfortable about hurting somebody. I felt good enough about it then that I felt terrible later."

"You did make a believer out of the school that night," Willow assured me. "They all understood after that how you could walk away even when people were calling you names."

"I need to dig a bit of information from you, if you don't mind," I requested. "It has bothered me for better than half a year, which is why I really need to ask, and because nobody has ever quizzed me about it, what does the student body think about my altercation with that coach last fall?"

"Altercation?" Willow giggled a bit and smiled. "I heard it was more of a cake walk. Anyway, in response to the question, at first, some of the kids thought maybe you had hidden behind the door and sucker punched him, or something, but Jack Leubenthall and 'Big John' Terrell swore that you were able to overpower both of them at the same time and you locked them in those storage areas. Big John, as you affectionately call him, said that there was nobody that he knew of that could take you, and Jack agreed. Also, what you might really enjoy is that John and Jack told some kids that even though you did not hide and sucker punch the coach because you did not have to, that it would have been justified if you had."

"Jack and John were sent by the coach to force me to clean the gym of shoe marks, which I refused to do," I informed her, "and their instructions were to physically restrain me from leaving the gym, hiding in the dressing rooms or elsewhere. They tried to restrain me and I threw them both in the storage compartments and locked them in. I was told that his putting two other students on me is why the coach was fired."

"And why the principal ruled that you acted in self defense," Willow added.

"Plus the fact that Julie Terrell and I both stood firm and stated that he had assured me that he had boasted regarding the paddle board that he had, 'I have a weapon and I know how to use it.' He brought his weapon back in the visitor's shower where he was trying to force me to clean it. He swung the thing at me and, from a view in a mirror, I stepped away from the blow and he hit his hand against a lavatory. He screamed curse words and threats at me that were the worst that I have ever heard. I punched him with the heel of both hands until he was standing motionless in the middle of the floor, then I threw him across the room, hurting him enough that he had to be removed by an ambulance."

"Actually, I was attempting to bounce him off the wall for a body slam maneuver but hit a lavatory instead. May I ask another unrelated but important question, Willow?"

"Of course, you can, but be careful." she assured me, "or I may not allow any more after this one."

"Why are we stopped here on this hill at a fork in the road overlooking half of Morgan County, the Tennessee Valley and Redstone Arsenal?"

"Hmm, that's a lot more than I feel like I can answer without some time to think," she pondered a bit and added, "could I do the 'stopped' part and get back to the place and the scenic value later?"

"Okay," I agreed, "a multi-part question can be handled one part at a time, I guess."

"I stopped," she responded, almost apologetically, "hoping I might get a kiss and some sort of expression from you of your eternal love for me."

"What," I screeched in pretense, "a kiss? What is this that a regular, everyday, run-of-the-mill, sweetest, most awesomely outstanding and beautiful girl in the world should expect to pilfer a kiss from a basketball half-time entertainment star?"

Willow got what she stopped for without any resistance at all. Not being so very experienced at enjoying the type of kiss that Willow is capable of, that one raised the bar and she knew it.

"What do you think about that Mr. half-time star?"

"Tough question," I admitted, "how about I get another sample to be sure I can give you a qualified answer." Willow made certain there was no lack of samples from which a qualified judgment might be made.

"Damn, now I think I passed out and missed the second kiss," I spoke as she flashed her smile of satisfaction, or triumph, or whatever that fabulous smile was intended to indicate.

"Nope, you got it," she assured me, "but in your weakened condition my kisses are just too powerful for you."

"I think I'm too weak to do the next walk," I told her, but got only a smile, a shift into reverse and a drive-away to the next exercise session.

"Hey, on a serious note, girl," I spoke as seriously as I knew how, "this thing with us started a day ago on a low, low note, really for both of us, and you have taken yesterday to be the most meaningful day of my life, while today is starting out to be so much better, and we joke about me being overpowered, and I am thinking it is like a dream to me, something almost unreal, while I know my pains are real but I am excited to be allowed to withstand them just so I can share this time with you and you are sitting in the driver's seat thinking that I am serving you up a bunch of romantic bullshit, right?"

"No, I am so sorry, really," she begged, "I was soaking it up and enjoying every word, and so what if it is a bunch of romantic bullshit, neither of us have had enough experience with relationships such that we know just exactly how to say or do things."

"We're having so much fun together, laughing and joking and kissing and saying 'I love you,' and we are no more than a couple of kids who are wrapped up in each other and the adults will tell us not to take it serious."

Willow hit the brakes, hard. The tires locked up. "Look left and tell me what you see," she instructed me.

"I see about 200 acres of plowed fields, actually it is 203 and I know because I have plowed every acre for the third year in a row," I declared, "so what is your point?"

"A kid did that?

MY WILLOW   65

"I love you, Willow."

"I love you too, young gentleman, and we are going to have to take this thing with the two of us and carry it together and protect it from ourselves and from each other, and fight off other people, the elements, society, . . . ! Don't say a word, we can joke about it and cry about it, even lie about it, cheer it, lament it, and do whatever we want to do about it, because it is ours, and it has to be kept by us for us. We can do it, because it is ours."

"I don't have a lot of confidence because I don't have experience, I guess."

"I love you and you love me, and we love each other because we believe in each other. You do believe in me, right?

"I do!"

"I now pronounce us, . . . ," Willow joked. "As two people who have confidence in each other, believe in each other, because I will be with you forever and always. How about that for your confidence? And, I know you want a kiss but you are not going to get one because there is a lady coming across the road who I have to get out of the car and go greet!"

-0-

"I am so sorry, Ma'am, he's hurt and can't roll down the window." I am Willow Preston . . . ,"

"Louise Landry, his mother's absolute best friend. I just came from there to see how he was doing." The two just opened arms and embraced, making me feel good about both of them. That was easy! Willow was the greatest for all the reasons that are good and Louise was best described as a character and a half. Louise was the fun friend who kept my mother off my case many times, especially the many times that I might have gotten out of line, those that Mama knew about.

Willow and Louise chatted for a short while. Willow opened my door, rolled down the window and pushed the door back closed again. "Hello, Louise," I greeted her nicely, "you owe me a kiss because you just cost me one, you know, bouncing your butt across the road at just the wrong time when her lips were all fired up to lay one on me."

"Your mother told me that there was not a damned thing wrong with you, just mean oozing out of a few little extra holes, little cuts and abrasions," Louise laughed. "She told me that you are milking a few little marks from a bit of a fracas, trying to hit on this pretty little innocent girl here."

"From what you see so far," I asked, "don't you think she is worth me pretending that I got hurt real bad?"

"Yep, that little girl is a prize alright, but I actually know how bad you are hurt, silly boy" Louise admitted, "I had to take Danny to school this morning, late of course, and Ms. Haggerty told me how bad it was and how worried her husband was about you." She hesitated, "and the girl," she giggled a bit, "Dr. Haggerty said he had never in a lifetime seen anyone who was so devoted and attached to someone as she is to you."

"Yeah, the doctor said, 'since we can't get rid of her we have to take advantage of her,' and she is doing all their rehabilitation therapy work for them, under their direction of course. We have to go to the doctor every day and she takes me through my exercises, like a pro would do it."

Sensing that we had a schedule, Louise opened the car door, rolled up my window and suggested, "you two go somewhere and catch up on all those kisses that you are missing." She looked at Willow, "be assured, Willow, that we all love you for what you are doing, and if you don't mind, give him a couple of extra kisses to make up for the one that I caused him to miss."

Willow shook her head from side to side and said, "But he gets so weak and passes out, or pretends that he does, and says he doesn't remember me giving him a kiss, and I just have to do it again, over and over."

"When I get over this, I'm going to have them do it again so Willow can take care of me."

Louise closed the door, and Willow and I headed to the bluff for the routine exercise routine. Well, we started anyway. Willow suddenly jammed the brakes. Looking at the rearview mirror, she said, "Louise is waving." When the car stopped, Willow got out to go back to meet Louise.

The ladies chatted a bit. I waited, thinking. Daddy said that talking to Louise was to be called "wacky-yacky" because Louise was so funny.

To me it seemed "my Willow has found another fan in Louise. That woman was strangely normal for Newton's Bluff and she kept telling me that I am the one that is normal and that these others who seem to be at odds with me were the screwed up ones. One can never be sure, but I feel comfortable around Louise and my entire family loves her."

"Hey, Louise wants to walk with us," Willow said as she returned, "so I told her that we would both love that, okay?"

"Super," I agreed, "and you can use some help getting me in and out of this thing."

"Louise is going back to get her Jeep and follow us," Willow told me. "She said her husband put seat covers on it yesterday and she is dying to show it to you."

"Yeah, her Jeep and my Studebaker have both been shared projects of her husband David, my dad and me," I informed Willow. "David is a great body man and not a very knowledgeable mechanic but Daddy could direct him and he did well to get the old Army Jeep back to running and looking good." With Willow seeming to show an interest, I continued with the car talk. "They got the idea to move Louise's Jeep down to our barn and we all had to get it finished and running before we could get mine out. It was great fun, and Daddy ran lights down to the barn for us so we could work at night."

"Now that reminds me," Willow interrupted, "do you sleep?"

"Okay," I admitted, "so David and Daddy worked at night, except on the weekends and it was mostly David and me doing the body work on this thing here, speaking of my Raymond Loewy designed Studebaker Starliner coupe."

"That we love so well and call a 'thing'," Willow added.

"No, that we like so well and call a 'thing'," I corrected. "I have to use up all the love that I have inside me for you."

We were arriving at the bluff, Willow stopped, looked me in the eye and asked, "so you really think you love me, huh?"

"Nancy and I believe so, yes!" She kissed me again. "Wow! Methinks if this is not love then somebody is going to have to come up with a better word to define it."

"Then why, my love," Willow pleaded, "did we have to go through all that back at the fork in the road?"

"Because you are where you are in our society and I am where I am," I argued, but it was more like a discussion, "and I have no confidence that I can keep you and I don't want to spend another minute on this planet without you being in that tiny little segment of time."

"Where am I?"

"I am at the bottom, Willow," I assured her, "and you are far above me in every respect, as rich as the day is long, never having to see a dark cloud in your life, beautiful, sophisticated . . . , and I sit here . . . , I sit here and this is what I am."

"I am with you and that is all that matters," she promised me. She sat erect, "let me explain it to you this way, my darling one, you have my heart and I have yours, and where ever either of us go we will be together, and I can't imagine any other reason to come to this exact same spot except to pledge ourselves to each other. It's the spot, where we pledged ourselves to each other, we didn't speak our love but we expressed it because we didn't know how to say the words, Nancy had not yet trained us," she added.

"You are a part of me and none of me wants to sit in the car and feel sorry for any other part of me," as she ran around the car and opened my door, gave me a monster kiss and a huge triumphant smile. "I have you right where I want you right now, young man, and I am giving it to you straight, you are stuck with me and you had better learn to live with it because wherever you may think I am, socially or otherwise, we are together, come along for the big ride, relax and enjoy."

"Okay, so I'll relax and enjoy," I agreed, "but please understand, honey, that this is so much and it is so good, so wonderful, so unbelievably awesome that I am going to have to lean on you to keep me under control."

"You do the same here, deal?" We nodded agreement in unison. "Now we seal the deal with a kiss . . . , and you can get your butt out of the car.

-0-

It will take a bit of time for Louise to get here, so while we wait I'll tell you one that she and my mother got me into, or maybe I got myself into it and they didn't get me out of it. Yeah, that sounds more like what happened.

The farm is two miles or more from the church and couldn't anybody hear the tractor, as loud as it was, but I dreaded coming home Sunday's listening to the list of who came by, from church, and what each individual non-sinner had to say about me and the reflections that seemed to be placed on my parents' ability to raise kids. My life seemed dominated by the bitchings and the whinings of the church folks doing no more than compounding the frustrations.

With my bad attitude, I usually told my mother to tell certain ones of them that I knew about their week-day sins and would have to testify to knowing, which is why I didn't make it to services on Sunday morning. The biggest part of what contributed to this ruckus, for which I was putting a slice of the coincidental blame on myself, was that I had no idea of how to suspect that Fats Terrell, he is JD's daddy, would be the one designated to be the house caller, the one to be coming by to jump up and down on my hind end.

"These tales of the troublesome Terrells just keep on coming," I related to Willow.

"I know you have told me that before, but I couldn't be sure you had told me what the sin was, but Fats Terrell came by with his Bible, I think last Sunday," Mama said, "and when I told him that, he said, 'why, that little son-of-a-bitch' and I let him have it up 'side the head with my broom."

"Is that why you keep that broom handy, Mama?" I asked.

"No, just for sweeping, but I busted his left ear and the upper lip on the other side."

"Hold on Mama,' I asked, "did he stay around long enough for you to assess the damage?"

"No, but Louise was laughing about it one day when she came down to bring me some quilt pieces."

"I'm wondering if Louise Landry didn't come down to tell you about the damage and used some rags as an excuse to visit, thus to tell you," I suggested.

"Well, yeah, maybe," Mama admitted, "but she comes down here so I can teach her how to quilt, anyway."

"And to get her cigarettes that you two hide in my room," I added.

"That way we can blame it on you if her husband catches her," Mama again admitted with one of her patented I-got-you giggles this time.

"She likes me, too," I added in respect, and she knows that I would cover for her if necessary. But I need to know one more thing," I requested, "does Louise Landry know how being hit with one broom can cause severe damage to two sides of the face all at once."

MY WILLOW

"Well, no, she didn't know how many times I hit him," Mama assured me.

How much time I expended laughing, I couldn't even guess, but I was getting my fair share of chuckles, and Mama joined right in as if to allow me to know that she and Louise had spent a bit of time themselves laughing about the ruckus. "Mama," I asked, "did you have to beat the man with a broomstick?"

"No, I didn't," she assured me, "but I must have not been thinking about it much 'cause I kept on hitting him until he got out to the road so he could outrun me."

Laughter was overwhelming but I found a hint of respite and asked, "Please, Mama, tell me that you didn't lose control so badly that you ran after your victim and beat him unmercifully after busting up his face."

"Naw, I didn't have nothing' to do with bustin' his face. No, I didn't," she added. "I hit him once when I busted that ear and maybe three or four, maybe more, times before the got out the front door and went across the porch and busted down the porch rail there," as she pointed straight toward the front door, "and I think he busted his upper lip when he went face down in the front yard when he busted down the porch."

Knowing that I was to fix all that was fixable around the house, I went to the window and drew back the draperies fully expecting to see a broken porch rail section in the front yard. There it was. My thought was simply that it had to be repaired and I wondered why my mother had not told me about it, yet I knew that I would never use the front door until I finished plowing or cultivating.

The laughing had stopped, anyway. I dreaded having to fix that porch when I didn't really have the time to go by the lumber yard and get the pieces. I thought for a moment, released the drape and turned to my mother. "Mom," I carefully planned my words, "you know you used a weapon and followed the man into a public street and used that weapon on him in public, or so it can be said?"

"Your daddy told me about that," she replied with a smile, then let go with an arousing laugh. "He said the Sheriff might be coming by," she bounced with laughter. "He drove up in front and I didn't even see or hear him 'til he knocked on the front door. I just went to the door not thinking that I might be the one in trouble, opened it up and said, 'John ain't here,' and he come back with, 'we come to see you this time, Ma'am.'" Thinking that this might be the spot where Mama was to realize that she might get in trouble, I anticipated that she might quit her laughing and giggling, but she tried to just continue her story that was thoroughly riddled with interruptions of laughing and giggling.

I interrupted. "Wait a minute, Mama," I pleaded for an answer, "did you not realize that you might have been arrested for what you did?"

"Ha! Me arrested? Are you serious? And, for pounding the crap out of some busybody for coming into my house, calling my son a son-of-a-bitch?" Certainly, my mother was thoroughly comfortable in her status, so much so that she was not at all bothered by my attempt to break her spirit as she continued, "And, as me and that sheriff and his young deputy was laughing that day, I could have whupped his fat ass right on into the judge's house, had I wanted to, and wouldn't have been no way that charges could be brought against me."

"Then why did the Sheriff even take the time to come by?" I inquired.

"Your daddy sent them by to explain it to me," she assured me, "because he knew I wouldn't believe what your daddy told me."

"So, Daddy did contact Sheriff Brown just to be certain?" I asked.

"Yeah, he did," Mama said, "but the fact is, everybody just about in this whole county is laughing about it and the Baptist Church is really ticked off at us, calling us heathens and saying stuff about the bad things God is going to do to us."

"I guess what they are saying, Mama, is that they are going to do things to us," I suggested.

"Well, your daddy has already talked to that sheriff about it and he talked to that Baptist preacher, so I think everybody knows what they can and can't do," Mama assured me, then she started to giggle again. I figured she just had so much built up from the fun stuff before and had to let it out but she told me about the Sheriff going to see Fats Terrell. "That young deputy told me about this one," Mama said. "He told me that he and Sheriff Brown pulled up in front of the Terrell's house and Fats came running out like maybe Fats was the one who called for us to come over, but the Sheriff got out, made Fats put his hands on the hood of the car and the Sheriff said 'spread 'em.' Now this deputy said," as Mama continued her story, "that he was bustin' a gut trying to keep from laughing as he patted Ol' Fats down for the Sheriff to see if he was totin' a gun. Then he said the Sheriff told him that he might have to come back and put the handcuffs on him and take him in."

"Hey, this is getting to be fun, Mama," I interrupted, "and I'll bet that scared Ol' Fats Terrell, didn't it?"

"I guess it really has got him scared right now," Mama explained as she giggled, "because they told Terrell that I had not made up my mind yet about whether or not to file charges."

"Yeah, but you hit him, didn't you?" I queried.

"I did that but, it seems that the Sheriff has got Fats convinced that he committed assault by cussing you," she assured me, "and that's what he calls verbal assault and that made me hitting Terrell be in self defense."

"It makes sense," I agreed, "but I might think that it would be a big old mess of a thing to prosecute if that one ever came to court."

"Oh, I'm guessing that's why the Sheriff is handling it the way he is," Mama explained, "and he's trying to get those church people to leave you alone."

"I'm not worried about those people, Mama," I said. "Ever since they got that fat-assed preacher to come in here three years ago, they try to power over everybody in an effort to try to run this neck of the woods, it's been a battle between me and him and he's been pumping up the congregation every Sunday to jump on either Daddy or Lloyd Marshal or me. Some of it actually has been fun and I know we are

MY WILLOW

laughing about this latest thing with Fats Terrell, but it could have gotten serious and still could get out of hand if allowed to do so."

"Let's see what happens Sunday," Mama suggested. "Sheriff Brown has ordered Fats to go testify at his church and tell everybody about calling you the bad name and starting the fight with me, and he is to apologize for what he has done to this family and what his preacher has done."

I agreed that the Sheriff had done a rather admirable job but I didn't believe that Fats would testify to his congregation about these few little sins.

"He better do it," Mama argued, "since that little deputy is going to be at the church on Sunday to hear what he says, and he thinks I will file charges against him if he doesn't do it like the Sheriff told him to." She hesitated for a moment, looked at me and inquired, "Do you really have something on Fats Terrell that he is afraid you might tell?"

"Yeah, he caught Bob and me taking a peek at the business between him and a girl in the bushes down by the rock quarry," I responded.

"A girl? What kind of business was he doing with a girl in the bushes?" she asked loudly, rather demandingly.

"Fifteen dollars worth, Mama," I replied.

"And, he's scared you are going to tell on him?"

"Of course he is, Mama," I told her, "otherwise he wouldn't have over reacted when you told him that the reason I didn't come to church. Bob and I both promised him that we wouldn't tell and he thought I had broken that vow." I was not at all certain and I likely shouldn't say anything, but Terrell is trying to make it sound like there is a feud between us so that if I say anything he can say that I made it all up like I do with all the other lies that I make up against him.

Mama shook her head as if to denote a discovery, and said, "then he would have been right."

"Like you said, the tales of the troublesome Terrells just keep on coming in," Willow agreed. "Will we ever get this thing stopped?"

"Not as long as there are adult Terrells who refuse to direct their kids properly," I answered, "and the pulpits keep preaching hate and using fear tactics as a way to control the masses."

Suddenly Willow speaks, "here comes Louise, is that purple?"

"Out of the West come the thundering Goodyears, a cloud of dust, and a hearty 'hi-yo-purple,' the Rose Ranger rides again! It only hurts when I laugh or when I don't laugh. Actually, my love, her husband David and I mixed the paint and it was supposed to be rose, but when David sprayed it . . . , oh, well!"

CHAPTER SIX

Encounter of the Other Kind

When four people are found in a place well suited for ambush, then ambush may be suspected but in his condition could he protect his love from physical harm, or himself, or his friend? What about his enemies and would they need protection?

LOUISE WALKED AHEAD for some reason. She stopped, looked back and put a hand up to indicate that we should stop, and placed a finger over her lips to quiet us. They had walked down to the 2640 stone and had come back almost all the way back to the bluff. I had made plans to show Willow the little lagoon.

When Louise walked back to inform us of her concern. "I heard a car door slam and I think it was a female voice but I need to investigate before my paranoia makes us all nervous."

Willow agreed that under the circumstances that we were likely better off to play it safe, "This river is infected with Terrells and Johnson grass, so his daddy says."

"I have an idea," I suggested. "Through the brush just past those rocks to the left is a tiny path that will wind you through a sassafras thicket to a clearing. Straight ahead is a beautiful oak tree and you will find a path to the right that goes straight or directly to the bluff."

Louise trusted my directions and started to go toward the oak tree but stopped. We all agreed that the best approach was for Willow and me to be very casual and walk slowly. "Are you okay," Louise questioned?

"My legs are fine, bruised and cut but functional according to my hero here, named Willow Preston, Miss Sympathy USA," I rather whispered to the two companions. "Willow and I will goof around and go in the direction of the little whirlpool bayou that the local kids and I adopted a couple of summers back."

"You cannot move your left arm at all and the right one is not a lot better," Willow was argumentative and quite demanding in her assessment of my condition, "so what are you going to do if they attack you?"

"Kick some ass," I said, "and I apologize for the language in your presence, my love, and for the disrespect that I may seem to show that is not the respect that I have for you, I love you, Willow, but anger brings out these things in me."

"It's okay and I understand," Willow said as she pointed to Louise peeling off the trail toward the bluff.

Louise turned toward her companions with a thumbs up when she found the trail by the oak tree. The second thumbs up communicated that she had found the other trail was going up to the bluff. She didn't tell Willow and me what her plans were but we assumed that she was going for help.

I told Willow about the trail that the kids and I had cut through to a little whirlpool lagoon not realizing that if anybody wanted to ambush us, that would be the place least likely for them to be seen. We also kept watching for sight of Louise on the ridge where the trail ran.

"There she is," Willow pointed. "She is giving a signal. I laughed because it was so typical of Louise and her fun way of doing things as a routine. The first signal was to push up her breasts, then with both hands made an imaginary line blow both knees . . . ,"

"Women," Willow giggled to make issue about her ability to decipher hand signals. Then Louise showed them three chop signals, which Willow interpreted to mean three women, then she ran toward the bluff again. They watched for a moment and saw that Louise had hidden behind a tree for a while, then she stepped out and signaled by pointing down and spinning the hand in a circle.

Willow waved back to indicate that we had seen her. "She is signaling that the three women are going down," Willow interpreted. "Does that mean that they are going down to the whirlpool lagoon?"

"Obviously, they are local women and they are just as obviously up to no good or they would wait on the bluff or somewhere out in the open where they can be seen," I told Willow as a word of caution. "I imagine also," I told her, "that Louise may know that she can block the path of the three women if they try to escape. I knew they could go out through an old iron gate that the Wheeler Wildlife Preserve had installed."

MY WILLOW | 75

Instead, we saw Louise as she ran to her Jeep. We couldn't see what was happening but felt then that she was going for help. The Jeep didn't move, however. Willow and I waited. After a moment, Louise stepped out from behind her Jeep and gave a two-powerful-fists-in-the-air type of signal.

"That means that we have help coming, and that it is powerful help" Willow interpreted.

"How do you know these signals, love?"

"Would you believe that I am brilliant."

"Of course I would, then if I had said 'no' I would be afraid you would push me into the river."

"How about if I said I was trying to impress you so I could get a kiss?"

"It worked!" These two were really getting good at the kissing business. Willow was awfully good at it and I was a really good student, thoroughly dedicated to my practicing.

"You held me with your right hand," Willow noted with surprise.

"I wasn't thinking and I wanted to hold you so badly that I think I just did it," I assured her, "but according to the list in your pocket, today is when I have to start arm exercises, anyway, so I don't guess any harm was done."

"We're supposed to start on the next walk and we have to do two miles this time."

"I can do it," I assured her, "I can do anything with you."

"Then let's go kick some butt," Willow joked though she acted serious.

"I'm game," I said. "but I don't think with three women there is going to be any butt kicking, just a whole lot of bitching and screaming and threatening me with their husbands. With women my love, there is pushing and hair pulling but that would only be if two of the women couldn't agree as to which of their husbands they got to threaten me with the most."

"What about me?" Willow asked in a manner that seemingly indicated that she was looking for my approval, and I knew I would bury the first bitch who ever tried to lay a hand on Willow, whether it be socially correct or against the law, it mattered none whatsoever. Or, she might have wanted to know if I could physically protect her if the women tried to attack her.

"No pain is great enough that I wouldn't protect you, honey," I assured her, "but these are women and women only talk, bitch, threaten and scream."

"Louise only saw women," Willow said, "but there may be husbands or some of the boys who attacked you or both."

I stopped for a moment. I assured Willow that I did not believe anything was in the offing but it was too late to do anything other than to walk in on it and find out. "We have about 40 yards to go and we have to go over some rocks to the left and then we can see down into the lagoon, I said. "I suggest that if there are a lot of people down in there that we wait for the power to show and that may take some time but it could be in short order. I know, Willow," I assured her, "that my mother will be appearing on the bluff in just a moment unless the sheriff is not already on the premises before she can get here, and I assume that is what Louise meant when she gave us the power signal."

Willow and I walked toward the lagoon. We could see the bluff when we rounded a slight turn in the river's edge. Mama and Louise gave us the signal to note that they were there and on the job and turned to walk away. "They know where the iron gate is and we can be certain that they will be in the lagoon by the time we are, or no more than a moment thereafter," I said, "so that is the power that we need, I am hoping."

I could not be certain that I was understanding what I was seeing but Willow was appearing to be excited about arriving at the lagoon and I was battling a personal quandary as to what to expect and how to handle it. I was confused and was concerned as well. Willow turned to me as I was negotiating the rocks to get to the top of the six feet or so of rocky barrier that surrounded the little lagoon. "I can see four people," she said, "one huge man and three women. It is just a slight grade down to the water's edge so when you get to the top, I am going down there and address the people."

"Please, Willow," I pleaded, "let me handle these people, and I might get hurt but if you get hurt, I will surely die trying to kill all the people."

Willow did not hear me. Willow did not heed me, at any rate. I looked down the grade toward the water and she was already by the water's edge and taking control. "Hey, sir," she addressed the man, Shorty Terrell, the biggest and so he was convinced, the baddest of the Terrells, "go over there and take yourself a seat on those rocks," as she pointed as she made her stern yet courteous demand and pranced about like could be imagined the drill sergeant would do, purposefully placing one foot ahead of the other with all the authority that goes with the command and some borrowed.

Terrell looked across the lagoon at the tiny little sweetheart of mine and mumbled but didn't move. Willow continued her deliberate entry toward what surely was a position where she may establish a control point. She is woman and women do control, I was quite aware of that. Were I not then my Willow was giving me a strong lesson in the way that it is done to perfection.

"You sir, I repeat," Willow demanded with much more authority that even I could imagine would ever be issued from that tiny little precious example of womankind, "sit your fat ass on those rocks over there or I will sit your fat ass on those rocks over there, and you may mumble quietly if you choose but you shall not address the group or me here except with my permission. Sir, am I making it clear to you that you may speak when I address you? Sir, sit where I direct you to sit and I am insisting that you sit there."

I was not able to completely comprehend what I was seeing, and that was a huge 300-pound bully being pushed around by someone, and female at that, of

MY WILLOW   77

about one-third of the total mass. Shorty sat but was slow about it, maybe even not to be sure himself what was happening and that he was doing it.

It is sort of like he acknowledged but just enough so he could deny it later if he needed to, so it appeared. Too, it must be known that I knew Shorty. Furthermore I knew that what was going through Shorty's mind at the time was "ain't no little tight ass telling me what to do."

Reasonably well astounded, I surveyed the group. There was Shorty and Shorty's wife, Emma Thompson Terrell, as the kids and the other men around affectionately addressed her. Then, there were her two sisters-in-law, the wives of the two Terrell twins named Fats and Jim. No, no, not the wives. They were named Lois and Denise.

Willow turned to the women, inasmuch as she had walked on past them as she focused on Shorty, "Ladies, especially the one married to this fat piece of shit, please come on over here and sit with the man who was ever so gracious as to allow himself to lower his slow-motion fat ass down to that rock that he has one hand on, and did not cause me to have to expend the energy to seat him," as she quickly turned and with lightening speed flashed a potentially devastating spin kick about two inches from Shorty Terrell's nose, and his hind end caressed the rock where he was seated as he was instructed to seat himself. Shorty's eyes showed maximum surprise and mine were slightly larger.

As the ladies advanced slowly in Shorty's direction, Emma Thompson Terrell lagged back slightly, and I had not advanced to the much wider area of beach over to the side where the one I totally and completely worshiped was taking complete control, so I needed to pass by the ladies to get to Willow. I might have bumped Miss Emma Thompson Terrell ever so slightly, but somehow or another, she tripped and fell into the cool pool of April water.

Willow turned in the direction of the horrible scream, then in the same motion back toward Shorty likely to see the reaction of Shorty to his wife accidentally falling into the water or to check his position, maybe even to see if he had remained seated as she had ordered. Whatever the reason she turned, Shorty bellowed out an unmentionable and charged in the direction of Willow. She dropped in the sand with a spin maneuver from her back side and firmly planted her left heel what seemed to be maybe a foot deep into his fat gut, then with explosive speed, rolled and flipped behind him. Extending the same motion, Willow put both feet into that horrible man's hind end and launched him, kicked his fat ass into the middle of the lagoon, conveniently placed in the proximity of his cursing and sputtering wife.

Needless to say, I was dumbfounded! I could only look at the skill of Willow's maneuvers as if choreographed for dance, and mutter, "Son-of-a-bitch, where did she learn those maneuvers?" I muttered a couple of other things as well, like "this is the reason she was anxious to get into the fray, so she could surprise me, or maybe she just wanted to try this stuff that she had learned on a human, or maybe she just wanted to kick some ass. Actually, she had said that but my eyes didn't know what my eyes have now seen."

Willow bounced up from the beach and began to brush the sand from her jeans, slowly and deliberately, rather demonstrating to her audience that this was the routine that she followed all the time and though it was a boring routine, it had to be repeated. Different audiences reacted differently, but the routine was so commonly performed there just was so little excitement left in what was accomplished. Ho-hum.

However, as Shorty righted himself chest deep in the little lagoon. The water was only three or four feet deep, so Shorty popped straight up gasping for breath with two eyes that looked the size of a wash tub. He looked at the wonderful and tiny little 115-pound Willow who addressed him, "Sir, I am certain that we all here assume that the reason you dove into the pool was to save your clumsy wife from drowning, so please get her out of the water and let's see if we can find out why you all came down in the typical Terrell fashion by the pool to greet us, you know to ambush us."

"We know about ambushes with our recent experiences," Willow calmly and purposely announced to her small audience, "but all are not as damaging as the one yesterday. Are you with me, folks? I am referring to the ambush that your family members conducted yesterday with the love of my life as your victim." Willow put the back of her hand to my cheek for a single affectionate stroke, and yelled as loudly as she could, "the one that got me this pissed off!"

Willow then turned to the two women, Lois and Denise and said, likely loud enough and demandingly enough but it was at the top of her lungs anyway, "now . . . sit . . . your . . . asses . . . down . . . and . . . listen . . . , both of you!" The women seated themselves.

My mother and Louise stepped out onto the clearing, both doing all they could possibly do to hold back a horrendous laugh. Willow was entertaining, actually scaring the daylights out of some people, me included.

Louise said, "Ida and I will gather some stuff to start us a bonfire so those two can get all dried off." Louise pointed out at the same time for Willow and me, "there are no vehicles up on the level of the bluff that these people could have driven themselves here in, so there possibly could have been a motive as we suspected before I split off to flank them. Ambush, Willow, is the correct word."

I surmised that Louise was establishing that they had suspected an ambush attack and that they had prepared for it. Whatever her motivation, I seemed to grasp the idea that Louise was assisting in her own way to scare these people more than they might have believed that they could be scared.

"You two," Willow addressed the wives of the Terrell twins and pointed to them, ladies we can all talk and figure out what is the urgency of this meeting or what it is all about. I want to remind all of you, however, that I am in complete control and I will not yield that control to anyone until I am ready to yield, or in

MY WILLOW

79

the event you decide that you can physically wrest it from me." She didn't slow, but continued in the confidence of control that she likely picked up from her preacher father.

"Mama can start the fire," she addressed Louise, "and you have your Jeep, Louise dear, so could you please grab a couple of blankets or quilts for these two," pointing to Shorty and Miss Emma and holding her keys to the Studebaker in case Louise chose them instead of her Jeep.

Louise was wonderful. She went with a huge smile pasted all across her face as Mama chattered with all of them like old friends, as she lighted the pile of leaves and branches with Louise's lighter. I recognized it because she always hid it in my room so they could tell her husband that it was mine. Willow, me and my mother were functioning just exactly like nothing was happening other than a bunch of close friends out for a friendly picnic.

Willow had center stage. Having spent considerable time with Nancy Bradley, she knew how to handle center stage. "My name is Willow Preston," she announced, "and I am here to take care of the one for whom I have more love that I know how to define, so let's leave the amount as simply 'immeasurable' and go on. I understand that everyone knows everyone else so I would like my patient and love object to address the group and tell me about each of you. It is not that I want to know so much but that I want to know it from his view."

Moving to center stage, I spoke. "I will start with the man, whom I know as Shorty Terrell and know no other name but Shorty who runs Newton's Bluff." I spotted Louise coming down the trail with blankets and mentioned that in his own manner, "Mr. Terrell gets the first blanket so he can put it around his wife, and he can have the other one to put around himself." I assisted both of them to demonstrate that I was fitting into the aura that Willow had established.

I continued. "Ms. Terrell is the wife of Shorty and the one we refer to as Emma Thompson Terrell, the town cryer, who runs around with her two sisters-in-law in tow announcing ill findings and what is to be done about them. Now these other two are Lois here, the one who married the twin Terrell brother before he got so fat and Denise here who did the same routine with the twin brother Jim but he is neither short nor fat, just Jim, and my Daddy likes Jim best of the bunch."

"My mama here," I continued with my introductory trip around the group, "you know her, but I can tell you that she is the one who slapped Lois' husband here up 'side the head with a broom one Sunday afternoon a couple of weeks ago for threatening me, calling me a sumbitch for plowing on Sunday, except maybe he was thinking I was getting back to his wife about doing that $15 whore that comes through here on Thursday. The Sheriff said he was going to have to tell you, but I see from your reaction that he did not. I apologize ma'am."

"Denise here doesn't say much but we should be able to hear from her a little later on, but she follows Emma Thompson Terrell and makes Emma appear to be more powerful by the numbers," I continued.

"Running right along, Louise here is Mama's quilting buddy and the one that I would never want Willow to ever know how much I love her. I steal all of her jokes and she lets me."

As I was going back around the group, I said, "I must assure you that before I came to town Shorty and Emma Thompson Terrell here ran the town of Newton's Bluff, Alabama. Now Emma, it is said, can sniff a dog fart and tell you whose dog it was and which direction the fart went in before the dog's owner can get his hand up to hold his nose." The Terrell's stirred a bit but Willow walked by to ensure that any movement beyond a stir would be addressed.

"Shorty called me a sumbitch when I was 14," I told them, "and Shorty said the only reason he didn't climb down off his tractor and beat me to death at that time was because there were laws that protected stupid-assed teenagers. That was the same reason he sent all his nephews and his wife's brother out to get me yesterday, too, I guess, but Willow is covering that part for Shorty here."

"Everybody is so quiet that it makes this easy," I told the group, "but I need to tell everybody about Willow. She is a bastard half-breed Penobscot Algonquin from Old Town, Maine and that ain't even the entire reason why I love her so completely, so now that we are all acquainted, I need to mention the seven cowards who were sent to attack me yesterday from ambush, no less, were the brother of Emma here, two sons of Lois here, two sons of Denise here, and Phillip Terrell and his little brother, the sons of the other fat-assed Terrell brother who lives about half way between here and the school house. Where is their mama today?"

Willow stepped in, "I have two questions: why Mr. Terrell did you send seven boys out to get six in trouble and to get the same six of them hurt really bad so they could ambush and hurt the person that I love more than life, and what is the purpose of this gathering?"

I met Willow at center stage and she retained her business-like demeanor as she whispered to him, "I am about to bust a gut to keep from laughing.

"Let me take over for just a second." She agreed.

"I had a question in there before Willow asked her two, primarily the whereabouts of Phillips mother, father or both, but I believe they are still trying to come up with bail money" I announced. Just for effect maybe, I hesitated, but didn't really slow down, "the reason," I said, "that Shorty sent the kids to get themselves hurt really badly . . . , excuse me, but I must digress for a point of information because you are wondering why we keep mentioning getting the boys hurt really badly and you are thinking that your boys didn't get hurt really badly, but this thing just started with your kids yesterday and starting and being over have time between them. Just for fun, don't tell them how pretty Willow is."

"Lois, can you tell us why Shorty sent out the kids?" Willow requested.

"It wasn't just Shorty but my husband was in on it," Lois responded, "and that preacher, too. They all went over there and helped that fat-assed preacher pack up and get out of town night before last and all the boys helped out. That's how it come about."

Willow asked, "Who is JD's mother?" She acknowledge Denise, "Ma'am was your husband and two boys in on the planning of the ambush attack?"

"They were all in on it but the plan was to rough him up a little bit," Denise admitted, "but Phillip was the oldest, and had to go to high school an extra year, and he had an old score to settle, he said."

"Miss Emma," Willow addressed Emma Thompson Terrell, "was your brother Clint in on any of the planning"

"No," Emma was surprised that she had to answer, "but he wasn't arrested or nothing."

"He wasn't arrested Miss Emma, and the Thompson side of the family needs to know this," I interrupted to announce, "Willow and Clint saved me from a lot more pain and discomfort than I have had to endure, and had Clint not gone to my classroom to get Willow then it is not much telling how long it would have been before I would have been found, and there is a small chance that I could have died had they not have gotten some good help quickly."

"I think," Willow spoke to kill the pause, that we have settled the one of the three things that Bud and I had in mind and that is why Phillip's parents were not here. Now how about why the boys were sent and Shorty . . . , now Fats, Jim, the preacher, and I don't know how many others, sat on their coward asses and sent their kids out, so I am going to make note that all these mother-fuckers are chicken-shit cowards and see if one of you will tell me why we called this meeting, or . . . ," Willow raised her voice, "listen to me people, did you come down here to ambush us in the known Terrell tradition? Don't mumble because I may want to insist that you remain here until I get an answer to that question."

"Louise, Willow and I felt threaten." I insisted rather loud as well.

Shorty perked up. So far he has been quiet, but maybe he had gotten dry and warm. "Girly, now when your boyfriend pushed my wife in the water and I got up to help her and you pushed me in, I took it like a man, but unless you can come up with a whole lot of backup, I done stayed here and listened to your crap just about as long as I plan on it."

"I have explained to you, that you may bring your fat ass through me any time you want to, Shorty," Willow assured him. She waited a moment or two for him to react. The man didn't move.

"She's got enough backup, Shorty," Mama says as she and Louise stepped into the clearing from off the trail and about half it seemed of the Morgan County Sheriff's department followed them. "I think about all of ya'll know Sheriff Franklin Brown, but I love the kid here, Deputy Becker, and I never even met the rest of these boys, but I met this good looking young man when Lois's husband was busting up my house, threatening my boy and cussing him, knocked off one whole side of my porch, and I whacked him up 'side the head with my broom.

"Yeah, but not necessarily in that order, Mama," I stated in a hushed voice but otherwise stayed quiet and noted the surprise on Lois' face to likely note that what happened was not related back to her in the same way that it was the first time. Oh, well! The way Mama put it, it was rather a better story, as I saw it.

Deputy Becker spoke, "As a newer member of the force, I have joined Sheriff Brown as a lawyer rather than an officer of the law, and my objective is to assist Sheriff Brown in doing all that he can to avoid any more arrests than are absolutely necessary but about half the Terrell clan is making it difficult to avoid Sheriff Brown having to feed you. Technically, . . . , what is your real name Shorty?"

"Travis Terrell."

"You had better come up with an answer to Willow's question or I have several sets of handcuffs for your . . . , pardon the expression, but I love it the way Willow said it . . . , for your fat ass. Now, I am a firm believer Travis 'Shorty' Terrell that you and these three women were here to ambush these people and this is the second day in a row."

"Do not interrupt me or I will interpret the interruption as due cause for the handcuffs and we can continue our discussion at another time and place." There was quiet but some noticeable sounds as some of the deputies spread out around the lagoon, with a couple of them moving close to Shorty, maybe as a threat.

"If I may continue, there are no cars above around the bluff belonging to a Terrell person, therefore, you purposely conspired to have yourselves delivered here for the attack that you planned for Bud and Willow, but you arrived to find Mrs. Landry here and apparently you considered no threat regarding your plans."

"No, no, no," Miss Emma was begging and that cast out in just a short instant all the power that she had been exerting over the people of the community. She spoke up, "Lois and Denise came down to our house and begged us to come down and talk to them and try to get them to drop the charges against their two boys and get them to help to get them out of the mess that they are in."

"Ma'am for one," Deputy Becker advised, "the purpose for coming here when you did we consider an absolute lie or you would have had no reason to hide in waiting. Furthermore, the charges are criminal and the six boys that we arrested are expected to go before a grand jury for consideration for trial." Miss Emma began to cry aloud. "For another thing, three were 18 and legal adults in Alabama, and three were 16 who did the criminal deed and crying is not an effective approach to business at this time." Deputy Becker continued, appearing to be unmoved by the emotional display.

"We need to answer some questions and all of you need to work with me so that I can assist Sheriff Brown in meeting his objective, and that is to arrest the fewest people possible."

"My son JD," Lois speaks up, "never intended to hurt anybody but just to rough him up a little."

"What is intended does not play a part in this, ma'am, rather what is done is the crime," the deputy assured her.

"Can my husband get arrested," Lois asked?

"Yes, of course he is involved in the planning and execution of a crime, which is considered organized crime by the letter of the law," the officer explained, "and let me clear up again what we want to do, but first allow me to tell you, that enough laws are broken such that I can arrest each of you today and I have not done so because I am struggling to try to find a way to avoid doing so. I am struggling for your cooperation to help me to protect you, and it is a take-it-or-leave-it option if I can ever get that far."

"While I also have to protect the integrity of the force that Sheriff Brown represents and the laws that he is dedicated to enforcing. Allow me to explain it this way, we can do what we do to avoid arrest by presenting evidence to the Grand Jury in a manner whereby we try to convince the Grand Jury that there is no benefit to the people for prosecution, therefore, no harm for the transgression and no advantage for the transgression to be interpreted as a crime," the deputy explained, "or we may even convince the Grand Jury that we can't prosecute a crime.

"The Reverend Foster is in custody as is his son. I can keep them for 72 hours or charge them. I am issuing a verbal warning to Mr. Travis "Shorty" Terrell that we will slam his fat ass in jail in violation of organized crime statutes at the drop of a hat and I have enough evidence to do so but we have a couple of twin brothers and three wives that we will be forced to prosecute at the same time. This, damn it, is what I am trying to get you to help me to avoid."

"You got their asses in a crack, Shorty, because of their ignorance, and I don't think these people are criminals. I think you are, but I am not so absolutely certain that I can prosecute you an let them go clean without getting a deal made somehow. Do any of you see my problem? I didn't think so."

Apparently Deputy Becker expected a response but didn't get one, so he continued. "Now you wives are sitting there wondering what you did but it is what you didn't do. There was a crime planned, you knew husbands and sons or nephews were the perpetrators of the crime and you did nothing to prevent the crime or to notify the authorities to try to prevent it. Basically, what I got out of JD's mother is that she was okay with the planned attack because she thought her son was only going to rough him up.

"Now, you know you can't be forced to testify against your husband or wife but your brother-in-law and your sister-in-law, nephews, et al, is another story, so stay close and allow me to strike fear into some people, because if there is any lack of cooperation we will return to the letter of the law, because Sheriff Brown does not have to have me or anybody like me and you had better believe what I tell you, because I am still not convinced that you did not come here for any other reason than to lie in wait and to do harm to these two young people here in ambush."

"While I am on the subject, allow me to let you know how long we were here and what we saw and heard. Mrs. Terrell stumbled and fell into the water and Mr. Terrell blamed it on Bud and Willow and attempted to charge Willow who moved out of his way, thus allowing him to fall into the water. I am convinced that there was no contact between the little girl and the big man or the big man would have already been in the slammer on assault charges. Is that what you saw Sheriff?"

"Exactly, in every detail," the Sheriff agreed, "now all of you who are being kept out of my jail need to figure out how the medical bills are to be covered for the young man here and the legal fees for your kids. On the legal aspects, Lois and Denise, if you want to help your kids get off easier, you and your husbands be in my office at 9 in the morning and we will discuss the advantages of states evidence. All four of you have to be there with the kids, all four of them.

Sheriff Brown continued. "Mr. and Mrs. Travis "Shorty" Terrell shall meet Deputy Becker and me at 9:30 in the morning in his office, where it will be explained to you Mr. Terrell your arrest or how your full cooperation can allow you to take your meals at home instead of at my table."

"Bud and I have a doctor's appointment," Willow announced. The pair walked up the path toward the iron gate.

Mama and Louise walked with Willow and me and told us how they had worked out the signals and how Mama had already called the Sheriff when she had seen the cars drive toward the bluff and drop off the people. Mama had climbed up the ladder on the barn so she could see the bluff. When she saw Shorty and Emma were dropped off and their car was driven away, she believed with a strong certainty that they were there for an ambush.

"I went to my Jeep and flashed the lights," Louise explained. "I saw Miss Ida on her way here and that is when I gave you the two fist pumps." Looking at me, she added, "your mama was coming up the path that y'all use to sneak out, so I ran down and met her, which is when the Sheriff and the cars arrived and I flagged them down and told them about Willow. They parked down by the woods and we sneaked them up to the bluff."

I inquired, "Then you knew about Willow?"

"Yes," Louise agreed, "Willow and I knew that she was planning to kick Shorty's fat ass as soon as she got the chance."

"And, I didn't even know she had the skills," I admitted, "and I was so worried about her when I should have been worrying about the people who might get in her way.

CHAPTER SEVEN

Private Lessons, Yesterday and Today So Far.

He knew that they would have a better time going through this were he willing to accept the status quo and if you don't lie about it you will have to fight about it.

"WHERE DID YOU learn it?"

"Nancy and I have been going to Huntsville two or there times a week for private lessons, actually it is in Whitesburg, just across the river."

"I noticed that you have some of the stuff down rather well," I reminded her, "but I was wondering if you had gotten around to 'lard-assed son-of-a-bitch' yet?"

Now I have to try to find a way to stop her from laughing so hard. "Hold it, hold it, hold it," I demanded in fun. "Let me get through the other part first, 'I apologize for the language in your presence, my love, and for the disrespect that I may seem to show that is not the respect that I have for you, and you are my Willow and I love my Willow."

"You added the last part to stop me from laughing, didn't you?"

"I did, but I love the way you laugh and I really do love you thoroughly and completely, actually."

"I thought your face was going to fall off when I told Shorty to sit his fat ass down or I was going to sit his fat ass down," Willow laughed. "I was trying to get as many fat-asses in as I could, if for no other reason than to see your face with each repetition."

"Really, that was an unbelievable performance," I assessed, "so how about telling me about the martial arts lessons, now"

"My best response to that question is to announce to you that I had every intention of kicking the lights out of that organized crime boss." Willow admitted. "It was a premeditated kick-ass and I enjoyed it much more than I feel guilty about it. My martial arts instructor warned me that I would feel guilty if I ever did the premeditated attack on somebody but from the time I learned about his role in your life and ultimately in you injuries, I have planned it, as is said, premeditated it."

"And, you feel guilt?"

"For what I did to the man, no, but for planning and executing and attack on a human being, I am a lot like you," she admitted, "I don't want to cause anybody any pain. I don't want to fight. Nancy and I took the lessons for self defense." Willow explained. "Our instructor is the father of a former North Korean military officer who defected to the South during the war, moved his entire family here and teaches at the Army training facilities on Redstone Arsenal."

"Ooo, those North Koreans are some nasty people, so we are told," I said, "of course I have never met anybody from the North."

"The soldier could be a nasty person," Willow corrected me, "but the father is gentle as a lamb and with his training techniques emphasizes the defense aspects and sportsmanship of the sport of karate, primarily I believe because most the other students that he has are involved in competition."

"Then you don't compete?"

"No, Nancy and I pay for strictly private lessons and take off during the school day. Nancy's Mom has made arrangements with the school to get our physical education credits with these lessons," she explained. "We go for two hours two days per week to get out credits then go back sometimes on Saturday." She went on to explain, "they tell us that we are required to have 15 units of credit per week, which takes three hours and forty-five minutes and they give us a receipt to turn in at the office."

"You know, the strange thing about this, is that I always sit at lunch where I can see you . . . ," I confessed.

"And, what you might think is strangest of all," Willow admitted, "I always insist that Nancy and I sit where you can be sure to be able to sit where we can see each other."

I laughed! "This is crazy and I am not laughing at us to ridicule us, but then again I think I am laughing at us to ridicule us, but we have likely not been successful at hiding our love for each other from a single person in that school except each other."

"Furthermore," Willow continued to admit, "we did an exceptional job at that." She stopped, but flashed a note of discovery, I did almost blow that thing last month when you were practicing for that play that you were doing and I caught you back stage."

"Wow, we were walking in that aisle way, I was going one direction and you were going the other and there was room for just one to pass," I related the scenario, "and we both just kept walking and met in an embrace and a monster kiss."

"I have never been screamed at so much as I was that next day," Willow admitted, "Ms. Lawrence, you know Emma Lawrence's big sister teacher at school, was very tight with that Ms. Garrison, your drama teacher who caught us and broke up the fun, the two of them took me into Mr. Abbott's outer office and read me the riot act, telling me about how you and your brother would find out who was putting out and that was the next girl that one of you had out on a date, because that is all you were interested in."

"Now hold on . . ."

"Let me finish," Willow quieted me, "and you will find that we are likely in full agreement. Anyway, Rebecca Lawrence told us about the time that you took Emma to a movie and groped her and tried to tear off her bra."

"That lying bitch . . . ," I defended.

"Please let me finish or I will stop the car and whip your skinny butt."

"Not a word out of me."

"Since Nancy's car is that little rose colored Chevrolet and it is so noticeable, we drove it and parked it at Emma's house so that when Rebecca came home from school that day it was to be most apparent that Nancy and I were there visiting Emma. Now this is the fun part, Rebecca wouldn't even come up stairs to her room, knowing that Nancy and I were there, so Emma had the idea that we go down with her and let her do all the talking so that the issue was a family issue rather than a school issue, though it related to what happened at the school."

"We found Rebecca in the kitchen and asked her to sit. Emma said, 'I want to tell you about a date I had.' Rebecca nodded acceptance of the discussion subject. Emma named you as her date and said 'I am likely the only person in your school that he has dated and I had Sara Terrell ask him to take me out. He was a perfect gentleman and you told Willow that I lied about him. Why are you slandering your own sister in your sister's own school?'

"Rebecca began to defend herself, 'that is the wrong way . . . ,'

'That is the only way that I have,' Emma interrupted, 'to defend myself from a lying sister who is a teacher in my school from slandering me and colluding with another teacher to slander other students.'

'Now, you wait just a minute little sister,' Rebecca demanded, 'you are not going to make demands of me as a teacher.'

'I have not yet spelled out my demands, Rebecca and that is exactly what I am doing, which is making demands of you as a teacher in my school, otherwise, I shall as a student file a formal complaint with the County Superintendent of Education for formulating a lie for the purpose of slandering me and colluding with Ms. Garrison in the formulation of a lie to slander and defame the character of two other students.' Emma turned, picked up the phone, slammed it on the table and said, 'I hope that damned thing still works after I slammed it on the table in anger, because if it does not, you are going to high tail your ass over to Garrison's house and get her over here because Willow and I have some discussions with the two of you and the two of you have some demands that will be met I firmly believe before 4:45 today, which allows us 15 minutes to get to Willow's house to call the superintendent before his office closes at 5:00 O'clock.' Emma left the room and Nancy and I followed."

"Don't leave me hanging! The story was just starting to get exciting," I demanded but in a jovial manner.

"We giggled about what we had done or what Emma did. The phone worked and Rebecca Lawrence was reasonably confident that Emma was not bluffing, and I believe she might have known the Bradleys well enough to know that Nancy wasn't there to see any white-capped mountains. Had she not known for reasonably certain why Nancy was there or assumed that I was with Nancy because we were usually together, then she would have casually strolled up the stairs to her bedroom."

"No, it appeared that she knew she was wrong and was being challenged," I agreed, "But it is beyond what I can imagine as to why half the people in my world hate me and the other half is at the other extreme. What I should be concerned about is the thin skin that I have but I work hard to meet society's highest standards, and I am naïve to believe that that part should work in my favor."

"Because they can't shove two fingers up your nostrils and drape you over their shoulders so they can parade you down through their road of life as that which they have lorded over and dominated to defeat," Willow informed me. "You are the type of person, as so many of the people of the world see you, as the type who will break off both fingers and shove them up their own noses. It's not that you are not likeable, you are feared."

"Rebecca Lawrence was on my case from the first day she went to work at the school and I didn't understand it," I said. "I accepted it that she was a snooty socialite and I was a filthy dirt farmer in her assessment, in mine a 'snooty bitch' versus a . . . well, versus a filthy dirt farmer but a damned good one."

"I had a study hall with her, last period," I continued my explanation, "and Principal Abbott often requested that I break from the study hall to help him run errands because he would not trust anybody but me to drive his pickup. She lied to him and told him I could not help him on this particular day because I was on discipline. I think it was about the third time he asked for me. When she did, I stood and asked to see the paperwork and she couldn't produce it. I enjoyed helping Mr. Abbott that day. She then came up with one of her own for disrupting the study hall but Mr. Abbott rejected it when she turned it in to his office and sent a note back to her that he accepted full responsibility for the disruption. She carries the vendetta today."

MY WILLOW 89

"Of course, because we challenged the two teachers the way we did, off campus sister to sister, Garrison blamed it all on Rebecca and the lie she told but they both apologized for the misunderstanding. Emma and I rejected the apology and made them write it and sign it with a commitment to get off your case and mine, yet I didn't concern myself with what they might do regarding me. I guess you know we didn't even get disciplined for the kissing."

"It wasn't the kissing, Willow," I advised her, "it was the *who* you were kissing."

"True, of course," she agreed, "and on the *who*, when we do the girl talk, I believe people make it so hard on you because of the 'nigger lover' label that you have been tagged with. Not another person in the school is brave enough to agree with you, but I'll venture to say that most of them do agree especially with the notion that Mr. Abbott presented to cause the ruckus last week, we need to prepare because we don't have the choice."

"I know that I would have a better time with having to go though this were I willing to accept the status quo," I said, "but I just can't bring myself to lie about what I feel so strongly about and if I don't lie about it I have to fight."

Willow asked, "so we know what you fight about is there anything you want to kiss about?"

"About all the time when you are with me. You are with me all the time now. Then the answer is all the time. How did I do?"

"You did just fine," Willow told me, "but do you think the people in Dr. Haggerty's office will see us kissing in the parking lot?"

"If they look they will," I suggested.

-0-

"I honestly don't know how you found her but you are one lucky young man to have this girl," the doctor said as he entered the room.

"You are right about my being lucky," I agreed, "but she found me actually."

"I can't help but marvel at it," the doctor added, "but the thing with you two is such a deep love, none of the kid stuff that we might question the validity of as adults, but the thing with you two is so very strong and you don't pretend to hide it. I'm just a romantic, but I think it is wonderful, so how long have you two been together, you know as sweethearts?"

"About all day yesterday and today so far," Willow responded, and smiled quite strongly to know that the response would draw a comment of surprise from the doctor.

"What? Impossible! You two are pulling my leg," the doctor said.

"Yes and no," I admitted to the doctor, "we have had this tremendous affection for each other for three years but just couldn't figure out a way to break the social barriers. Then, when Willow learned that I had been hurt yesterday, she broke all the social rules and she took control, got help and wouldn't leave me."

"Wouldn't leave you? That is an understatement," the doctor volunteered, "When I arrived I asked everyone to wait in the next room, I looked at those pretty blue eyes of hers that were spilling the tears down her face and she said, 'I won't go doctor, I can't go, I have to touch him.' I was so stunned by the love that she was giving to you, with the tears and the touch, yet she seemed to be so well in control of her emotions, except the tears were there. She looked up at me and almost brought me to tears when she strongly stated, 'Doctor, he means life to me, like I live when I touch him and I if I can't touch him now, I don't know.' I choked a bit, because I had never seen so much love and the sincerity with it. I let her stay."

"We waited so long to touch each other, Doctor," I commented, "that we can't let go right now." I added, "she slept in a chair beside me last night with her head on a pillow, touching me, and it may seem silly to others but I feel that my life and her life is one life right now, and life has to be transmitted back and forth between us with the touch. I understand as silly as it may seem to some the 'being as one' term, now."

"Nothing between the two of you is silly because it is so beautiful. Now we have to check all these wounds."

Whatever a "topical" is the nurses used it and kept me from crying like a baby as the wounds were cleaned. Bleeding the first day was for bandages so they were discarded many of those for patches and stick-ons. They explained things as they went along, but they mumbled a lot about the right ear. Mumbling caused worry. The doctor and the nurses went out for a while, maybe to look at X-rays or charts or something,

There were some concerns but thoughts of Willow were the strong ones. I got the credit for bravery when Willow was my strength. I felt she was my entire life in one little girl.

"You know, Willow," I spoke so very seriously, "you are the one who has been in my visions and at my hand essentially every moment since I awoke from my ordeal and I don't want to imagine ever changing anything from the way it is. Can you work with me on that?"

"I like the way you say it and I love you too." She made sure I felt a tightening of her hand on mine as she looked up and smiled a triumphant smile. "You had better be stuck on me because you are stuck with me; I am never letting you go."

"How are we going to live when I can't even afford my medical costs here, and I just realized that I had not even thought about that until now," I said, "and Mama reminded me to see the girl out front about the bills."

"The school is insured and you were on the school grounds," Willow told me. "Speaking of the girl out front," Willow added, "I checked to be sure I could report back to your mother and she told me that a number of people had called her to offer to pay the bills for your injuries, including the Burtons, the sheriff's department and the Bradley family. Now, there is so many people who feel so strongly about you so can you tone it down with the concerns that the entire population doesn't worship you?"

"As we learned from the Sheriff a while ago," I suggested, "he is pushing the Terrells to accept the responsibility for that which they should be responsible, but I don't worry about the money, but we had just not thought about it."

"While you have all those who hate you, you must surely feel that there are many of us out here who care."

"I have known about both sides all along, except for you, but have never understood what I could have done, or anybody else could have done for that matter, to cause the opposition, or why I have to be on the defense all the time," I explained, "or it is just that I don't need people to take care of my bills because I made good money my first year on the farm and didn't do as badly as most farmers last year in spite of the drought. With my father working for Ford Tractor, it supports the family so what I earn on the farm is clear. That is family money," I said, "but I just happen to be family, too."

"Nobody is offering charity, I want you to be sure to understand. You are a different person than those who may need cold impersonal support. The Burton's you have told me about rather taking you and a friend on for teaching you self defense skills, so they want to offer some support, you understand the Sheriff's motivation and I love you so much that I am blind to feel any need to argue about money being offered from my family, and I know nobody thought about the negative implications of the charity word because I know my family. My family would be offended to have somebody accuse them of making a charitable donation to you. It was to me and it is there if I need it."

"Okay, so the insurance, and the others," I agreed, "take care of expenses, so I don't worry about that, Willow, and we are pledged to each other for a lifetime. There are other steps in here, you know. I never thought about charity. Poor people may. We don't. Simply, Willow, we are not all that poor, but my family chooses to live close to the land and society has a grading system I guess."

"For us you mean, as in fairy tales," Willow joked. "and they shall live happily ever after?"

"Exactly!"

"I know what you are leading to and we have to discuss it and to make plans and agree on everything, like which college do we go to, if we go to college, do we do it now or later and all the rest of the steps that we have to go through, like where we want to live, our career goals, bla, bla, bla."

"Omigosh," I said, "those are some other things that we have to talk about and decide." Willow laughed. That sweetheart is not a pushover on the jokes, I could tell. "No that is exactly what I was talking about."

"You know, I have looked forward to getting us into these types of discussions," Willow responded, "and we have the time on our hands."

"You are a good healer," Dr. Haggerty said as he re-entered. "That right arm doesn't need to lift anything for a few more days but you can hold Willow with it if you don't squeeze her too hard."

"He cheated, Doctor," Willow laughed as she tattled, "he lured me to this romantic place on the river today on our noon walk and gave me my first one-armed gentle hug."

"Let's try the left one then," the doctor said, "and tell me how much pain" as he lifted the arm to about parallel to the floor."

"It is very painful when you do it and I feel no pain when Willow does it, and I am joking, but the pain is tolerable," I joked.

They laughed, which is what I had wanted. Dr. Haggerty asked if I was ready for him to release the arm and test it without support and Willow's reaction was one of what might jokingly be referred to as "a full-body knee jerk." She waited for the doctor to respond to her reaction because she knew I had seen it and she was a bit self-conscious.

"Come around to the left side, Willow," Dr. Haggerty suggested, "and help me by holding your hand a few inches below his so that when I release it and it falls, then you can catch it."

"I'm ready," Willow held her hand about an inch below my arm but the doctor pushed it down to about four inches.

"Hold it steady if you can and tell me the pain level," the doctor suggested. "Okay, here goes," and he released it.

Willow flinched. I felt a surge of love for that girl that I couldn't imagine, simply because of the flinch from her and none from myself. "The pain is almost unbearable," I said, then the longer he held it the better it was but the strength was minimum and I had to lower it to touch Willow's hand and stimulate a beautiful smile.

"How many times can you do that?"

"I can take the pain," I assured him, "but it started to ease quite a bit and I lowered it out of loss of strength rather than the pain."

Dr. Haggerty gave us exercises that we could do with both arms. He wanted to work the left arm most because the right would have to heal the bones while the left had muscle and ligament damage. All the exercises were light but the doctor included Willow in every movement, just as I wanted it, Willow involved in everything.

He sent us away with his blessings, and I asked him to thank his wife for her interest, "and allow her to know about all that Willow is doing," I requested.

"Tomorrow at 2:00 is our next one," Willow informed me as she helped me into the car.

As she drove out of the parking lot I addressed her, "Willow, you are the most amazing human person that I can imagine."

"You are not so bad, yourself" she replied, "and I love you too, for one reason because you have the sweetest way of saying that you love me."

"It's not that I try to create all these new and unique methods of describing my love for you, Willow," I told her, "but it is just that you keep putting so many unique opportunities out there in front of me."

"If I'm doing so good I certainly don't want to change anything but would you like to tell me what I did this time?"

"Why, the full-body knee-jerk?"

"Ah, the pain that I felt for you when he told me that he was going to release your arm?"

"That's it, exactly," I assured her. "You can say you love me, Willow and I know you mean it, but you feel my pain for me and you prove it, most assuredly."

"I felt I was going to have to jump up and grab you to keep the pain from driving you through the ceiling," Willow assured me.

"Now, do you know," I asked, "what that does for me?"

"It makes you know for an absolute fact that you love me?" She giggled triumphantly.

"Yes, and that you love me," I agreed, "but I was thinking when you did it that your reaction verified what we have been talking about, picking at each other about, and just kicking around, it is about like the two of us are one."

She asks, "You want to make a point?"

"Yeah, the doctor warns me of an impending pain and you flinch, like what I termed a full-body knee jerk. You feel my pain for me, like you are a part of me."

While all the jabber was going on and all the talk about love and being one and knee-jerks, all I really wanted to do was to hold her, then my thoughts went to the three years that we never told each other anything and now we can, so it is easy to wonder why I don't just tell her what is my problem. I had not lied to her but I had uttered words and more words and had not said what I wanted to say. I don't take any of the words back, but I ached to hold her. I wanted to squeeze her and hold her tight against my body like I had dreamed of for three years.

"Everything you say has been said, but I love to listen to you say it, so I sit and quietly encourage you to say more and more," Willow said, "but I know you want to say something that you won't say."

"Okay, here it goes," I said, "so get ready to laugh at me, ridicule me to the end of ridicule, but I will say what is bugging me. Back there we talked about the arms and therapy for the arms. I get the arms working and I can hold you Willow." I couldn't help it, I began to laugh at my silliness and the tears came. "I am laughing at me and crying at me, or for me . . . , whatever. "I want to hold you, Willow," I said.

"I know you do," Willow agreed, "and I want to hold you, but while the crazies gave you me and me to you, they put a little hitch in our ability to do all that our desires cause us to crave, but I have a plan."

"I'm anxious so I don't wait to ask, what's the plan?"

"We have to walk two miles as soon as we get to the bluff, so what we do is start with a kiss and as much of a hug as we can do, then go to the 2640 stone and do it again, then . . . ,"

"What about the 1320 stones, and the 3960 stones?"

Willow asked, "did you mark all those stones at the quarter-mile marks just so you could take all those opportunities to hold me tight?"

"If I had thought about holding you tight, my most wonderful girl," I assured her, "there would be a stone with a number painted on it every ten feet."

"We're almost to the bluff, get ready to learn how to hug me and get me all worked up," she giggled.

"We have to talk about that, too," I told her.

"I know," she said, "but you will have to let me take the lead, because you get started and you will babble all the time like you did this time, and all you wanted to do was to hold me and I knew that because I want to hold you all the time, too."

"I really wish I could hold you now," I told her.

CHAPTER EIGHT

Not Long Enough to be Ashamed of It

The total time in each day being spent together was making every minute become a memorable time and the pace was contributing to the intensities, the intensities were growing to challenge the ability to maintain a line between right and wrong or to recognize one if it was there.

TIME PASSING WITH unconsciousness here and there and the chemical knock-out on occasion to numb the pain and get some time out of the way that heals, and there was absolute bliss in the conscious times. Willow was with me! That was the first day. I was trying to count the time the second day, or the third day, no matter. It had been an eventful period, with the ambush, Willow in my life, and another ambush.

Willow was so impressive the way she handled those people on the second ambush that it really wasn't an ambush, or at least it didn't work out to be one. It appeared that Shorty and Emma Terrell figured they could get that little cutie and a beat-up sweetheart of hers hemmed up in the lagoon and force them into some kind of an agreement, maybe any kind of an agreement that would let Shorty, his dumpy little wife and the other dozen or so family members of his off the hook. They had been getting off the hook for everything they had done in the past so a little bit more getting off the hook for some major transgressions against the lesser people of that neck of the woods could be expected.

My expectations were to be recognized as not being among the lesser people. Certainly Willow was not and she had earned some recognition.

They could expect to get off because it was the normal routine for them. It seemed that it was about the normal routine that these people were thinking because about like that was maybe the only way these people were capable of thinking. Working a scheme, yeah, that's what they were doing, scheming.

Three excursions with the doctor and me and I was in good hands. That made me feel certain that I was into the third day. I kept refusing the pain medication, but Willow did succeed in putting one of Dr. Haggerty's knock-you-out-on-your-butt sleeping pills down me. I hoped she could sleep, in a chair with a pillow on my tummy. I was starting to worry about my Willow. I hoped she never gets fed up with me like all the other people do, as I ran thoughts through my mind as the chemically induced sleep was being called up for a short period of welcomed peace. I slept through the night.

Days were spent outside. The sun lured Willow, it seemed, and where Willow went so went me. She was so very dedicated to my therapy and our time outside lifted both our spirits and kept our thoughts far from the pain that I endured and Willow shared the endurance.

There was never anybody on the bluff, nobody frequented the place much until after school let out for the season, so we didn't expect to have anything but privacy on our regularly scheduled trek. Willow loved those treks. I loved Willow with a trek or without. Willow picked the parking spot and helped me out of the car. I saw the sneaky grin on her face, "I got a monster kiss that I have been saving up just for a special moment," she teased, "so is that moment going to be the one where I get my first 2-hand hug of the year?"

"Hey, I'll bet if you help me with the left arm," I bragged, "then I can hold you." I held her with the right hand and she assisted in getting the left around her to the waist. I couldn't hold her tightly with both arms but the right one kept me close as we kissed and the left one started to slide downward. I released her with the right and reached for the left and held it up, then squeezed her again. I could hold her. What the heck, that was about all I really wanted to do anyway, so it was a big event, to me at least.

We held each other for awhile. It appeared that Willow knew that my arms were not so good for an extended period of messing around so she gave in to my pain and released me. "This is temporary," she said as she helped bring my left arm down from her waist. She then added, "I thought for a moment that you were trying to put the left one on my bottom." She laughed.

"I was, but it just does not have the strength to move where I want it to move," I said knowing she knew fully well that I would not take advantage of her, "but I'll be able to do better tomorrow."

Smiling she asked, "you will put your hand on my bottom tomorrow? Is that a promise?"

"If that's too long to wait, I promise I will try harder before the day is over. Is that good enough for you or maybe we should try it again now?

"Okay, but your quest for today was to be able to hold me and you did that," she told me, and you need to see if you can do better this time."

We held each other again for awhile. I didn't even attempt to use the left arm because this was love and the therapy could wait. Her cheek was so soft and warm against my own as she held it there for awhile then kissed me, long and sweet. It was just not long enough, not forever and ever which maybe would be enough or close to it.

"We have work to do." Willow wasn't smiling as she looked at me and said, "I am in love with you."

"I love you, Willow," I assured her. "It's my favorite thing to do among all the exciting things going on in my life right now."

"Then, let's find the 2640 stone." She turned and walked but didn't go far before turning back and putting her arms up in a come-to-hold-me gesture.

"Willow the con artist," I named her.

"I know what you like, you like your Willow and you like to hold your Willow and I have to encourage you to use your arms to hold your Willow, so 'come along with me the best is yet to be,' as the poet tells us," Willow teased.

"I love my Willow the con artist," I chided, "and my Willow the tease."

"Next, you will be saying, 'I love my Willow the slave mistress,' because I know how I may enslave you and put you under my command," she continued, but she let me walk right into her arms, just like I did that night behind the stage when I kissed her and caused her to get yelled at.

It seemed that we were getting much more comfortable with each other, quite deep into beginning to believe in what we were telling each other. The part about we really were in love and we planned to be together for as long as we lived. I knew certainly that I had to have her with me always and the teasing was an element that was coming out in our relationship that allowed me to believe that she was as comfortable with the idea of forever for us as she stated she was. Not that I thought we were lying to each other before now or that we were merely caught up in the moment and the moment would go away or start to subside in intensity. It was just that the feelings were being accepted as permanent, no questions, no doubts, done deal!

There was some feelings that the intensity was growing, actually. Willow had said something on the way back from the doctor's office about getting "worked up" and I felt the term was meaning "sexually aroused," and I knew she went serious on me for a moment and started the tease routine soon after. Another thing I knew is that I am the "perfect gentleman" according to her and the girls who are her closest friends. At least that is what they came up with in the discussion regarding the back-stage kiss. From that conversation I got the idea firmly implanted that this type of thing is very important to Willow. Well, yeah, to her friends as well, but they didn't matter. Willow mattered. Willow was just about all that mattered.

The way things were going, the time we were spending together, our pledging ourselves to each other, in general, the feelings that we had for each other was about to start to hint of a stronger sexual need that we were getting into having to deal with. I couldn't step over the other line, so it was most apparent that I was not about to step over this line, the sexual one, of course. "Gosh," I spoke to myself, "here I am crazy in love with this girl and have no idea what to do about it, and even if I did, I would not know how to go about doing it." Maybe I laughed at myself because I couldn't keep from doing it.

"Now you have to tell me what that laugh is all about," Willow broke her silence. "You have been walking briskly with the left arm hanging and you have been being quiet."

"I know but so have you, so I was thinking."

"About me?"

"I will be as honest as I know how, Willow, my love," I spoke seriously, "I don't really believe I can have a thought any more without having you in it."

"She skittered in front of me, put both hands gently on my shoulders, looked me in the eye she growled in a comedic manner, and asked, "and are you going to tell me that you can laugh about that?"

"No, of course, I was thinking about you," I defended, "but I was laughing about what I was thinking about you, because it was another one of my silly things."

"Did not the doctor tell you today that there was nothing silly about the two of us? Not wanting to get to a subject change, but are the blue rocks the 1320 stones?"

"Yeah," I answered, "a quarter of a mile."

"Okay, you need to rest a couple of minutes," Willow advised and we sat where we could look up river. "Now, what were you thinking that was silly and so funny, but you made me promise a kiss at the 1320 stone?"

"Easy to love and hard to negotiate with, huh? Okay, let me see if I can let myself back onto this embankment in the grass and I will relate word for word my silly thought," I agreed.

"I won't help but I need to hold my hands on your shoulders in the event the effort is too great," but as I rested on the grass, she kissed me and held me. I could hold her with the right and did. The holding had just become a necessary part of the kiss. I was really proud of myself for adding that, if for no other reason, it made me feel I loved Willow even more than I thought possible before. Yeah, about like I was giving her credit for magic therapy, about like nobody else could make me feel as well as Willow did. That was certainly a fact.

"What are you thinking now," she asked, "about how to get out of telling me what you were thinking before?"

"No, but I was thinking about how to tell you in a way that it would not upset you."

"Well, I guess we are back to my having to explain that we are two adults so to speak who are in love with each other, who have pledged ourselves to each other for always, so I know of nothing that we can talk about that should make the other one angry or to get upset, only maybe how we do it, but the love we have for each other will not allow that." She gave me another kiss, then said, "that kiss was an extra one just for me, to make me strong so I can endure what you have to say that is so silly and funny, too."

"Okay, here we go," I warned. "What I was thinking was, and I quote, 'here I am so completely in love with this person and don't know what to do about it and even if I did I would not know how to do it.'"

I looked at her and saw that she wasn't laughing and it gave me a bit of a fright, to say the least. I was so afraid that I had crossed a line that could kill all that had been built up between us. I knew I was naïve, inexperienced, but I trusted Willow so I just came right on out and said it. I can't take it back now, it is done. Like Ol' Charlie said one time, "my father told me long ago that his father warned him, that when you release the arrow, you can't go get it back before it hits the mark."

Willow spoke to break the silence, "we do have to think about that one and we have to talk about it like two adults have to talk about everything."

I spoke, seemingly relieved that I could let go of the fear, "then you are not upset with me?"

"No, but I would like to know why at this particular time?"

"There have been other times but I got caught this time."

She asked, "was there a reason maybe that you had it on you mind at this moment, maybe like you knew of the terrain, the privacy and the soft grass by the 1320 stone, and you might have believed that maybe you could get me to show you a thing or two because you don't know anything at all about how to have sexual intercourse with a girl?"

"I don't see you that way, Willow," I defended. "I see you as someone who can discuss these things with me, and if we agree that sex is something that we need to consider between us, and it is absolutely certain that we need to, then I could have those thoughts, but we had not gotten into the subject until now. I could not have plotted and schemed any such idea. I do like the idea, however, and like the way you pitch it right out in front of us and declare it as important dialog."

"Let's walk and talk about sex so you don't change your mind while we have nice soft grass," Willow suggested as she stood and reached for the right hand and smiled, plenty enough to let me know that no harm is done in getting into the subject matter.

As I stood I told her, "to ensure that I am fully honest with you, I must admit that I am aware that you got 'all worked up,' as you define it, back at the car."

"You did, too," she accused, or at least made me aware that I couldn't hide it.

"Guilty, as charged," I admitted, "and again to be totally honest with you, Willow my love, there is lots of times that it is on my mind. Most of the time, actually! I believe it is a part of being in love, correct me if I am wrong in your view."

"Neither of us have experience," she admitted, "so we have to use all that we have learned from some of the right sources and some of the wrong ones, put them in our minds and sort through them to come up with something that is good for the individual. In that context, I want to know if you believe you love me enough to allow me to feel like I have trained myself properly."

"I love you enough, I know that," I promised, "but I need to know all about your feelings, and we have used the words like sex and sexual intercourse so I need to know where you stand and I have promised you that I will respect you in every way. You know I will."

"All of those years in the church, at least from the time I knew what 'to abstain' meant, I have believed that it meant to me that I should protect myself from being used by a man in that way," Willow explained. "I have lived with those standards and by them, then you come along and I question them, at least I am questioning those standards in these recent days when we have discovered the extent that we are in the lives of each other, that we are in love with each other and have been for years."

"Do you think," I asked, "that sex is necessary between us now to ensure that our relationship is one that is everlasting?"

"No," she answered, then she said, "but I am not sure."

"Could you take my hand and lead me back to the 1320 stone, so we can get so . . . , how is it my father says it . . . , so we can get wound together as tight as a couple of copulating copperheads?" When she didn't immediately take my hand, I continued with my lesson, "Willow, you didn't take my hand so I have to honor your need to feel, how do we say it 'unviolated' or 'pure,' I think that is the proper way to say what I have to make reasonably clear."

She nodded with appreciation in her light smile and said, "now you are making me believe that I can love you even more than I have to this moment."

I continued, "we have pledged ourselves to each other and we have sealed it with a kiss and we both feel that this can be as everlasting as the wedding pledge, and you do not have to have sex with me to maintain the strength of our bond. Simply, I want to love you for what you are what you want to be, not what I can change you to."

She came to me, opened her arms and held me warm and tenderly as she kissed me and shared with me the heat of her passion. I walked her to a soft spot on the ground beneath the pine trees just off the trail. We sat and she assisted me in laying back on the soft cool pine needles on the ground and continued the kissing and the sharing of the heat of her body against mine. I felt her knee move across my body and felt her knee find my throbbing erection. We moved our bodies together to comfortably place ourselves together in a most appropriate manner, my left leg between her legs. It seemed as if she was trying to tear through her jeans and through mine to get to what was throbbing to penetrate the layers of cloth. She squeezed with her legs and found the perfect spot to move herself against me slowly and rhythmically, squeezing and rubbing. I placed my working hand on her bottom to feel the rhythm and to aid it, until her body began to react and to react again and again, as she held on tightly and moved more quickly until the end became apparent. Her body rested against mine and she kissed me gently.

I felt her attempt to move her bottom and I held more firmly to her for a moment, then reluctantly let her go. It was a gesture to show her that I approved, I think.

"Then you don't think I acted like an uncontrollable child," she stated almost like a question.

"I feel like you are a full grown woman who needed a release, that you have kept in so much emotion that you had to turn it loose," I told her and then I quickly added, "and if there is blame being handed out, I was in on that too."

"And you don't think less of me for it?"

"Willow, honey, I think more of you! Now, slide over and hold me, because I think I feel like everything we do just makes a bond stronger and stronger between us," I attempted to assure her.

"I know all this holding does," Willow agreed, "because it gives us more places for our bodies to touch and our love can just pass to each other better." She giggled and pulled and squirmed to make more contact of the bodies.

I asked because it seemed the opportunity would be gone forever if it were not used at that most appropriate time, "What do you think if we try it by taking our clothes off and see if we can feel a different sensation?" I got a quick little kiss on the lips and she rose to reach for a hand.

"Good idea," Willow agreed, "tomorrow, or maybe someday. We overdid it today."

"Nope, I disagree."

"We still have a mile and a half to walk plus exercises, and we have used up more than half the time," she said, "and that is overdoing it."

"I thought you meant we overdid our love."

"No! Overdoing our love is when I say I love you, I love you," she assured me, "when all we need is one 'I love you.' So, I love you, now lets exercise.

"I love my Willow, I love my Willow, I love my Willow . . ." She put her lips on mine and I couldn't say anything. Though I loved the lips being there, I was aware that Willow was feeling some shame for what she did, and the lips were used to slam the door on the type of position that I was taking regarding what had just occurred.

CHAPTER NINE

Way to One Side

In the times that we experienced the morality that was used in judgment of us, we worked hard to protect ourselves within the standards of life rather than to circumvent or to make changes.

SO THAT THEY might be certain that Willow would sleep better, she moved my reclining chair over to my little sister's bed and Willow and Mama fixed the linens so she could sleep with her pillow at the foot of the bed. That allowed my right arm to be next to her and it was a lot more usable than the left, and we could kiss. Willow loved her kisses. I loved my Willow and my Willow's kisses. That seemed simple enough and it just about settled everything, at least everything that is of importance anyway.

It had been a busy day. We had been gone the entire day and it had been an eventful one. I knew for certain that Willow had not been able to sleep well the night before. Nobody could have, and she showed it at dinner by actually nodding. I did, too. I was tired and the family was all worried about me instead of Willow.

Willow was exhausted, I knew it and had an opportunity to feel concern for her comfort. It was a good feeling for me knowing that Willow was so totally dedicated to putting her entire self into me. It was my chance to feel something in return, if feeling was all that I could do. Even busted up bodies could feel.

We had laughed rather hard and that tired us. I could see that Willow was not laughing as strongly and ask to allow her to retire. Mama had to tell everybody

103

about how I "accidentally" bumped Emma in the water and how Willow put Shorty in the lagoon with a kick in the gut and brilliant spin-over and double kick in the butt. Then, made him sit his fat ass down, and how the Sheriff scared their wits out of them and impressed upon them the fact that it ain't over yet.

To impress the family that we are the clean-cut American kids with the highest morals, Willow and I must impress them that we are not sleeping together, but are merely staying in the same room during the night so Willow can be with me to take care of my health needs, when the actual truth is she can't keep her hands off of me and I can't stand not to be able to touch her or have her touch me. We just didn't explain it in exactly that manner.

They all knew Willow and I loved each other but they also knew that Willow and I had respect for each other just as much. We both sleep in our clothes, at least fully dressed and the doors are always open so they invite movement to check on us.

The little kids helped to get Willow reverse tucked into the girl's bed in her short shorts and athletic jersey, each with a kiss on the cheek for her, and I into my recliner close enough that Willow could touch me but I got no cheek stuff from the little ones. Dang it! She had given me my knock-you-on-your-butt pill, but it worked slowly. Willow was asleep long before me so I had some think time.

I was personally looking forward to seeing what happens with the meetings on Wednesday, and if I knew if I guessed right, Deputy Becker and Sheriff Brown will have complete control of the outcome of those meeting. Look for Shorty to accept a lesser charge and likely get off with something akin to contributing to my assault and he will agree to plead guilty and Phillip will agree to take the rap for the whole big deal. These things usually get plea bargained anyway, but plans to get my hind end out of the area and take Willow with me if she will go. Otherwise, I will not go anywhere and it can be carved in granite that I will kick some ass and nobody is going to venture the weakest of doubt Willow will want to be a part of it.

I had thought enough about what I wanted for the tomorrow years, the time after I get out of high school and have to go into the world and fend for myself. I have earned the money that my family has in the bank over in Decatur, and there is enough for a good start, and there is no doubt that some of it can be taken to get a start, pick up a small farm somewhere away from here, even take one of the tractors.

I didn't mind farming. I did mind farming here. The fact is, I loved farming. I hated farming here. Yet, while I mulled these things, Willow is the only thing that matters in my mind, the absolute only thing, and I know she wants to go. I want to go, Willow wants to go. If it is the other side of the river, the other side of the mountain, the other side of the world, then Willow has a follower or a leader.

There was not even a month left to make plans. Any plan will not include this farm. I decided that graduation and Willow are the only finalities in my plans, whenever I could get around to making some. I have the Methodist scholarship offer that I really don't want to take but may need to in order to buy some time to make preferred plans, that is if Willow will go with me. Army, Navy, Air Force, Marines? Whatever, but I won't be taking military anything that is not with a commission and Willow must approve it.

Yeah, I was thinking that I may end up in Old Town, Maine on a Penobscot reservation if it means that is what I have to do to be with Willow. Maybe Vineland, New Jersey raising grapes. Maybe now but not this time last year. Willow's grandmother had asked the FFA to come out and prune her grapes since they had not had a professional in the vineyard since they bought the place two years prior. I was the only person around with any knowledge whatsoever of grapes and that is what I had learned in one lesson at a seminar at Auburn University and a little that my grandfather had showed me about how it was done in the old country. But, the grapes needed work badly.

I took a crew out, maybe close to 20 kids, the entire class, and they worked the entire day on the huge vineyard, about 40 acres. Grandmother Preston was at the Agricultural Building the next morning when I arrived at school. In short, the lady was unhappy though pissed is a much better word. "That kid was in charge," she said as she pointed to me, "and he destroyed my Vineyard." The pissed-off old lady made it very clear that none of us were to ever appear on her property ever again.

That was January. At the end of the season, the same old lady appeared back at the Agriculture Building in a hugging and kissing mood. It seems that somehow the "destroyed" vineyard had doubled the production of either of the previous two seasons before it was "destroyed." She begged my forgiveness for her tirade and referred to herself as a stupid old lady.

I just had to talk with Willow, about Vineland, New Jersey or any other place that Willow may want to talk about. I don't know for sure if Willow will push for more time for us to be together here for nursing and rehabilitation. I know she has said she wants to stay but it is not exactly Willow's or my choice, completely. Willow will have to push for getting more time with me. Though it is decided, that part is not approved.

After all, we two are at some time or another going to have to teach ourselves how to spend some time away from each other. We are both afraid to think of that and Willow feels the same, but life is such that it will have to happen somehow. As I get better capable of taking care of myself it will allow us to accept separation from each other temporarily on a short-term basis, extremely short term. Yeah, probably with some kicking and screaming in the mix.

Willow slept maybe seven hours. I awoke and found her lifting and caressing my left arm. "You were moaning and the arm had fallen to the side of the chair and you couldn't raise it so I had to do it," she said.

I responded sleepily, of course, "I woke you? I am so sorry angel, but I was dreaming that I was moving over to make room so you could lay beside me and I guess my arm just fell or I pushed it out of the way for you."

"So that's why you are all the way to one side." She walked to the right side of the chair and pushed her bed aside. She then positioned herself beside him in the recliner and snuggled close. My right arm was around her and I could hold her close.

It was the first time ever like this, so we kissed and I held her. "You know somebody will come through the door and you and I are in bed together and we will be in deep trouble," I cautioned my Willow.

"The light just came on in the kitchen," Willow announced. "I'll be right back."

I could hear the sound but couldn't hear what was being said.

Willow returned and into the position that she left from. "I told Mama that you were having a bad dream and caused your left arm to fall and you woke me making noises from the pain. I told her that I thought I could get in the recliner with you and get you comfortable and if she thought it might be a good idea. She encouraged me and said she would be in to help me."

The door opened. Mama said, "look, Willow, I have another quilt to put over you two because there is still a chill in the air." Mama loved those quilts that she and the others made. They were works of art.

Willow and I had made certain that she was atop my cover to ensure that it could be seen that we were not in bed together, but more like she was sitting with me and we were reclining. Mama felt of my brow, like to see if I had a fever and said, "son, let her sleep if you can – she hasn't slept much the other nights – and she needs it. She stays awake nursing you. I'll keep the rest of them out and explain if I have to but I won't allow anything to be said bad about Willow. She is too trusting of you."

"Because she knows she can, Mama," I assured her. I told Willow, "see, we all love you! 'Go to sleep little baby, go to sleep little baby . . .'" She smiled and kissed me. I held her so close while she slept. We both slept past the time when everybody was gone, the kids all off to school, Daddy at work and Mama in her huge garden that she puts together every year. That was what Willow liked about this place, Mama's garden. It is rather well known that if she had the time Willow would be on her knees with every plant on the place.

Mama had laid out some clothes for today; I found them in a chair when I awoke. Well, maybe not just when I awoke, but after I awoke and found out how wonderful it was to have Willow snuggled on my right arm and sleeping so well. She seemed so comfortable with our arms around each other that as much as I wanted to kiss her 'good morning' and share the wake-up time with her I was perfectly content to feel her against myself and her arms around me and to see her comfortable in her sleep.

With everybody gone and the house quiet, I had hoped Willow would sleep long but actually we had both slept a long time. When I woke her earlier with the problem with the arm, it was already at Mama's wake-up time, and I was usually

MY WILLOW | 107

out at the same time to feed and care for the stock. Little brother Frank was on that job no doubt. He was such a great kid. Before John escaped to the Air Force we used to joke about wishing "we could be as good a kid as Frank is when we grow up."

And, the paper route? The fact is, there were a lot of wage earners who did not do as well as Frank and I did with the route, which was a little better than $40 per week. With both of us working at it we shared the money and did well. We had money to buy and keep the best bikes around and I had put enough aside to get the Studebaker to its current state of running around so Willow and I could call it a thing. Frank and I even took care of our own lunch money at school and at monthly collection time would offer up grocery money for Mama never to turn away.

Maybe it is strange, but I never thought much about life being a good life until it gets close to the time to leave it and to make a new one. The family was thought of as being poor but we were far better off than almost all the people around and we certainly had lots of love in the place called home. Willow had notice that and had noted it.

"Ah, my Willow! My wonderful Willow! I love my Willow! She has the little gang here wrapped around the little Penobscot finger." I said. "The big part of the family, too. I love to see the way Mama inches toward her when they are together. Daddy comes right out and says, "that one is a keeper." I think Frank is almost as much in love with her as I am. Then there is the little sister. We refer to Linda as little but at thirteen she is mature, extremely bitchy but mature. She and Willow are "both teenagers, so who says we can't be best friends?"

"Things are better when we see them better, Ol' Charlie Wolf told me once. I understood. Having what I was having in my arms to awake to this morning makes everything good. It is a new experience and me and I am selfish enough to want it every day of my life and I can hardly wait for Willow to wake so I can tell her. I wanted to squeeze her to wake her but felt the squeeze from her instead. I kissed her on the nose and evoked the smile that he wanted to wake to every day from that day on. We held each other so tightly and for as long as it was socially comfortable.

I asked, "you slept well, didn't you?"

"Yeah, but first 'I love you,' because I want to try to be the first to say it every time," Willow told me, "but the best part was that I slept with you."

"I love my Willow, too," I said as I corrected her statement, "but you didn't sleep with me, no way."

"I was in your arms and my arms were around you."

"I know that, but all that happened is that you sat in the chair with me and you dozed off. Honey, that is not the same as sleeping with somebody."

"Now that we have the official story down pat, how well did you sleep with me?"

"In the most simple terms, I have waited for you to wake so I could tell you that all the rest of the days of this life I want to wake in the morning and find you in my arms and I want to start believing in an afterlife so I can do the same there."

"We can do it," Willow agreed, "in this life, but we have to force ourselves to miss a few of those opportunities while we make arrangements. I have thought about it and I see it as a sacrifice that we have to make so that we may get ourselves into the position so that everybody is happy with us so we are happy together."

"That is some of the stuff that I have been thinking about while you were asleep," I told her, "things like we have to train ourselves to be separated for short whiles. We have to decide on what our future is to be, like where we are going after graduation, to college, a career. Willow, we have to discuss making arrangements for us to be together."

"But, that is decided!" she said in a manner that included the silent 'please believe me.'"

"We can make it legal in this state when we turn 18."

"Don't you have to propose?"

"Marry me, please Willow, when we turn 18."

"I will, because I love you, and we don't know what the hell we are doing but we will figure it out." She hugged me, kissed me and squeezed me and marveled at the fact that I had gotten out of my sleeping position all by myself.

"Willow, we have to do it legally for everybody else. And, I can't imagine how we are to make it in the life ahead of us with nothing to sustain us except each other and love."

"I want to keep our plans secretive for awhile, if you don't mind," she requested, "because I have to get my mother back to Vineland or Old Town or wherever she plans for the two of us to go. For us and our legal aspects, we can go to Georgia where everybody goes from here because the legal age is 16 there, and we can still keep it a secret."

"That way," I suggested, "we don't even have to wait until graduation."

"You are in a hurry," she teased.

"You are in a hurry," I corrected. "After yesterday, I am not so sure you will allow me to remain a virgin past noon today."

Startled, Willow covered her mouth, "am I still a virgin?"

"Does it matter?" I queried.

"No, I guess it doesn't if it doesn't matter to you," she responded, seeming to me relieved, "but the question had not gotten up there among everything else in my mind and started to messing around with me."

"Forget all the labels, Willow," I asked or requested, "we are throwing the old ones out anyway so we can be together. While you were still asleep, I considered all the others and they were not important either."

"How long were you awake before me?"

"Maybe half an hour," I guessed.

"That's a lot of time to think," she said, "so don't try to tell me everything right now because we have all day and a very busy schedule that we have to meet so you can tell me all of it as we go through the day.

"A busy schedule," I asked, "what is on the agenda today that is going to keep us so busy?"

"Being together, holding each other, kissing, touching each other, looking at each other, smiling at each other, telling each other 'I love you' and explaining it, walking, your exercises, and we have to repeat those things so many times and then we have to go to the doctor at 2:00, then we have to repeat and repeat all the other stuff so many times."

"I'm exhausted just talking about it," I said, "can we just lay back down so I can hold you again?"

"We have to shower and get dressed."

"Can I shower with you?"

"No."

"Can we get dressed together?"

"Sure! That way you can look at by breasts, then at my bottom and the other private parts and you can lust after me and show me disrespect, that way I can be like a stripper and you can put money in my panties, or like the girl who comes by the rock quarry on Thursday and charges $15. Am I worth fifteen?"

"You are worth more than I will ever see, and I love you more than you can ever know, so cover your legs." I got a monster kiss for saying the right thing.

"Do you want to talk about caressing my breast while I was sleeping?"

"Do you want to go back to sleep so I can caress it, the first time, because I did not caress your breast and you are making a joke, right?

"I was joking to let you know that I might have approved of it if you did," Willow told me, "because you would have to use the left hand and arm in the position we were in, and it would be worth it to see that you could use the arm." She giggled, "You see, this is real love when I will offer my body for your rehabilitation."

"Bolt the door securely so I can't peek at you in the shower," I suggested, and pretended I was trying to pat her on the bottom. The again, it might not be certain that I was pretending. I had the idea that her bottom has to be the most perfect bottom on a human being. Actually, that was nothing wrong with anything about Willow, according to me, exceptional in every way.

-0-

Starting late for our outside excursions, we walked a bit more briskly. I had been told that day three would be easier and that the left arm would show some progress on day three. I was amazed that I could move it a little. I felt like I was moving it some when I woke Willow after 5:00 to 5:30 but couldn't be sure. According to Willow's therapy chart I was supposed to try today and later in the day try again but not to expect too much. Doing it for Willow I expected more. I wanted to impress her or wanted to impress the doctor or Nurse Nan with what Willow was capable of getting out of me.

There were things on my mind from earlier when I had the time to think and allow Willow to look so cute sleeping, and on the trails today, I had on my mind the fact that the Terrells were on the hot seat with Sheriff and his deputy as we were walking. Willow and I had talked about it but felt they were at a loss as to what they could do or have done. We enjoyed the event in the lagoon but that had nothing to do with the Terrells and the hot seat, merely that Willow and I, with the help of Louise, had entrapped them there for the Sheriff because they had the idea that the kids, Willow and I, would be fear struck when they came to the lagoon and found a large number of large Terrells.

Willow walked to my left and held the left hand. Her instructions suggested that the arm motion be started with the therapist moving the arm. they were impressed that I could endure the pain when she moved it but disappointed when I tried to apply my own muscle power to make it move. We stopped at the infamous 1320 stone. She removed my shirt then a tube of something from her pocket. "I was likely supposed to do this the previous two nights but the people in Dr. Haggerty's office forgot to give me the instructions."

She rubbed the shoulder thoroughly. It felt like an athletic balm. It felt good. Willow got in a couple of kisses and I was like a horse ready to trot. She wanted me to swing the arm. I did it! I surprised myself that I was capable.

Walking briskly now, Willow was reading her instruction sheet. She swung around to my left side and instructed me to turn the left palm forward and make a fist. I did. "Now, open and lift your hand up to touch mine," as she held her hand just above my waist. I endured the pain and she cheered me. "I will have you driving in two days." she assured me.

"That is exciting, my love, the more exciting part of it is if I can drive I can hold you with both hands."

"And, put both hands on my bottom, I assume, am I correct?"

"Why certainly, I will do the best I can, you know, anything to make you happy." Of course I was grinning the big grin but realized we were at the pine thicket where we were yesterday. I turned into the spot where we lay, seated myself in the soft pine needles and waited for Willow to respond. She didn't. She waited on the path. Knowing I had made a huge mistake in deciding I could make a joke about a sensitive experience, I hopped up as quickly as possible and moved in the pine thicket along the path ahead of Willow, made my way out onto the path and stood as if I had been waiting for awhile.

I watched her as she stood looking sadly toward the spot where we were in the pines, then began to walk back toward her being as noisy as possible, pretending I had waited on the path for awhile. When she spotted me, she ran toward me and put her arms around me and gave me a big kiss, and a very special one at that.

"I love this place along here because I get more love here than any place in the world," I announced.

Willow began to cry. "I thought you were ridiculing me for yesterday, and I was feeling like you might be thinking like I was the cheap little girl who would do it again because I was just a cheap little girl, or something like that." Tears and laughter can work well together. She was so very beautiful laughing with her tears, and she was so perfect for caressing, so vibrant, and I was so deeply in love with my Willow.

"You could beat me up for a bad joke," but she couldn't because I was holding her too tightly, "and what happened yesterday we did because we love each other and we expressed our love in a physical manner, not a lot differently than we are right now. Our bodies are together."

"I know but yesterday I lost control and it was like we had sex and didn't take our clothes off," Willow explained.

"Willow, my one and only love ever in our lifetime, there were two people who had compounded their love for each other for three years and it overcame us before all the things that needed to be done to justify it were done, and that's all."

She started to speak and I interrupted, "Willow, this three years that we avoided showing our love got terminated at an instance, the years of not showing, honey, when Clint Thompson came into that room. It didn't make the love any larger or smaller, just more real, just that it had to be recognized and dealt with in an emergency, thus no more avoiding showing it."

"That explains how, Willow," I continued. "I can't explain why and don't want to even know. I want what we have and nothing else. I want our love making yesterday to be the highlight of our relationship, and I want it to prove that we love each other so much and so completely that even our silly little trip-ups can make our devotion to each other stronger."

Willow didn't release me but she did lean back and looked me in the eye. "You had me convinced that it was more than a silly little trip-up then you label it a silly little trip-up, what gives?"

"No, honey, that was another silly little trip-up on my part," and I defended both, "but I was talking about my trying to make a joke about something that was sensitive to you that was a silly little trip-up, but it might not have been so little."

"I'm okay with it now but I thought we had misunderstood each other, you thinking of me as a cheap tramp with no concern for self control and me thinking that you were the stereotypical man," she explained, "when all along we are just two people with so much love we don't know how to accept and deal with every aspect of it."

"How I see the problem is that there is a couple of 17-year-old kids here with a love big enough and complicated enough for a couple of adults twice our age and we have no knowledge and no experience with it, yet we are convinced that we are in an unusual situation, with confidence in our love for each other, but we test it."

"For awhile," Willow said, "you had no solid confidence, and now we find that I am not so confident as I pretend I am."

I asked, "This doesn't do anything to delay our trip to Georgia does it?"

"No, but it's doing something for your therapy," Willow noticed, "and that can get us to Georgia faster, you know as soon as you are well enough with those two arms."

"I was so afraid that I was getting in trouble with you over my really bad joke that I strained the left to get it around you," I explained, "but it won't move again. You're stuck with my arms around you forever and ever, kind of like lock-jaw with the arms."

"Then I will smother you with kisses and hold you with both arms."

"Keep it up but I have to ask if you know how scared I was when I knew I had made a mistake on my joke?"

"Probably about as scared I was when I thought you didn't believe in me."

"I just know I'll be more careful about joking around because nothing can happen between us" I admitted. "Had you turned to go back toward the car I would have gone nuts, and I knew that it was my fault." I went on, "It was stupid of me to make a joke about your expressing your love the way you did, where you did, and if you will please forgive me this time I know it will not ever happen again. I love you just too much."

"I love you too much too, and we are trying to pack three years of loving each other into a few days of showing it and we will be sensitive sometimes, so forgive me for being stupidly sensitive and I will forgive you for your stupid, insensitive joke."

"Does that mean we stand here in the middle of the path holding each other or does that mean we have to stop holding each other and continue therapy?"

"Yes."

Willow and I continued our walk holding hands.

CHAPTER TEN

There Were Things I Never Did Get Around to

The things that I never get around to is telling you that we have nothing in our future except that we are planning never to be separated, no career plans, no aspirations of career goals, nothing, only each other.

"YOU CAN FEEL relatively comfortable," I questioned Willow because I loved to confuse her and cause her to want to play, "that the question is covered about as well or better than it would have been had we covered it the way that we knew for sure was not the best way, don't you think?"

"You are probably right," Willow agreed, "but do you know how well you have to be before I beat you up again?"

Willow was so beautiful when she pranced in triumph twisted her little perfect body and turned her face to the breeze to allow her raven tresses to flow from her face and expose that open brilliant smile as she teased and laughed just enough to excite the living hell out of me and cause me, no matter where we were or among whomever we may be, to want to pull that little brown body of hers so close that it could be a part of my own, inseparable, just as we were, never to be parted. No way, no how, no matter what, Willow and I were one. It could be no other way. It had been seen, shown, proven, that we could close those little gaps of slip-ups. We would close the big ones, too. We wanted to and we would.

"I don't know how well I have to be, but it won't matter much after we go to Georgia," I informed Willow. "I'll be legally yours and you can beat me unmercifully on your own schedule, at you own whim."

"I can hardly wait." Willow stopped suddenly. "I just thought of something else," she said. "After graduation when I have to deliver my mother to New Jersey or to Old Town, Maine, where ever she decides to go, then you will belong to me. I will own you. Ha! Then you will have to go with me. Ha, Ha, Ha!"

Damn, I loved the way she laughed and teased. I was thinking, "I have to copy that ha, then the ha-ha, then the ha-ha-ha routine, if I ever want to be a comedian." I was thinking too, that I liked everything about this little girl anyway. I just really liked this little girl.

She walked backwards ahead of me. "What a tease," I thought, "just enough for me to show that I would come for her if she got as much as a step away from me." She did not disappoint. "Laugh if you will, wonderful one," I told her as her arms closed around me. I helped her a little, "but I would put that ring in my nose just to get to go with you. After all, how far out of town do you think you would get without me before I would come looking for you?"

"Ever how far, you would meet me coming back for you," she admitted.

It was a question that I had been hesitant about asking but asked anyway, "How to you think your mother is going to like me or accept me?"

Willow thought for a moment, "I know she remembers you from the vineyard incident and she speaks very highly of you. I told her like a bit over a year ago when you pruned those grapes that I was in love with you, when my grandmother was at your throat, yet I will never know until we put it right in front of her face how she will accept you, primarily because of your position on religion would be the only thing that I believe she could consider a negative."

Being the first time Willow had commented, I felt I needed to get it into the open air, "What is my position on religion as you see it right now, Willow?"

"Oh, I think it is exactly like mine," Willow assessed, "much like it is for social involvement, otherwise useless."

"You said it better than I could, so now let's go back to talking about your property, me. Your mother is expecting you to stay with her wherever she goes, right?"

"Yeah, but she will have no say in the matter when we are married and I am thinking that it is one of the things that justifies."

"Plus the fact that it keeps you from tarnishing me sexually." I allowed her to giggle a little and pretend that I was foiling her fiendish master plan, and continued on the subject at hand. "Then, for example, what if her choice is to stay in Vineland and she insists that the two of us stay in Vineland with her, the vineyards, your friends there . . . , accepts me as your monkey boy, lap dog, bear rug, and all the rest?"

"Now we may be taking the ownership thing too far because I will be as devoted to you as you will be to me, your cheap whore, your cook, your . . . , property. I love you."

"You said the right thing that time. I love you, so what if she wants both of us to stay and don't ever be my cheap whore, always charge me, make me pay, even if it is just to keep me working as your love slave until I am so weak that you can fold me up and roll me up into a little ball and hold me against your breasts until I can decide which one is my favorite."

"Eeeek!" Willow put her arms around me, held me so warmly and said, "that is about the most exciting thing I have ever heard! Can we talk about it?"

"That's what we are doing now, my precious love."

"I mean talking about the lovemaking until we can no longer talk about the love making."

"I'm not sure we need to talk much about that or you are going to get all worked up again and you know what happens, only the next time I rip off all your clothes and take you to a time and place in your heart that you have never ever been, or me either, but I had such a good sales pitch going there I didn't want you to find out that I probably couldn't do what I was popping off about doing."

"We do have to stop this love making dialog and go back to serious business," Willow decided, "or it will get out of hand and I won't be able to give to my new little child-like husband what I have saved for you for these past three years."

"You put it that way, my little child-like bride-to-be and I have to help to keep you off me," I told my Willow, "as bad I hate to at these times of almost uncontrollable lust."

"Ah, the beauty of lust," my Willow waxes most poetically, "while it has so long been critically reviled as the ogre of the heart at this time in one's life rises to be the second most beautiful word."

I asked, "the second most beautiful, then what could be the most beautiful?"

"Orgasm," Willow responded, and we both laughed almost unjustifiably.

"No," I disagreed when I was able to take a rest from the laughing, "I think Willow is the most beautiful word and I am trying to get my Willow off the track toward enjoying her word and saving it for later, and in a way I hate what I am doing."

"You're right," Willow agreed, "I guess we do have to stick with the bad decisions after they are made as she embraced me again and kissed me warmly and held me so very closely. I held her and held her some more, feeling first hand what the mistake of the decision was all about, denial, abstention, yeah and protection of wonderful Willow.

"I loved this little precious one, and lusted so badly after her," I spoke to myself. I felt so right and so wrong about what we were doing and what we were not doing all at exactly the same time. This is crazy. This is love. I didn't have any experience with the love part but I felt good about it and it appeared that Willow and I together were doing what had to be done to protect it. There was just that bothersome batch of concern that considered if it might be just as well protected to go the other way but I couldn't dwell on that or it would allow things to get out of control. Then, were it wrong, then it is done and cannot be undone.

"We were at the point," Willow redirects the chat session, "to where we were deciding about deciding about New Jersey assuming that my grandmother is shooting in the direction that we think she is aiming.

"I think you know New Jersey and you need to decide," I suggested.

"But that would be your decision," Willow assured me.

"My decision is that you should make that type of decision or at least let me know what you would like to do about it, because I want to be with you wherever, whenever, however . . . , you know, all the evers."

"Has Nancy said anything to you about Grandmother calling?" I nodded negatively since I had no information as to what was coming down and wanted Willow to continue. "It's uncanny that you bring this up, and I was discussing it just as if you were a party to the conversation that Nancy and my grandmother had. My grandmother thinks you are an absolute genius now and wants you to come to New Jersey and look at the vineyards. She says you did magic to the ones here and the ones there need you."

"I knew you couldn't go right now and was not certain that you would go if she wanted you there, you know, permanently, I mean. Then again, I was afraid I didn't know how to ask you if she wanted to lure you there."

"The way you ask me anything, Willow, the better half my heart, is just to ask. Get it into your precious little Penobscot noggin that I am yours, heart, soul and mind."

Willow continued. "Okay then, mine, Nancy told me that when she came by to bring my clothes and I called her when you were in the shower the next day." The place is a wreck. My father was supposed to have been up there for preparation and to decide on what is pruned but nothing got done and it is too late now. My father made so many trips up there that there never was a professional caretaker hired. There's several hundred acres."

I responded, "I know, you have told me about it. Tell your grandmother that we can be there next week if we have to but I want her to find some laborers somewhere and put them out there with whatever tools are necessary and clean all the weeds, grass, whatever, that can potentially grow up to touch a grape. I know nothing about fertilization, water needed for the zone or what to expect of the weather that may factor into production. These are things that we can learn and we can get the place back in shape in short order."

I suddenly realized what I was saying and figured I had better get myself back in line with reality. "Willow, honey," I pleaded, "I know nothing about growing grapes."

"The thing that you don't know is that you know a lot more than you realize, because growing one plant is not a lot different than growing another and you know how to grow the others. Furthermore, my grandmother loves you about as much as I do."

"It is true to an extent that if you can grow one thing you can grow another, and I have had a little training on grape production at a seminar that I took down at Auburn, and I know about how to ask questions but the main thing I know is to keep the vineyard clean, and that actually goes for any type of plant. Now we are almost back at the car," I continued on my role as a pseudo vineyard manager, "so why don't we go home, call your grandmother, and find out what she is doing and find out if she is trying to talk you and me into relocating in Vineland and working in the family business and if so to start talking money, residential facilities, universities where you and I can go to school and . . ."

"And, what were you about to ask?" Willow was itching all over to say something.

"I was yielding to you, my angel," I said, "because I thought you needed to have some input before I start making decisions on something I know nothing about."

"I am about to explode with excitement," Willow announced.

"Excitement? I had hoped you would cool down by now," I joked, well, sort of joked. I thought I knew why she was excited but I was trying to pretend that I couldn't imagine anything that could possibly make her happy other than what we had already decided, and that was to live happily ever after in each others arms.

"Everybody is leaving me but you. Nancy is going off to Tuscaloosa, and you are essentially playing into my dreams and I don't even have any, but more like you are making dreams for me and playing into them. That's where the excitement comes. I mean, really it looks like to me I am getting so much as I am getting you and I have little to give you, so much like it is not an even type of deal."

"Then it looks to me as if I am getting so much in you and I have so very little that I can give to you, just the bare minimum me, like you are fulfilling my needs for me before I can't even sort them out and know what they are."

"We might be good for each other, kind of matching up it seems."

"The things that I never did get around to telling you this morning that I was thinking about while you were sleeping," I continued, "was that there was nothing in our tomorrow. No career aspiration, no college hopes other than that one year of non-renewable Methodist scholarship, and it appears that your grandmother is calling for us."

"Let's get you in the car and go call Grandmother."

When she talked to Nancy and her mom, they told her, "Willow has been in love with this kid, the one who did your vineyard last year, since she got here and she has fallen into a situation where she is not going to ever leave him now. Then my grandmother replied, 'tell them to get their love-stricken asses up here, then.'

My assumption is that she wants you on a permanent basis and I have another assumption now that you liked the idea and I got excited about it."

"Let's just call her and find out," I suggested.

We arrived at the house and I offered to get myself out of the car. I did it! Yea! "Call your grandmother," I said, "and figure out what would be the most ideal situation for her and I will agree to every detail as long it keeps me with you." Then I backed down just enough to say, "I trust you to handle the details, not that your grandmother is not trustworthy, but you and I are one entity now, just a common pile of two humans making up one blob."

Willow searched her purse for her address book and started to flip. "Grandmother will be at the trucking company office about now," she mumbled, and she dialed the operator and gave her the number.

Grandmother answered. There were the typical cordials, then Willow went direct and said, "grandmother, he got hurt really badly and I am here to take care of him and I guess I just went over the edge or something. I just refused to leave him or even to go so far away from him that I couldn't touch him." Following a moment of silence she spoke again, "Grandmother, we talked about what we had to do to satisfy our society and we did discuss it but we are not yet in the position to start telling people anything until we get it all lined up. Maybe it is our way of saying that we will find out what others want and put as much as we can into getting done what we have to do."

I listened but getting only one side of a conversation is tough on an eavesdropper like I profess to be, so I put my arms around her and tried to hear what her grandmother was saying. No luck, but I did get some rather good snuggle kind of loving.

Willow spoke again, "We are leaving here, no matter what happens anywhere else, for the simple reason that all these people know is fighting and hurting other people, like it is a whole different world here, Grandmother." She listened for a moment, "that stuff is lots of fun at first, Grandmother, but neither of us enjoy hurting people and we both want to just go away." Grandmother talks. "We want to go to school and we can do that there, so we have decided that we can run the vineyard and get our education, and begin a long life of never being separated from each other." I had to assume that Grandmother was talking. "We will be there within two days after graduation. I love you Grandmother and Bud does too even if he hasn't said so because he knows already that you love him, and you are loveable you know."

"Grandmother's lawyer up there suggested that she set everything up in a contract, much like a sports contract, since we are here and she is there and we have to relocate and it can function like that until my father's will is probated. She will deposit $10,000 in my account because she can and I can get you on that account. The $10,000 is half a signing bonus of $20,000 and we will get the rest when we arrive in New Jersey and can open an account there. The estate will pay

MY WILLOW

for our education as an operating expense. Our home can be either the caretaker's residence or the guest wing of the big house with maid services provided for either of the places we choose. Our annual salaries will be based upon the vineyard income and my grandmother's accountant says we will earn somewhere around an additional $14,000 for the two of us for the rest of this year. If our efforts prove fruitful, pardon the pun, then the limit is sky high."

"I can add and that is about $17,000 per year or three times what my father makes and that ain't shabby," I said, now how long so we have to decide?"

"We are committed," Willow announced and I knew she was holding back on the celebratory explosion or thought she was, "and you earned us that by pruning 40 acres of grapes for my grandmother. You are unbelievable." She kissed me.

"We leave the day after graduation," I told her that he had overheard as she was talking on the phone to her grandmother. "Also," I added, "I think you were telling her about our secret plans?"

"With her it is like putting it in a vault," Willow assured me, "but I didn't give her the details like we were going to Georgia and when, I mean it's like we don't even know that.

I have to call her back when I talk to you, so I'll call her again tomorrow. I'll tell her what you told me on the advice as to how we can get started before we get there."

"We have to get back to school so we can graduate, Willow," I offered, "and we just have to show up some to do so, I think. Shall we try it tomorrow?"

"I am a bit nervous," Willow admitted, "if you don't mind my being strange about this situation we are in. I can handle the bad that might come to us but there is going to be so much good that we are to be, and should be expected to be, overwhelmed. My devotion to you last Monday and my staying with you is expected to stimulate a world of questions. We have to answer them somehow. What do we tell them?"

"The truth!" I thought for a second or two and continued, "we have to tell them just enough to cause more questions, I am certain, but we can drive away to New Jersey with many of them unanswered. Like for example, we can tell them that we have decided that we are inseparable and figure we will marry or people around us will accuse us of that which does not please them. We have to tell them that I have been offered work in another state where I can work and go to school, and you will return home to New Jersey. We may not even want to tell them that we are going away together, just at the same time.

"What we tell them is that I shall walk away from the life here. If it provides people great joy to say I am running away from a fight, then they can have the great joy. We don't have to mention that anybody who tried to interfere will provide us the great joy of busting some asses."

"If we can have Mama get us out at 6:00 in the morning, we go to my house, I get dressed for school and you find out about whether my mother will love you as yours loves me. We can end today of the old life and begin tomorrow as the first day of the new life."

When she said the significant things, Willow seemed to always have her arms around me and she could add emphasis to words or impact to statements as she held me a little tighter and work in a little squeeze here and there at certain instances. "Gosh, I love you, Willow."

"You beat me to it," she said as she squeezed, "I love you, I love you, I love you." She pulled away just enough so that he could see her eyes in front of mine and said, "I have a new pledge. I pledge to do my best in every way to love you more every day, to tell you more every day, and to make every day better for us." She kissed me. That's a Willow thing that I liked just about the best of the many things.

"Now help me if I need it," I said, "I pledge to do my best to love you more every day and to tell you I love you more every day and to make our love better every day for us. Close enough?" I kissed her to complete the routine.

With Willow, everything gets sealed with a kiss. I wouldn't have it any other way. "We haven't seen Louise in a couple of days," Willow noted.

"We haven't seen Louise in one day," I noted with corrective satisfaction. "We have the doctor at 2:00, and we need to stop in on her and maybe she will want to do another exercise run with us after that. What do you think?"

-0-

The doctor was amazed at the progress that we were making, or that Willow was making, toward getting my body parts back to functioning. We told him that the nurses who took care of changing the bandages were the miracle workers. They were already working so it was a chance to thank them in person with a compliment.

Dr. Haggerty chatted a little into more detail than the standard doctor-patient chit-chat. He said, "we look forward to having you two come in every day at two, rather like the spirit of the two of you rather lift the spirits of all of us for the afternoon."

We talked of lots of things about us that we were discussing in our expanded time together. We told him of our plans to relocate and fact that we knew we were expected to get married. We felt almost like we were lying about that part, because we were so enthusiastic about it, but being only 17 we had to act mature about things. Dr. Haggerty told us that we should sneak over to Georgia where the age was 16 for consent. "We talked about it," Willow admitted, "but we will both be 18 in July."

I told the doctor a bit of our situation,. "About everything was dumping on us for awhile it appeared. Willow had lost her father. Her grandmother has already moved away and her mother is waiting for Willow to complete school to go away herself. Nancy Bradley, your Nurse Nan's niece and Willow's constant companion, is heading off to Tuscaloosa. That leaves me, and you know some of what I am going through and you have seen only the tip of the iceberg."

"You could say fate did it. Nah, Willow and I were so mad about each other that we waited and we were ready and willing when the time came, and it came to us because we wouldn't let one of us get far enough away from the other. It wasn't fate or luck or anything accidental, she was here when I went down and she picked me up."

"And, he is picking me up at the same time, so he gets to be my hero and the hero of my family. My family has a vineyard in New Jersey," Willow told the doctor. "My Grandmother went there when we sold the house and found it had been neglected. We're going there to do our best to turn it around just as Bud did the one here. Whatever we do will be better than it is now. My grandmother loves him almost as much as I do. Now I have to find out about how my mother is going to feel about him tomorrow."

"So, your mother has never met him?" Dr Haggerty asked.

"No she has seen him while he was working in the vineyard a year ago," Willow told the doctor, "and she does speak highly of him, but that could be because of the controversy we had and how he came out on top with the vineyard pruning and my grandmother. I told her that I was secretly in love with him, so he is known as a mother and daughter would do girl talk. We have done some girl talk, too, where Bud is concerned."

The doctor was almost apologetic, "I hope you guys don't mind me asking questions but I sort of head up the Bud and Willow fan club around the clinic here, and you two are like cult heroes. Other patients come in here with stories of both of you and the nurses feel important because they have met you."

"We really haven't done anything actually," Willow admitted.

"I know," Dr. Haggerty agreed, "but it is a wonderful love story about the two of you, and you did whatever it took to generate the story about how Willow beat up the big guy and you knocked his wife in the cold water."

"It's not the official story," I corrected, "but it is the true one and I know how you got that one, from Danny Landry, Mrs. Haggerty's seventh grader."

"Yeah, Beth came home with that story last night and we laughed for hours about how the kid told that Willow spinned, flipped, rolled and kicked his butt out into the water," the doctor laughed. The three of us laughed, actually.

"The bad part about this," I complained, "is that I am the one who is supposed to be known for kicking butt around here, then I get mine kicked and little Willow here turns instant ninja princess and makes us both heroes."

"This even makes it more fun," Dr. Haggerty laughed and looked at me, "you didn't know she was a ninja princess?"

"No! Not a hint! And she and little Danny Landry's mother planned what I termed a premeditated kick-ass and I knew nothing of what was planned or what we were getting into," I assured our doctor friend. I was scared about half buttless, to use one of my father's terms, and Willow just pranced right in among those waiting for us in ambush and started to pushing them around. I can't repeat the language she used, doctor."

"We heard about the ambush," our doctor chuckled a bit on a serious note, "I can't believe these people had planned to attack you two."

I assured him, "we are most certain that they planned to scare us into making some type of agreement to get their kids off the hook for beating me up. Thanks to Willow and her friend Louise Landry, the plan got reversed on them."

"I don't mean to break up the fun talk," I was apologetic, "but I need to know what is my chances of getting your okay to attend classes tomorrow."

"My only problem with that," Dr. Haggerty advises, "is that it could be quite painful with hallway bumps and I would want you to put your left arm in a sling, during the time in school only, just to allow you a little more freedom of body swings for maneuvering in crowds, and if we could get you to wear upper body scrubs, you would be a lot more visible to those who will need to avoid contact." He nodded approval, "and I will have Angela here get the scrubs for you, two, because the two of you will be together and I know that. Tomorrow again at 2:00 and bring me a good report."

On the way out Willow needled me, "some hero you are! Louise and I do all the work and you get to share the credit, while all you did was act like a decoy."

"Decoy? We need to get you one of those duck calls, so you go 'wack-wack-wack" and I come in a hurry."

"Or," Willow suggested, "one of those piercing whistles so I can blow it and you come running and drop at my feet and pant and slobber, then I pat you on the head and give you a bone."

"I'm curious," I asked, as we drove out of the parking lot, "why would we use those things when I will be touching you at all times anyway?"

"And, I will be the one slobbering and panting at your feet," Willow adds.

"We are a couple of silly kids but a couple of happy kids, are we not?"

"We are! You know," Willow adds, "I have never been so happy in my life."

"Most of my life I have been unhappy. Too poor, people on my hind end, don't like the weather, working like a slave, and if the weather is good you pray for rain to get to rest. Today, just as it has been the past few, I am happy, like in a wonderland of everything good. I am committing to begin tomorrow by holding you with two arms forever and ever because today we quit on the old life and start the new one tomorrow, remember?"

One of Willow's favorite ways to transfer her love is to touch the back of her hand on my cheek. As she touched me she said, "I remember, but I will let you renege on that commitment if you hold me twice as much with the one arm, okay?"

"Okay!" How could you beat a deal like that? Everything is going like it is a win-win life that I am living now. Oops! A reality thought hits me suddenly. The cotton needs to be planted. Who is going to plant the cotton. Bill and Chuck McWorter, maybe, they always help me whenever I need them, but I haven't even slowed down enough to ask them. I haven't even seen them and I know they would have come to see me as soon as they heard about me getting my butt whipped. They would have laughed at me, with some kind of garbage like. "me and Bill could have done a better job than they did."

Aching and paining and complaining have taken what little time I have been able to spare from total dedication toward loving my Willow. There has not been a lot of time away from Willow and thoughts of Willow, with loving and planning and planning and loving, which just means a hint of planning mixed in with the lots of loving.

"Oh, Willow, my most wonderful and sweetest and most loving . . ."

"Your wonderful Willow who interrupts you when you start to tell her about a boo-boo that you have made?"

"Yeah, that's the one and only."

"Tell your sweet Willow what it was you did so I can begin my search for the time and energy so that I can forgive you long before it interferes with our hugging and kissing routines."

"I have 135 acres of cotton that has to be planted and I can't do anything about it but think about it and I even forgot to do that."

"When your father comes home about 6:00 this evening we have to collar him and make some plans that . . . , well, you couldn't even help by driving a truck or tractor."

"Good idea, now let me add another one to that one," I suggested. "The McWorter family lives in the only house on the left if we go past my house around the curve to the school and turn right, then another right at the baseball field. We can go see Chuck and Bill and their little sister Adelaide, we call her Addie, and you will love this little girl. Well, Chuck and Bill may not be home yet but Addie is almost always home taking care of her mother."

"Oh, I thought you were talking about a little girl, you mean small like me."

"No, she's little," I assured my Willow, "maybe about . . . ," it was difficult to show her how tall in the car, so I suggested, "maybe waist high to the two of us."

"Then she must be about ready to . . . ," Willow interrupted herself as she was driving up to the McWorter home, "she couldn't be old enough to take care of a mother could she?"

Willow stopped and started to run around to help me out when the front door opened and Addie came out. Willow stopped, forgot about me and ran to Addie McWorter, dropped to her knees, they embraced, and Willow said, "Addie McWorter, I have heard so much about you from Sara and Carrie Terrell and Bud's Mama, nothing at all from him because he was surprising me and I was letting him, but I feel like I know you already, I am Willow Preston, the one I know you have heard about who is so madly in love with him," as she turned to point at me. I had made it out of the car on my own and I got me an Addie hug, too.

"Oh, Willow," Addie excitedly addressed her, "you better believe we have heard about you and you might be as beautiful as we have been told."

"Not even close, Addie," I corrected, "this girl is so awesome in every way that nobody can come up with words to describe her."

"Oh, we've heard the story about how you two have worshiped each other for three years and finally got united and now you can't be separated," Addie explained. "Really, You two are the talk of the countryside and it is all good talk. Oooh, especially the part that Louise told us about when Willow kicked Shorty's butt into the lagoon."

Yeah, they got the idea that they were going to ambush us and little Willow ganged up on all four of them," I laughed as I explained.

"I heard that Willow is almost as good as you," Addie teased.

I don't know, but I know one thing for sure, I am glad she is on my side," I assured her. "hey, where are those two little brothers of yours?"

"Three," Addie corrected, "Bill and Chuck, they are little like me for Willow's information, have been up in Tennessee all this week stubbing out some houses for their big brother, and Sid is driving them back. They should have already been here.

"I need to talk about planting cotton then immediately follow up with the corn," I said.

"That's why they're coming home a couple of days early," Addie assured me, "so they could have three days to plant, then Sunday if they can't do it in three days, and I think they figure on planting corn next weekend."

"You folks are the best friends I have in the world, Willow included in that." I got a big smile. Addie and I had dropped her from our business conversation and Willow had to be in all my conversations, all of my everything, actually. "and, Willow has been delayed from her visit with Louise Landry. They met and I am afraid Louise is going to take my Willow away from me."

"I doubt that," Addie assured me, "I have heard the stories about you two and there is not any way that either of you is going to be taken away from the other. Furthermore," she added, "any other two people waiting for so long for each other would have given up on the other had there not been a much stronger feeling that could have been held in just a normal devotion."

"We don't try to explain how we did it or how it happened," Willow said, "but it did and neither of us is going to let anything do damage to it. We've discussed it and it is like it that it happened and we're satisfied and don't even care if there might be something or somebody better by some other standards."

"We will all see you after about supper time," Addie waved us away so Willow could do her promised visit run, Louise Landry.

CHAPTER ELEVEN

Getting Some Requirements Out of the Way

Requirements established for my Willow are to get the graduation out of the way, yet we are presented with the requirements of others and that is to allow them to bully me around some more.

MAMA GOT US out about 6:00. I got a quick shower while Willow and Mama made breakfast. We ate fast and ran out. We had to go to Willow's house first and I had to meet her mother. Willow had run out of clothes. "I want to see myself in my own mirror," Willow decided. "I think your little sister's mirror flatters me and makes me look too happy and vibrant," she joked.

I sat thinking on the way, as Willow drove to her house, touching her hand, holding it, tracing the veins, feeling that there was not a tiny little spot on the girl that was not perfect and precious.

We took Willow's car. She wanted to offer it to her mother but she knew her mother usually refused to drive, having the maid at the big house drive her where she needed to go, which was not hardly anywhere. Willow knew that she and I could ride the bus back to the bluff and have my car for us to drive, "you know, the thing," she suggested.

Willow and I looked forward to the day we dreaded. Okay, so we dreaded the encounters yet we wanted to see friends, get the requirements out of the way that were needed to graduate, go through the proper motions. We felt that school was going to make it a bit difficult to continue the touching in the same continuous mode that we had been in, but knew we had to do it. There were some sacrifices to be made in the preparations to make it permanent, to be able to hold each other for the rest of our lives. Yep, we were working on it and it was going to happen. We were making it happen. I thought, "Wow, I love this girl."

So much had happened in the three days that we had been away that it seemed so much like half a lifetime. Everything was new on this particular day that was the same old stuff last week. Willow and I were different people today. We had damned well better be. We were responsible today for a single entity. We were not a couple yet, not by legal standards that were laid out for all to adhere to without question or complaint, but we had accepted adult responsibility.

Not being man and wife legally, we were not what society recognized as anything other than two separate people. What did society know? We were one people. Yeah, one. That's it! It's a new day that was the first of those that for all the rest of our lives we were as one. One what? We didn't care that it was not defined. We would get to that.

"Are you sure we can meet your mother," I asked, "answer her pointed questions and avoid getting killed before school today?"

"My mother will be okay with everything that we are willing to tell her," Willow promised, "which is the end result and we just have to assure her that we are saving the matrimonial plans to let the family get in on making the decisions for us, you know time and place, etc." She lined up a thought or two, "our Georgia trip is for us and if they want to have a formal wedding for us when we are of legal age here or New Jersey, then we can do it in the formal manner that will make the others happy. You like that?"

"I like that and I like my Willow," I said.

"Well, I love you," Willow was emphatic with the 'love.'

"I love you, my wonderful Willow," I said, "but I wanted to let you go first because you make it sound so much better when you do, you know, with the dramatic stuff. You like saying 'I love you' first."

"I do," Willow smiled and gave me an extra squeeze and the back of her hand on the cheek, kind of her silent way to say 'I love you.'

Willow drove on. I pondered. Thinking about the introduction coming up. Meeting a woman you fear is not easy for an injured man, not at all easy for an injured kid. Maybe fear is a bad word here, but I was nervous about meeting the lady who was to have me integrated into her life and she had no choice in the matter. It was Willow's choice and my choice and Mama Preston was out of the decision loop. I kind of felt bad. I got my thoughts going in that direction and began to feel sorry for the lady and start to feel less fear of the lady and fear the situation that Willow and I had gotten ourselves into.

I decided that we were a couple of selfish kids who thought of nobody but ourselves. Yeah, we did. We thought of Grandmother Preston. Well, Grandmother Preston thought of us and we responded to her thoughts and maneuvered her into

MY WILLOW | 127

a commitment that was to serve Willow and me quite well when the time came to prove that we were the hotshots as Grandmother had decided we were. Okay, so Grandmother maneuvered us. It still sounds right.

While Willow and I were doing for ourselves, we were not forgetting the needs of the family. Overall we were not, but what about Willow's mother? I didn't know. I really hadn't gotten into thinking about her. I had not met her. I wondered if I could use this as an excuse. Maybe I could say, "ma'am, I was personally waiting until I could be formally introduced at which time I could engage my thought processes to consider that the decisions that Willow and I were making would begin to include considerations for your well being."

Ah, that was good, or so it sounded, but the formal language would need to be toned down a little and allow the context of the thought and consideration to be more spontaneous. Then again, maybe a lie would be good, like, "yes ma'am, the decisions that we have made include provisions to insert considerations for you and your opinions prior to their being finalized." Again a bit formal but could be toned a little lower to make it seem more spontaneous.

As Willow pulled into the house, I looked at her and admitted, "there is a flood of fear that's engulfing me and I feel we need to back out of the driveway and high tail it 'anywhere there ain't no mother' that could make remarks contrary to my expectations of our being together in love forever and always."

"How many chickens did you tell me that your daddy has every year?"

"Three hundred."

"Three hundred and one," Willow jokingly numbered, "counting you." She laughed her triumphant little ha-ha-ha. She continued to laugh at me and pick on me unmercifully for being a coward, willing to take on any man and fearing all women.

As we walked in the door, Willow's mother was standing just inside. My first thought was "Wow!" Of course, that one was not allowed in the normal context, but I got it straightened out in my own mind rather quickly knowing my Willow was the only female person of interest to me. Well, she was a beautiful woman and I couldn't deny what I felt when I saw her for the first time, she did look good. Anyway, back to the real world, Willow introduced us.

"We call her Annalee because nobody can pronounce her Penobscot name," Willow smiled proudly.

"I have wanted to meet you for so long," I think I must have babbled.

"And, you have been the subject of lots of girl talk around here for years," Annalee told me, "but her father never knew about you."

"Honestly," I admitted, "I told Willow a few days ago that I am glad this happened to me when it did because of what has happened that we found each other, found out about each other, I mean how we feel about each other."

'Nancy told me that it was the most beautifully serious thing that she has ever seen," Annalee admitted.

I looked her in the eye, "Then you are okay with it?"

Annalee asked, "may I be brutally honest?"

"Please," I suggested.

"Willow has loved you so long," she told me, "but I was afraid she would let you go away and never know that because she was so afraid that you might not feel the same way, then when you got hurt nothing mattered but you. She didn't have to tell any of us."

"The fact is so simple that I believe she could have never known," I admitted, "because I likely would have let her go without expressing my love for her because we were two kids too afraid to break the rules that had been pounded into us for three years." Before anybody else could respond, "then again, I was telling myself to go ahead and get the rejection that I knew I would get anyway and I was trying to go for it."

Willow finally contributed, "Same here, Nancy and I were plotting to see if Nancy would do it or if I had to do it." She laughed, "Nancy told me once that if I didn't confront you that she was going to beat both our butts." She hugged me. I was hoping for a kiss but figured it was best that we get to know the mother more before we start to show her too much.

We got a good chuckle at Willow and me. Annalee stood with us just about like she was happy to be there but I had this strange desire to hear the words that told us that we were being approved. Willow did too, it seemed, and she openly stated it. "Mom, we have to know."

"Know if I approve or not," She asked, "then I wholehearted approve."

Willow and her mother celebrated with a hug and I got left out. They did some girl chatter then silence descended for a moment. I didn't know what to say so I joked, "how do I get repaid for all the knots in my stomach for the fears that I had for meeting you, Annalee?"

"Welcome to our family," Annalee said, "and I would give you a hug but I am afraid it would hurt you."

"Thank you, but I think I will endure that pain," I told her as I collected a hug.

Willow gave both a quick kiss and said, "I have to take a quick shower and if I scream, don't come running in to see me in front to my own mirror naked." she looks at her mother and adds, "his little sister's mirror makes me look happy and vibrant when mine never has."

Her mother assured her, "you look happy and vibrant so I think it might be you, so shower and dress, while Bud and I talk." She had coffee and I didn't really like the stuff but told her enough cream and sugar and I could stand it.

We sat at the table in the kitchen. I didn't want to get into questions but knew I had to, so I allowed her to hear it straight and to the point, "I don't know how much Willow or Nancy or her grandmother have told you but Willow and I are

MY WILLOW | 129

committed to each other so long as we both shall live and you can fill in the rest of the blanks. If you want to ask questions or assume the details, that is up to you."

"Her grandmother has told me everything," Annalee began, but I interrupted. "The steel vault, huh?"

"Yeah, but I have a key," she laughed, "and Nancy has told me everything the two of you know and lots more that she made up as she was telling it. Nancy is excited about you two. She's taking lots of the credit for the putting of the two of you together, sort of like she engineered the entire love story."

"Without Willow here, about all I can add is that we have pledged ourselves to each other for as long as we live and promised Grandmother that we would be there the second day after graduation."

"You both have committed yourselves to each other," Annelee pointed out, "yet, you have agreed to the formal wedding at some time." She gave me a serious look, and added, "I am a mother and I need to know more about what goes on between the two of you in the time that comes between now and the ceremony."

"I thought you approved of us," I challenged the lady.

"I approve but I need to know . . ."

"Approval is trust while trust is not needing to approve. Then, whatever we do in the interim is between Willow and me," I was pointed in stating, "but I will tell you that I will not approve of Willow telling you of that which we might do that could reflect in a negative manner upon your opinion of me or of Willow, and Willow has not given her approval of me telling you anything."

"That's the right answer," she said.

"Willow says that." I thought for just a second and went for the surprise, "Would you like to know if Willow and I have been sleeping together?"

"That wasn't what we just covered?"

"No! I didn't know that was what you were asking about, but I don't mind telling you that we have been sleeping together. Yeah, she put her Willow pillow – she handed it to you when she came in the door – on my tummy and slept there all night the first night while I was sleeping in a recliner. The second night I had a dream and moved to one side in the recliner and my left arm fell. As she sat in the chair with me, with my arm around her, she went to sleep. My mother put a quilt over her to keep her warm and she slept with me for a couple of hours."

"You are laughing at me," Annalee accused, "but a mother is concerned about her daughter and you are absolutely right 'approval is trust' and I need to trust that my daughter can take care of herself."

"I am laughing at the social addiction that people suffer from who thrive on the control of others' activities through silly judgments. I must inform you that you need to trust that I will take care of her. We love each other enough such that we want to honor the needs that we have to maintain the highest standards of respect for each other. People can say what they will. I can't stop them, neither of us can. We have discussed that we don't care about what others want or expect. What Willow and I want is to be able to answer to ourselves and to each other. Answer for the standards of living and the morals that we have already recognized as belonging to us."

"Church and religion?" her mother asked.

"I am not sure we need to even talk about it," I declared.

"You and Willow have talked, then I must assume," Mama Preston offered.

"Yeah! Of course, the reason for my condition is that I have had to fight for my right to believe as I choose, like I didn't want people telling me that I was to go to church where they said and when they said. Those people saw me as a threat to them or so I was told, and I don't know why."

I was hoping that I was giving her enough reason for the conflict so that there was no need to discuss philosophy. There was just too much to the philosophy difference that there could be some big reasons for conflict, I knew that and I was hoping that could be avoided. Being religiously naïve, I certainly did not want to get involved with the crazy people who comprise those radical cults. Those were people to fear, as best I could know, and I knew Willow's mom was in one of those things.

I was sitting in a seat in Willow's mom's kitchen and I was thinking it was a hot-seat. To some sort of a degree, I was scared, suddenly. I had gotten myself into a line of questioning that was certainly going to lead to conflict. I had no doubts. I decided to ask her to allow Willow and me to work those things into our lives in a way that is comfortable for us.

Mrs. Preston appeared almost as uncomfortable as was I as she terminated the long pause that was sitting between us threateningly, "your church and your religion have to be the . . ."

I interrupted! "Please Mrs. Preston, allow Willow to know that I will wait for her in her car." I stood and began to walk toward the door.

She called me. "Please come and sit with me," she pleaded. "I am sorry but I made a mistake and I have an extreme need to reconcile it with you."

I turned back toward Willow's mother and told her, "ma'm, I have no desire to hear anything more of how I must live and how I must think and how I must believe. I have made the point to you that the reason my condition is such as it is simply is that I will not be taken into someone else's spirit for control of how I feel and think. I was of the mind that you approved of Willow and me, so be it, but you begin upon the moment of stating that approval to declare to me that I am another of the victims of your church organization."

I took a breath and continued, "I used the word 'victim,' ma'am," I courteously stated yet I was angry, "because that is how you people are trained to pounce on the next person that you deem to be of interest to you, and with your stated approval of me, I must assume that I am of interest. No! You took your option to assign your spirit to an organization for their possession and use, while mine is assigned to Willow and hers to me. We are one person; we are one spirit. You have to know that and live with it, yet we came to you today to ask that you understand and accept that, though it is of no consequence. In more simplistic terms, we want you to embrace the entity of us as one, but if you don't then we shall still be the entity of us as one." I took a deep breath, "I know it sounds rather formal but I was hard at work trying to avoid saying we don't care what anybody else thinks, because we do, yet it will not change our direction."

"Mama," Willow came in, "I heard only that Bud was to wait in the car so I stopped and listened. Everything that he has said is what he should have said about us, except for the assessment of your church organization and I must say that I can't even disagree with that."

I quickly interjected, "and I must apologize for that, I have no right to assess your church organization, except that was the point in question, now that I realize."

"Don't apologize, please," Annalee said, "I was the one who was out of line. I completely forgot who I am and spoke what I am trained to believe just as he said, and I am the one who is so very sorry."

Willow took charge. "Give each other a forgiveness hug and I will go get your scrub and dress you," Willow informed me.

We embraced. It was a sincere embrace and gentle. Annalee held on a little longer, just to let me know that she was sincerely sorry, and I certainly was glad that there were no animosities held. She meant so much to Willow and Willow was everything to me.

Willow came back in. "Hey, you two," she instructed, "cut it short and I don't get jealous." As her mother released me, she walked into my arms and said, "it's a good thing you are holding me with two arms, you were holding my mother with two."

"I promised you that today was the beginning of the new life and I would always hold with two arms," I defended, hoping that was my explanation was good enough to justify holding her mother, also.

Willow turned to her mother, "his mother and I have to dress him at home so maybe you would like to assist me here?" She began to unbutton my shirt and sneaked a little kiss, pretending that she was sneaking it anyway. She had her mother take the right side of the T-shirt because Willow was more familiar with the lack of mobility of the left arm.

Annalee gasped, "Oh, I have never seen a body more beaten and bruised."

'Those are bruises?" I joked. "I thought that was my quarter Cherokee."

"Cherokee are not black and blue, my love," Willow corrected. Her technique for putting my shirt on me was to put it over my left arm, the more immobile one, then over the head then the right arm in before rolling it down over the body. Willow told her mother that the bad part of my body was the stomach and around the waist where most of the blows were concentrated. She explained that the left arm was used to sling-shot the body into the side of the bus, thus the solid-bruise effect of the left shoulder is from muscle and ligament strain and caused the three small crush breaks in the right arm and damage to the ear."

Annalee asked, "And you two are going to retaliate, aren't you?"

"We have no plans, Mama," Willow assured her but we are hoping there are some opportunities and one has presented itself already."

"Oh, the word came back, Willow," her mother said, "and it could scare a mother out of her wits, but you took on four of those crazy people?"

"No, only one big one," Willow corrected. "Bud put the other one in the water, with a little semi-accidental bump, but we made believers out of the four, we are rather certain."

"We are hoping we can just make it through the formality of graduation or either get our diplomas and fade away into the sunrise, you know, East to New Jersey. Both of us are really excited about the vineyard," Willow assured her mother. "Bud has promised to teach me to drive his little Ford tractor. His big John Deere scares me, and I can learn to grow grapes and to help run the vineyard."

"Are you taking me with you?" her mother asked.

"That has been our plan," I admitted., "tentative, of course, awaiting your approval . . . okay, so that is what we hoped for."

CHAPTER TWELVE

Some Heroic, Some Villainous

Always there are some heroes and there are some villains, some villainous who can turn heroic, then there is anger and pain that can reverse the direction of the best of intentions.

OUR MAN TRAVIS "Shorty" Terrell found himself in the position of power in the little Baptist Church in Newton's Bluff, Alabama then found himself a preacher pal, with the same intent. The Bible gave them some power, the church gave them some power and the numbers of Terrells per capita was added force. They lined up forces against me, it seemed to me they did. Shorty's young brother-in-law changed over to my side, maybe too late, maybe not.

I don't know if I changed directions, nor did Willow. I never asked myself where I was headed with pain and anger and I never asked Willow as she suffered my pain and shared my anger. We both hoped that the conditions were temporary, yet we feared that we had little or no control over either.

The numbers of Terrell's, the ambush from the back and the front subtracted all the power that I might have been able to muster. That is, if I could have done any harm to amount to much in the open against seven of them. I wished I had been afforded a chance to know that. Anger was a big part of that wish. Where I was trying my best to grow up, anger was just about all that was guaranteed on any day, that and fear. I just had not allowed fear to get a good grip onto me. The pain had; the anger had.

Anger against these people put an attitude in me that I was not exactly proud to have, but I understood why it was grating on Willow and she had picked up on the attitude regarding her position in the fracas, or the several of them. I felt her desire for somebody to give her a chance to expose her talents. Not the kissing talent, nor the way she said "I love you" that caused me to turn weak and vulnerable, but it is all about her kick-ass talents. She had 'em, too!

Wow, did that girl have those kick-ass talents! She had about everything but she really had a unique kick-ass power. One that was unique in this pathetic neck of the woods, anyway. There being so few girls about who didn't have to give in to the force of the bunch of overgrown ignorant male pseudo-humans that seemed to want to overrun the population.

Not a lot of people had done much over the years about the exercise of force that some people applied to other people. I guessed that this allowed the people to have an attitude that they could continue and build the force that they so freely applied to others. It was not understood, nor was it accepted in the tiny little niche that I felt that I had carved in this awful thing we call society. Willow didn't accept it as I hadn't. Maybe our attitude helped with our bond. The bond and the attitude were certainly there.

Power can confuse, we learn, and force might not always be the power that needs to be applied at any given time. Willow parked the car in the faculty line, where she always parked anyway. Maybe her reason for driving her own car was for the implied privilege. Some power came with that. She could have parked at Dan Bradley's house across the road, allowing maybe 10 more steps to have to be taken to the front door. She took the privilege.

I could feel the anger in Willow as I saw several people react to the car being parked. Willow and I had not been to class all week. She was noticeable. We walked toward the front steps, about a dozen of the steps that brought us to the level of the classrooms about four or five feet off the ground. We didn't see any of the six Terrell culprits, yet there were cousins galore, and they didn't even have to share the surname. A few people gathered near the steps, a normal hangout to keep from having to spend any more time than absolutely necessary inside the school.

There was at least one smart-ass in the group who directed his words toward Willow, "looks like somebody kicked your boyfriend's ass, huh, bitch!" Several hangers-out laughed. It seemed that it took so little, so very little, to trigger the laugh track from the smallest of minds.

Willow and I stopped. Willow turned to the boy, "Yeah, it does, but how would you know? You're too stupid to be able to figure that out on your own. Who told you? She goaded him. Willow wanted a fight, and I knew it and I let her go so maybe I wanted one as well."

Coming from a little girl, senior status or size didn't matter, it was literally a surprise, thus it came with a reaction of silence with the crowd gathered. Big mouth saw what he deemed to be a little girl, something typical of that which he and his friends and family had pushed around, kicked aside and taken advantage of for generations. He knew women could talk and threaten but he could not visualize a threat coming from one, therefore, what he saw in front of him was a noise maker. He decided, "I want to get me a better look at the cuts and bruises on that boy, just for laughs, you know." His group chuckled. Apparently their minds were so underdeveloped that it took such a small thing to trigger them to laugh.

Willow warned him to stay clear and put out her left arm, essentially to mark a line between the boy and his quest. The boy slapped the arm down. Willow hit him full force in the face with an open hand jab that caused the face to explode and the boy to start to back away, stunned, hurt and blood gushing from his nose and mouth. Willow reversed and put her right heel into the boy's chest at full force, kicking his smart-mouth, his body and all across the school lawn. She followed and stood as if to dare him to rise, dropped to both knees and delivered a devastating blow to the breast plate of the smart-mouth and followed with the other hand to the stomach evoking a discharge and no other action.

Willow stepped over the boy and righted herself in a demonstrative motion as if to denote, "I'm though with this one; next!"

One of his smart-ass' buddies rose to the occasion and advanced blindly toward Willow. I sunk the left toe into his stomach and half-turned to reverse a heel into his shoulder as he began to back away. I missed a little and got too much neck. "Oops!, I got too much neck with my balance being off with only one arm useable," I likely spoke aloud as I paused for a moment to assess the damage of my error. Learning that I was not so very bad off my mark, I allowed him to turn to look toward his buddy on the lawn, then used a lot of movement with little force and kicked the kid atop his pal, his brother as I learned later

Willow and I put our arms around each other. I told my fabulous Willow, "you were wonderful."

"You were wonderful," she told me. "You were protecting me, watching my back and I think I am in love with you." She smiled and held as I held her. For the moment we were oblivious to school rules.

"I was thinking that I love you," I assured her, "right now more than ever, but I might have gotten too much neck on that last one, with my balance being off, you know only one arm moveable."

"I think he will survive," Willow said, as we stood together and waited for somebody to move. Our anger was there, so maybe we were daring somebody to move. While we felt triumphant, there was this deeper concern that our feelings that we didn't want to have to do this. Willow was not cheering our victory, nor was I. I didn't feel victorious and I was reasonably certain Willow didn't.

Our audience was stunned, it appeared. Teachers were gathering. The baseball coach appeared, and he was also a history teacher that I assisted later in the day, normally, that is. Being the only male to appear so far, he walked to Willow and me, looked at the crowd gathered, most of whom were laughing earlier with the two boys in support of the Terrells who had assaulted me in the beginning of the mess that we were in.

Coach Hawkins asked, "Is the comedy part over?" Not a word was uttered in response to the question. He continued, "I think all of you need to go to your home rooms." The crowd didn't move. "Now!" he barked, and everybody moved. Willow and I waited. Still the coach had not spoken a word to either of us. He turned to the two on the lawn and ordered, "up off the grass, you two go to the nurse in the North end of the Ag Building and stay there until I arrive and that may be an hour. Might I note, boys," the coach added, "I know who you are and there is a record of where you live, and if you leave I will personally bring the Sheriff to get you."

The boys rose. The coach addressed them again, "shut up and don't mumble to me, and you will bet both your asses that I will hear from your parents one way or the other because you will either be picked up from the jail when your bond is paid or your parents will come to the school for you." Following a purposeful pause, he barked again, "am I heard and understood?"

Both hesitated, just enough to respond courteously to the coach, "yes sir." Surprisingly, the boys had learned courtesies.

I personally realized that Willow and I were alone outside with only Coach Hawkins. The Coach spoke, "some of the kids had heard that you two were planning to come to school today and came in to inform me that kids related to Monday's gang were making the grand plans to wait outside and have a little fun at your expense. I saw the whole thing from inside the front doors."

Willow's mother must have called, concerned about just what happened. I had allowed a thought to enter my mind that I was not so very pleased to find there, but it was there and I felt a strong need to deal with it. I was strongly concerned that the coach knew nothing of Willow's abilities, which might have meant that his hesitation for interfering could have allowed her to get hurt. So I asked, "did you not think that you might have let Willow get hurt by standing inside the door watching?"

"No, not at all." I am her Phys Ed teacher and I am the only one who sees the reports come in from Trong." He giggled at my concern and was confident in his decision to stall before coming to her aid, then added, "I knew she had you," then he laughed. "I apologize," the coach told us, "I have been bursting to laugh about the kick-ass that you two put on those two and had to turn it loose." He turned toward us and pleaded with us, "please never tell a soul that I said that but," looking at me he said, "I saw what you did to that kid from another campus that day and wanted to see Willow in action."

We assured the coach that he was safe with us, but I had a question for Willow, "honey, did you put out your arm out as if to tell him where the line was and to warn him not to come any closer?"

MY WILLOW | 137

"For the record, yes," she assured me, "for the truth, no! I knew he would hit the arm and I knew that until he did I couldn't reconcile myself that I could, without a small sense of guilt, legally break his face."

"You are a beast, you know." I accused her.

"I am," Willow admitted, "now is that all you love me for?"

"No, forever, and for always, for damned sure and for all the other reasons for, including for goodness sakes," I admitted. "Sorry, Coach, we've spent four days trying to occupy our time and Nancy Bradley forces us to say those things."

"You two need to catch up for the last three years, anyway," Coach Hawkins said, "That's what all the talk is about, the love story. Everybody says you two have been in love with each other for all that long and wouldn't admit it."

"It wasn't our fault, Coach Hawkins," Willow suggested, "our families made the rules and we would have busted them wide open by the time we turned 18 anyway, so the trouble makers just gave us a jump start."

"I didn't care about anybody else and couldn't so long as Willow was around," I told the coach, "and it was starting to build on me. Yeah, I had way too much thinking time out there on that tractor by myself and I was trying to figure out a way to approach her."

"All the teachers and just about everybody here is pulling for you," The coach said, "and the scrubs are a great idea that I think will cause all the kids with sense to avoid bumping you, so let's go find a class for each of us."

"Thanks, Coach! Willow and I both uttered our sentiments. We went to the office, signed ourselves in to avoid the homeroom teacher having to do so, and enjoyed a big welcome from the teachers and students gathered there. I had completed all my credit requirements and Willow had only two half credits that she was expecting to complete. One of her teachers was in the office, so she killed off the excused absences and gave her attendance credit for the rest of school term, citing extenuating circumstances.

"Your grades are good enough which exempts you from finals and all we are doing is reviewing for tests," Mrs. Harris noted. "You need to go see Mrs. Young for that math class and I think you will get the same thing. We did just that and Mrs. Harris was right.

We came back by the office to see Mr. Abbot. "Following the incident this morning," he said, "I am afraid for the two of you. What I mean is, I am afraid the two of you will have to go to too much trouble just to get inside the front door." He laughed, "Coach Hawkins wanted to go out this morning to see you two do what you had to do because he and I knew about Willow's skills, we don't think anybody else did."

"She has been so wonderful to me, Mr. Abbot," I told him. "I have no idea what my family would have done, what I would have done, what the nurses or the clinic would have had to do. Willow is everybody's hero, the most fabulous human being that I have ever known."

"You two waited so long to get it past your little heads that you loved each other, and I am so glad to see that you have brought it out into the open for both of you," Mr. Abbot surprised us. "Yeah, even the teachers all knew about you two and we have all been talking about it just like the kids have," he added. "We always have had to concern ourselves with the courtships to give us a possible leg up on trouble and it got so noticeable that neither of you would get involved with anybody else and it was noted, "if those two can't have each other, then they don't want anybody else."

"Damn, the man is such a romantic," I thought, "and we have viewed him all these years as a hard-skinned totalitarian with no heart." Willow and I both thanked him for his thoughts. "You do surprise us, sir," I told him, "that you are expressing those types of sentiments."

"You would have known about my soft side later," he assured us, "now let's do a better one. You may both have your diplomas early. Nancy Bradley has told us that you both are likely going to move to New Jersey, eventually go through some ceremony like a couple of good 18-year-olds and live happily ever after."

We agreed.

"Willow has been a greater help than either of you could have known with what she has done for the school, which includes what she has done in aiding your rehabilitation. The doctor, sometimes the nurses call here every day about 3:00 and we hear all the accolades of Willow this and Willow that. She has opened up the hearts of this valley and yours as well. Anyway, what I am trying to get to is that we want to give a special award to Willow for her greater contributions at graduation."

"Thank you, sir," Willow said, "and I am most appreciative for the thought, but I am embarrassed to gain the attention."

"Would you do it," Mr. Abbot requested, "for us, for the school, accept an award?"

"Of course," Willow agreed, "I just don't do things for the credit or the attention and that part is a little foreign to me."

"Then both of you will attend the graduation?"

"Sure, we will," Willow said.

I agreed, "we have scheduled our relocation to the Delaware Bay area in order that we might get to go through it. We have worked for it."

Okay, Willow," Mr. Abbot closed with us, "your man here has a couple of things coming to him, also. So take care, and don't worry about a thing until graduation, but if you want to come on by, any time is great."

Willow drove us by to see the nurse. There was no waiting room. The place was so small that you opened the door and found the nurse working or found her patients waiting. The nurse was taking care of the big-mouth with the busted face. I looked at the other one, "Are you okay?" I asked.

"What do you give a damn?" the boy growled.

"Slightly less than before I asked, smart-ass," I responded. "Now, you need to sit there and shut up long enough that you can hear what Willow and I have to say. Otherwise we will allow Coach Hawkins to have your parents pick you up after Sheriff Brown gets through with you. Might I add that before Sheriff Brown gets through with you, you will have lost a year of school like the others who ambushed me Monday morning."

"Our interest is not in harming you kids because you are being sent out by your parents," Willow announced, "and our beef is with the cowards who will send their kids out to do their fighting."

The other one pushed the nurse's hand away and asked, "you think you want to whip my Daddy's ass?"

Willow asked, "Is he not the coward who sent you two out to get your butts beat? Of course, his is the ass we want to kick. I kicked Shorty's ass didn't I?"

"Uncle Shorty said he fell in," the boy said.

"He lied," I corrected, "she kicked his ass just like she did yours."

The nurse interjected, "she did this?" pointing to the kid's busted face, as if delighted to know.

The kid didn't implicate his parents with a direct answer to the question, but his reaction was one that suggested that he believed his old man was guilty. I knew there was family talk, family laughing at the fact that his condition was to the liking of the fans of the fat-assed Terrell named Shorty. I was ready to follow through. The more Willow and I kicked ass, the more I was dedicating myself to kick some more ass and I was feeling like the pain was getting to the point where I was ready to endure some pain just for the sake of dishing some out. That part was beginning to bother me. I am not the type of person who can enjoy inflicting pain, no matter to whom the part is imparted.

"You shouldn't take the punishment for your parents' stupidity by having to go to school another year," I said. "If you don't want to listen, we're out of here." I reached for Willow's hand. "Gosh, I love you, sweetheart." We walked out the door.

"I am dying for a kiss but this is school grounds," Willow said.

"I'm dying to put both these arms around you and I am going to get them around you regardless of the pain," I promised.

"Let me help you," Willow offered and ran around the car to open the door for me, "you know, the standard routine." She walked into my arms and I put them both around her. No kissing, but we were in the street, yet treated the kissing like it was needing to wait for a more private place. After all we were still students.

Thinking that I had heard a noise, I turned quickly to see the younger of the two boys. He spoke, "I don't want to have to spend another year in school."

"Coach Hawkins will be here any minute now. You two need to get your heads together and tell him that you were horsing around and you were in a group that were all just poking fun because family members had told ya'll that we or I was at fault."

"Well, that part's true," the boy agreed, "Uncle Shorty told us at church last night that you were shutting down our church because you hated Reverend Foster and that's why all his nephews beat you up."

"You're Billy Dean, right? Just tell Coach Hawkins that you and Larry Dale got into this mess because Shorty lied to you, and Larry Dale got pushy because he didn't know the girl could kick his ass all over the county. You need to trust me Billy Dean that I am telling you the truth because I am the one out here running free while all the others have either been arrested or they are the ones we are trying to keep out of jail. You are in the middle of a war that Shorty Terrell started with me better than seven years ago. He is sending out kids to do his fighting. He is lying to you, getting you hurt, maybe adding a mark to your record that can follow you the rest of your life, and if I have anything to do with it and you people keep up your attacks on me, you can be certain that I will make a criminal record for each of you who is so stupid that you listen to Shorty.

Willow stepped in. "I did kick his ass into the lagoon a few days ago, and as I understand, I am the only one to ever fight back against him directly, because he is supposedly too big and mean. He is not too big and the mean is quite a lot less now," Willow informed him.

"If you and Larry Dale don't take care of yourselves, none of those sorry assed people will." I assured the boy. "They don't care and have demonstrated that fact by keeping up with the routine of sending you out." I changed the course of the discussion. "Billy Dean, dammit," I told the kid, "the reason your preacher is in jail has nothing to do with me, but a rape charge that was brought against him in Louisiana."

Billy Dean never waned in defiance as he asked, "why do you give a damn?"

"Because so long as the adults are chicken-shit cowards and they send their kids out to get yourselves hurt, they will just keep putting out more kids, we keep kicking more kids asses. I have been shot twice, ambushed twice and beaten once and I am pissed," I made myself loud if not perfectly clear. "Then again there is two of us now, and we are going to kick some ass, and the rest of the county who ain't Terrell or Thompson, or whatever you are, is on our side, including the Sheriff."

"If that is not good enough, Billy Dean," Willow interjected, "I have spoken with JD Terrell's mother and the mother of those other two, other than Phillip's Mom, and they don't want you coming out here and doing Shorty Terrell's dirty work and getting yourselves hurt while he is lying to you through his green teeth. And, I don't enjoy hurting you. I did enjoy hurting him, because he got you hurt, and the others. We just did his work. We have more to do. Either you cooperate with Coach Hawkins, or as he commented, he will turn you over to the Sheriff like the others last Monday."

Willow and I seated ourselves in the car. The boy stood, likely thinking. I added one more thought to the mix, "Billy Dean, you are on the side that can stop this war that Shorty has lied and threatened everybody else into and has been enjoying up until now, laughing and popping off to his cronies about how he controls the ass whippings around here. That fat piece of shit is afraid of me and now of Willow. You can allow him to keep getting you kids hurt, because we are going to hurt you if we need to do so. Look at it this way, kid, I have been shot twice and have had seven of you guys beat the hell out of me and I didn't quit, yet I am trying to help you.

Why am I helping you? Because I don't think you are stupid enough to keep doing Shorty Terrell's dirty work and getting your ass kicked all over the county if you know the truth of what is happening. If you don't believe me, find out the facts." The kid didn't walk away immediately, so I picked up again, "you ask why I care, then maybe I am too lazy to want to have to work to kick the asses of all of you simply because you are too stupid or both you and your parents are too stupid to look at Shorty Terrell and tell him that he is a lying fat-assed piece of shit who is afraid of a 115-pound 'little girly,' as he refers to my Willow. Drive on, honey. This kid ain't worth my time."

"Coach Hawkins will be here in about five minutes. We are just trying to help you," Willow told him, "so get Larry Dale to cooperate with the coach. Get him to call your parents instead of the Sheriff."

She drove away. I pretended I was really pissed at the boy because he wouldn't listen. "Willow," I addressed the love of my life that I knew was the one for me to want to be with forever, "what do you think are your chances to remain a virgin until we can go to Georgia this weekend?"

CHAPTER THIRTEEN

Five Pounds of Self-Rising and Some Black Pepper

"Five pounds of self-rising and a 'thing' of black pepper," was what Mama sent us to the store to get, but we enjoyed the view and made some friends, among other activities.

BEING FREED FROM the classroom for a couple of weeks was not exactly what we had looked forward to but maybe would have had we known that we might be able to expect it. A big surprise to say the least. Willow and I had no plans; now we have to make some.

We visited again with Willow's mother just to get the schedule down between them. She was conditioned to wait until after the graduation ceremony, so that left so little for debate. We also cleared it that she had no intentions of going back to the reservation, inasmuch as she and Grandmother Preston had determined that they were both needed in New Jersey.

Willow offered her mother the car. She declined the offer.

Willow wanted to see some different things that they had planned to see, like the island and she was most fascinated by the thought that she might get to visit awhile with Ol' Charlie Wolf and she was thinking that she might get to work in the garden with my mother for the afternoon. She had never done that since she was a child in the village on Spectacle Pond, and desired to see what it is like to cause things to grow.

We had to go to the drugstore for more of the balm for the left shoulder, then to the doctor at 2:00 and we needed to exercise the left shoulder. Though the schedule was reduced to twice per day for the 2-mile walk, we enjoyed it so much that we didn't mind getting another trip in. There were even thoughts about driving over to Triana and to Rock House Landing, just to see places that Willow had never seen. She was an outdoor person, alright, and I liked that. She wanted to see places where I grew up. I could hardly wait to do things with her in the vineyard. She was so excited about learning about things.

"Hey, I just thought of something, my love," I told Willow, "Chuck and Bill are planting today. We can go out and see what happens with that process."

"Now that would be the most fun we could have with our clothes on," Willow said then shook her head from side to side. "I don't know why I said that after what we did with our clothes on a couple of days ago."

"Please, Willow, honey," I implored her, "that was the most beautiful experience and you make it seem like we did something wrong."

"It is wrong to lose control and we lost control," Willow argued.

"I felt we were both in complete control and we expressed our love without violating any trusts between us," I laid down my point of debate.

"We sort of had sex with each other," Willow said.

"How do you sort of have sex," I asked, "is that like masturbating?"

"What? Two people can talk about masturbating? No!"

"We are not two people, Willow," I explained. "We were two people but we have been folded inside each other, squished together, stirred and mixed, blended, all the above and we are one. We have pledged ourselves to each other, several times over and sealed it with kiss after kiss. And, there is nothing between us that is mine or yours any more but all is ours."

"Now you tell me that we have nothing that is private between us," she summarized, "because there is nothing that is separate from the other. Do I have this correct?

"Right on, my precious one."

"You mention often that I have a nice butt, am I correct?

"That is a fact, my precious one, you do have one fine little posterior on you."

"And, 'nothing is mine or yours any more, but all is ours' which means that any time you want you get to see my butt, to touch it, to caress it, stroke it, tease it, pat it, play with it, maybe kiss it . . . ,"

"I really, really like the touching, stroking and caressing part that you are talking about."

"You have a little skinny butt like it is about barely worth sitting on and that is all I get in exchange for the contribution of this fabulous bottom of mine to the union that is now us, but I guess it is okay for serious kicking and more kicking, just enough to make it swell up and look a lot like a couple of melons and be very painful to sit on."

"Which brings me to the point I was trying to lead up to," I assured my precious Willow, "I mean that there are still things, though we are one, that are private to the person originally bringing it to the union."

"You had a great argument there," Willow agreed, "it is amazing how you figure out these complicated things, but there is one that I'll bet you can't figure out, and that is how in the world can I justify this extreme love for you."

"You call that 'extreme' while I have this love for you that was merely extreme before it compounded so many times. I win!"

"I'm better at kissing than you are," Willow boasted as she parked her car in front.

"You need some practice before you try to get into a real test with me, so since we are one now, I guess I will have to sacrifice myself for your practice."

"I am starting to like the part about making your little butt sore."

Upon arriving at the house we found that it was empty so we practiced on Willow's kissing. I wouldn't let her know how good she was at it for fear that I would lose out on the practice routines.

We found Mama in the garden. First off, she sent us to the little store for some flour, self-rising, she preferred, "and while you are there,' Mama suggested, "maybe you should pick up some black pepper." We decided to walk. It was such a short trip. Because we left from Mama's garden, we walked the back road or street if you want to be loose in the description of a graveled road. There were houses on the left and the Baptist Church was there.

We got to the end of that leg of the trek, which was about two blocks, and turned to the right to go back to the main road where the little store was located. It appeared as if a town could have grown up there if everybody had cooperated and followed the original plans. It was fun walking, fun talking and telling Willow about the people who lived in each house, my fourth-grade teacher, the empty parsonage. Yep, empty as a tomb. Word had gotten back that Foster skipped on a rape charge in Louisiana.

Arriving at the front of the store, Willow and I experienced a huge surprise, a startling one no doubt, not thinking about the fact that the Terrell kids who had beat me up were suspended from school and home all day, JD and Chip, JD's younger brother, were leaving the store as we arrived. Willow and I attempted to pass without speaking or acknowledging the presence of the two. It didn't work.

Neither Willow nor I had yet gone to the trouble of removing scrubs. They were noticeable, which was the purpose, of course, and Chip had, shall we say, a chip on his shoulder regarding what had transpired during the week. He walked toward me, "I'm going to get me a closer look," he said.

"Come too close and you might come up with a shortage of what it takes to take a closer look, Chip," Willow warned. As he ignored her and advanced anyway, I backed away a couple of steps to allow some space between Willow and him. Chip passed between us pushing Willow. I did a half spin from a step behind him and kicked Chip's legs from underneath. The maneuver worked about as well as if it were choreographed. Willow threw a left elbow to the side of his throat as he went down. I backed away two more steps and Willow accepted the signal and did the same to allow his brother to come to his aid. As JD bent over to assist his brother, I signaled Willow right and I went left. Her kick landed in the chest area from the left and mine in the lower stomach from his right side and lifted JD's body and his fat ass about six inches off the ground before he flopped onto his brother with a half-gallon carton of milk between them. Milk went everywhere.

Willow looked at me with only a slight smile and said, "I love you!"

"I love you, my Willow," I said, but added, "Gosh what one helluva team we are."

Mr. Sparkman came out the door of the store. The first thing out of his mouth, "Is that the little girl who beat the hell out of Shorty Terrell, Louise Landry told us about?"

"Mr. Sparkman, I want you to meet the girl who is the love of my life, Willow Preston," I presented her.

As he shook her hand and the two smiled with their best ones, Mr. Sparkman said, "it's Ben and everybody calls me Benny."

"Mrs. Sparkman came out of the store with another carton of milk and presented it to JD and asked, "are you boys going to need your Mama to come get you or can you drive."

"They can drive, that is if we give them a few minutes to get some air back inside" I assured the lady, as she and Willow introduced themselves. "I didn't hurt them that badly."

"The little girl didn't do that . . . , Willow didn't so that?" Mrs. Sparkman asked.

"No, this one is mostly me," I said, "but Willow did get an elbow into the first one and we shared the duties on the next one." I thought for a moment, "what I am trying to tell everybody is that I am hurt, Mrs. Sparkman, but I am not to be messed with any more, and while Willow is more than capable of defending me, I am capable of defending me and her as well. As you might know, Chip started the attack today on Willow and I defended her."

Benny addressed his wife, "Bud is saying, Ellie, that he is done taking off these people and he is kicking ass from here on."

"And so am I," Willow is quick to point out, "because we are one now and any attack on either is on the other or both. He has walked away so many times and he hasn't been the one to tell me about that. No more bullies."

"There have been times, Willow," Benny told her, that these kids would come into the store, they got a dime on Thursday, they told me it was because the peddler came on Thursday when they lived across the river. Anyway, I would give them each a big dip on a cone and three pieces of candy.

Buddy liked these little peanut butter candies with the stripes. Any number of times the Terrells, Shorty and them two big ol' twin boys would take their ice cream cone from them and eat it and laugh about it. What was you when you moved here, Buddy, about 10?"

"Actually, nine we figured out, because it was January of '48."

Benny continued. "Those big old grown men taking from the kids and the kids never was the type who would try to hold me responsible but I took charge and started to add seven cents for each cone and let the Terrells crow and argue, but I wouldn't let them out of the store until they paid full what I had them charged for. When they left I gave the kids another cone.

I started out lying to them and saying that the boys had never paid me for the cones that the Terrells took so they had to pay me. Then we got the idea that the boys would go outside and eat their ice cream, then come back in and pay me so I didn't have to lie to the Terrells."

Miss Ellie contributed to Benny's story. "You know the worst part was where the Terrells would take from the boys and never buy anything. Benny kept track as much as he could and made them pay. Then their sister and her husband put in a little store in that house over past the little post office, but I heard the Terrells came in and charged so much the Colburn man went broke. They still live in the store building but don't have a store there anymore."

"Ya'll come on in. I know you didn't walk down here just to kick some butt, so I figure you want something," Benny said.

"Yessir," I responded as Miss Ellie held the door for us, We need self-rising flour and a thing of black pepper."

As I paid, Benny mentioned that the parents would be coming around asking questions. "Tell them the truth, simply that we tried to back away from them, Chip pushed Willow and I kicked his ass. JD charged for Willow and we both dropped him."

Willow stepped in and said, "Mr. Sparkman, the parents are the problem. Had they not wanted to lie about me beating up big fat Shorty, those two boys would have known that I would hurt them for messing with either of us, and we gave them a wide berth to leave the store without even having to acknowledge us." Willow continued, "They couldn't handle it. They had to bully. While they were bullying the first ambush, they were too stupid to know that they needed to break Bud's legs instead of his arms. Furthermore, the reason I was obsessed with kicking Shorty Terrell's butt is that he is the ring leader of the pack and when we stop him we believe we can stop whatever is the problem with this bunch."

"They're coming," Ellie Sparkman came yelling from the back of the store, "looks like two of the big ones. Ya'll run to the side door and I'll let you out."

"No! No more running!" I said.

I did run to the front, out to the steps, and Willow came with me. I looked at her and told her, "I love you! I swear that I want to handle this but if I can't stop you, I promise you I will murder the one who puts a scratch on you."

"Get ready! I love you! I'm in this because we are one entity, remember?" She sat on the steps and I leaned against the post. The pickup plowed into the parking area and slid the tires in the gravel. JD's father was driving. Apparently, he had picked up Shorty. Willow looked up at me and smiled big, "you want to pick one?"

"Ladies first," I said.

"Shorty again," she chose, "he gave me the 'little girly' bullshit the other time."

I pitched her my sling and removed the scrub that I never seemed to stop long enough to rid himself of. The two bounded out of the pickup, both huge men each weighing about the equal of the two of us, Willow and me together. They spoke several profanities, lots and loud. Willow looked at me and said, "verbal assault." I raised a hand to the right ear indicating a phone signal assuming the Sparkman's were watching.

The Terrell Brothers arrived at the foot of the steps simultaneously and Willow and I just as simultaneously kicked, Willow from her sitting position with the bull's eye to the crotch of the one on the left and I shot a half reverse straight kick to the throat of the other, and it landed perfectly. "This is the last profanity that this motherfucker will speak for a few weeks," I spoke aloud, "hoping Shorty would try to speak and find out that he couldn't."

Willow had kicked mine and I had kicked her chosen one, so I allowed her to spin in the front of us so we could switch opponents. Working to get mine to stand erect so I could see his ass get thoroughly kicked, I swiped him in the left of the face then the right with the top of each foot, then not caring if he lifted himself erect or not, took a step or two up the steps for height advantage and with all the force I could muster kicked Jim Terrell against his truck with a heel to the upper chest, in an attempt to get enough throat, the kick landed perfectly. Seeing that big-assed Jim either didn't want to or couldn't get up, I turned for Shorty.

Willow was well in charge. She loved the crotch shot and delivered it just as I was getting into the position to mount the steps for a spin and straight kick to the forehead or chest and expecting to have bad aim and connect about throat high again. He must have expected it and turned with the kick landing full force southeast of the left ear. Shorty's body turned as if he was ramming his head into the side of his brother's pickup, but didn't make it that far. His head hit in his brother's stomach. They collapsed in a two-man pile.

Next, I was attacked by a 115-pound bastard Penobscot half breed who jumped up around my neck and tried to kiss me savagely but could not kiss me and say 'I love you' at the same time. She didn't give up and kept trying. Whatever it was that I got, a kiss of strange name or just a sloppy 'I love you,' it was what I wanted again, and many times over.

"You were wonderful! I love you, I love you, I love you!" I didn't want her to miss it.

"There's movement," Willow yelled and quickly released me. She turned to the two brothers. "Movement," Willow is most emphatic, "at this time is not what will serve to improve your situation or your condition." She walked toward them. "Shorty, did you want to say something sweet to the 'little girly' or do you think shutting your mouth would be better? I'm not going to tell you what to do."

I noticed out of the corner of my eye, Mr. Sparkman returned the shotgun to the store.

As his wife received it through the door, Benny said to her, "I wonder what I thought I needed this for."

"Are both of you guys comfy sitting in the gravel up against that pickup? I hope you are because if you move I am going to put you back there," I told them. "There is another thing I need to tell you people while we are gathered here This is the third time today. Willow and I have taken all three of what you might believe is the best you could send after us, handily we have taken them, too. We have time for three or four more today if after Sheriff Brown gets through with you, there is time to get some others out here lined up to take us on. Now, I am going to tell you that there is a lot more of you than there is of Willow and me. We work as one because we are one."

"Your brother here is in on this thing because he is stupid, Shorty," I continued. "He listens to you. Now, that is stupid! He listens to you and sends his kids out to get their worthless asses beat so he can sit at home and protect his coward worthless ass. What brings you out today Jim? I can answer that for you since you can't. You didn't think Willow and I would still be here and you came down to push Mr. Sparkman around. I'll accept that answer."

"By the way, the reason neither of you can not speak as that I have applied a rather expert blow to the throats of both of you that has caused a muscle to constrict and temporarily deny you the ability to speak. It will come back in a few minutes and you can growl. It will be normal in a few days and I might be almost sorry for that.

"Twice Jim, you have sent your boys for me. I sent them home to you today, when I could have exercised less restraint, in far better condition than they left me last Monday. Yes, Philip did most of the damage but your boys participated. Somebody is keeping Philip from me, or from Willow, and we haven't seen Fats' two boys yet. We will! Your boy Chip attacked my Willow this morning and she gave him a shot that he will not forget. JD, got humiliated like we are doing to you right now."

Willow stopped me and spoke to Shorty and Jim. "He's going to teach me the one to the throat.," then whispered in his ear, "Mrs. Sparkman didn't understand and called their wives to come pick them up instead of calling the sheriff."

"Perfect, honey," I told her aloud, then whispered, "tell her she did right, that I am bluffing with that part, anyway. Since they don't know we didn't call the sheriff just yet, I can use that to do what I need to do."

"Okay, the secretive stuff is done now so I can get back to Shorty. You have been on my ass since the day I got to this pathetic hole seven years ago. That's over right? Since I am responsible for your not being able to speak, I will answer that for you. It is over, Shorty. You may nod agreement. You will nod agreement of I will turn my Willow loose on your fat ass again and again." He nodded agreement.

I continued, "I don't know what will happen with the two boys you sent for us this morning, Shorty. Were those Lucille's boys? We left them in the hands of the school officials. Likely, they will be picked up by the Sheriff and will face the same fate as Jim's two boys, trial and a school suspension that will cost them another year in school. Because you are a fool Shorty, these kids have a year of their life that you should owe them for. Were I Jim here, I would take you home and whip your fat ass all over your own back yard. You are a fat-assed liar, and I have tried to explain this to your family members but so many of them are too stupid to listen, Jim being one of those."

"Again, were I Jim here, I would call up my twin brother Oscar, called Fats, and tell him to give you about a week, then he needs to come over and do the same thing. Maybe Lucille's old man a week later. For all the stupid shit that you have pulled, you need to get your fat ass kept under control by your own family because you have agreed that it is over between the two of us."

"I would say 'gentlemen,' rather I will say, you two pieces of shit, your wives have been called. I am here badgering and humiliating you as you wait for the ladies. I wanted to be here while you related to them what happened to you. No sheriff was called. That was a bluff, to make you think. Did you think? By the way if you can't speak to your wives, Willow will tell them or Mr. and Mrs. Sparkman can relate the details on how one of your victims only four days out and a 115-pound "little girly' pounded your asses, and how well they were pounded. Tell them that we humiliated you inhumanely but you were too chicken-shit to respond. Or, Shorty, you could tell the ladies that the 'little girly' kicked your ass so badly that you couldn't defend yourself from humiliation."

"I am leaving Willow with you for a moment, you pathetic pieces of shit. Don't be afraid, Shorty. The 'little girly' won't hunt you unless you move. By the way, if you feel too severely humiliated, think about telling me later on about what a good job I did. Willow will relate to you our plans for the future. I was hoping your wives would get here so they could hear about us."

Willow told them that we are one although they had heard that one before. "It didn't take a license to tell us that," she said, "but we have to live in this society so we will do as we are expected. We don't feel that there is anything stronger than our personal commitment to each other so the marriage ceremony is so private that there will not be any invitations sent out. Don't wait by the mailbox."

Willow went on. "We will graduate, both of us with honors. The following day we will leave for our new life managing the largest vineyard in the coastal foothills of the Appalachian Mountains. If we return to this piece-of-shit acreage, it will be because the State of Alabama forces us to testify against some of you and the kids that you threw at us with chicken shit all over them because you touched them. Or, that there might be some reason that harm was brought to our family members that we have left here."

"It looks like your wives don't want you," Willow jokingly assessed. "You need to get your asses up and go beg them to let you in the house. I hope they don't. If you need us to, we can call Sheriff Brown to give you a lift home."

"She speaks for me," I assured them. I walked back into the store and told the Sparkman's that Willow and I were so very sorry that we had to do what we did. I thanked them for their support and for their hospitality. Benny laughed and thanked us for the show.

Miss Ellie, or so it seemed, thought maybe it would be crude to say so but she even nodded approval. "Somebody had to stop those men and I think you and Willow might have done it today."

"That's all I have tried to do," I told the Sparkman's. "If you get a chance to tell them at the right time and place," I requested, "I would appreciate it if you would tell both of them that we really are sorry for having to do what we did, but they had to know how we were made to feel and we honestly believed that in the long run they would understand that we wish no harm to anybody, not even them."

'That's nice," Benny said. "I believe Ellie and I can handle that."

"Willow and I will make a special trip by to see you before we leave."

"We would be honored," Miss Ellie giggled.

I exited, and said, "come on Willow, "I'm starting to get jealous of you and Shorty. Shorty. Go home! Take your brother home!"

Willow and I walked away, Willow and Miss Ellie exchanging waves. "Wow," I said, "that Willow girl of mine is the most captivating person. Everybody falls for her. Certainly I have fallen just about as deeply as anyone can fall for anyone else. I hope she feels as strongly for me."

"Oh, Willow, my love, there is something that I have to admit to you," I added, "so promise me that you will love me endlessly even when you know I have done stupid things."

"You know I will love you forever and always, even when I am having to beat you up, so what did you do this time?"

"I think I must have compounded the injury to my left shoulder."

"My baby, my baby, my dumb and wonderful baby, I don't know what I am going to have to do to keep you out of those fights and you let me take care of those things." She had tied my sling around her waist so she untied it and shaped it and knotted it around me with my left arm in place. I told her that it felt better. She put an arm around my waist and reached the other across my chest and began to massage the shoulder until we got home. I had the flour in a bag, holding it with the right arm. "I couldn't hold my Willow," I complained, "but she walked me home with all the love a person could ever ask for. I was really nuts about my Willow."

We told my mother of the two incidents, basically one with the parents follow-up. I decided to tell her about our plans, Willow agreed.

"Three incidents today, Mama," I told her. "I really believe we have gotten their attention, yet if they keep bringing to us what they have in the past, then it is of no consequence, Willow and I don't much more than break out into a sweat. But I am tired of these people, Mama. I don't want to fight them. I just want to go away. I just want to disappear."

I went on to tell her, "Willow and I are as devoted to each other as two adults can be. We refuse to leave each other. We turn 18 in a couple of months after graduation, so what is 18 but a number. We want to go to Georgia where the age is 16 to get legal, that is just for Willow and me and our extreme honesty and respect for each other, to hold us until a socially acceptable ceremony can be conducted for the rest of our society, the two families especially."

I went on to suggest that we had two weeks to fritter away. "Two weeks," I said, "to fritter Away our lives dealing with the trash of the earth, the Terrells of Newton's Bluff Alabama or we could use the two weeks to make a future for ourselves.

"After graduation we are headed north for a job we are offered running a vineyard in the coastal foothills of the Appalachian Mountains. Willow's family owns the vineyards and Willow's grandmother loves me now as intensely as she hated me this time last year when I ruined her grapes and they produced double what they did the previous year." I went on to tell them that we could use the two weeks to piss away our lives in Alabama or to build a life in New Jersey. It is our choice. "I suggest that we go to Georgia tomorrow, have the private ceremony and go to New Jersey the following day. We can get our lives started there and return for graduation."

Willow agreed! "I will call my mother and make the arrangements to get out personal files from the compound and head out for Georgia, New Jersey and other points of interest," she said.

My mother felt the suggestion was the smartest thing that we could do. "Those people are not going to leave you alone as long as you are on what they believe to be their turf," Mama said.

"Ladies of my life, I know that I have overdone it today, but it had to be done and at least Willow knows this to be true, but the pain is working on me."

Willow put me to bed. She and Mama searched for the pain pills that I normally refused but I was game to take them this time. The pain was just a bit much. I don't know what I did, merely used the arm for balance knowing that I would end up with a foot down somebody's throat without the left arm free or I would fall on it and hurt it even more. I hoped I didn't tear anything more, that the pain was just what we were to expect from over exertion.

My wonderful nurse removed my shirt and massaged the shoulder thoroughly but gently with the balm-like stuff, then gave me what I called the silly pill. She put another shirt on me and moved me to one side. "Mama is going to wake us at 1:15 so we can get to the doctor at two. The pill will make you sleep and I want you to hold me while you sleep and I can hold you" Willow said. She didn't mention the kisses, but there was no time between them for mentioning much of anything.

It was decided that we were to go to Vineland and return for graduation. I really did like that idea even if it was my own.

-0-

The doctor was not at all happy about Willow and me allowing ourselves to get involved in three altercations in just a half day. There was nothing more wrong with the shoulder just a bit of pain to tell me that I had over reacted to the people goading me into a fight. All was good news. He was finished with us and we always chatted awhile.

"It may be the wrong decision, Doctor, but Willow and I decided that today was the beginning of our new life together and that we are capable of defending ourselves, so that is what we will do," I explained. "I am not happy that we have to do it but these people cannot be reasoned with, so what we have given them today is a taste of what they deserve, a small amount of pain and one helluva dose of humiliation." I went on to add, "we got two new kids, two of the kids who beat me up, the ring leader, and the father of two of the kids who ambushed me this past Monday."

Willow added, "we have only two more kids that we are committed to, so that we may get them all, and we will find them if the parents allow them to get out and about."

"Then," Dr. Haggerty asked, "you are not going to try to avoid any of these people any more, are you?"

"Let them call me a coward if it pleases them but I want to just fade away, but they won't let us do it. They blocked us from entering the school this morning, then from entering the only little store we have within miles of our house, and the adults came before we could leave the store. We don't have a choice so long as we are here."

"We just have to get out of here," Willow said, "but we can't just dig up and go. The school has given us class credits to free us for the two weeks prior to graduation. We could miss it but have worked 12 years for it and I don't believe it is fair to allow Shorty Terrell to take the goal from us. Bud has 203 acres with hired hands starting to plant it today and we haven't even been allowed the time to go check on them."

"Assuming the planting is done properly and all is well where could you disappear for two weeks and come back for the graduation," the doctor suggested. "I know Bud knows the Sheriff well enough, he would send a couple of his guys out to watch out for things during the graduation ceremony."

"Absolutely!" I was almost jumping with joy. "When you have a doctor as brilliant as I have, you follow his suggestions to the letter, right Willow?"

Willow gave Dr. Haggerty a huge hug. "We have to check with my mother, get her to packing, maybe just enough for two weeks or we leave here for two weeks. Let's go," Willow instructed.

"Can we do without you for two weeks?" I asked.

"Come back by after an hour," Dr. Haggerty told us, "or maybe tomorrow and I will have Angela give you everything you need, instruction and prescriptions for travel."

"Thank you, Doctor," Willow and I echoed as we hurried to the parking lot.

"The first things first, but we have to find out what to do to ensure that we are good with my mother," Willow suggested, "then we have to check on Chuck and Bill or your body will turn to salt or stone or something."

"You love me though I am a little bit weird, don't you?"

"I would love you if you were only a little bit weird, yes," Willow tried to keep a straight face but couldn't.

Her little joke earned me a public kiss on the way to the car. Public? Wow! That girl was so reserved that she wouldn't kiss the back of her own hand in public. I wondered what gives. I asked, "Is my love excited?"

"I haven't said anything and I play the game with the kick-ass because we are good at it, but I am so afraid for you, and I love you so completely, and we have a good life ahead of us together." She went to the driver's side of the car. I followed. She was crying. At least the tears were flowing. No sobbing, but I felt the pain with her.

"Three in one day gets your attention doesn't it?" I thought, "when one realizes three of what in one day and it does get to be a bit frightful."

She held me so very tightly and I wiped her tears. In a hospital parking lot, I guess such things are common so we didn't draw a lot of attention. Then, neither of us were very big on public display of affection, but special occasions are alright maybe. "These are a combination of fear tears and tears of joy, you know," my Willow explained to me.

"The tears of joy are okay I guess," I told her, "but the fear tears are what I have to take you away from."

'The tears of joy are because you are so wonderful and so willing to totally and completely wreck the life you have for a life for me and you don't even know where it is or what it will entail. You have no idea how to grow grapes but you will do it and do it well for me."

MY WILLOW | 155

"Because, Willow, I am so thoroughly in love with you that I will reach for any straw that I feel I can use to build a future that includes you."

"Hold me just a little longer and let me stop these tears so I will be able to drive and get us to my mother."

"Holding you is a natural thing for me I do it so well, do you note, with two hands."

"Okay, a quick kiss for you magic man and off we go." She gave me a parking lot quick one, a lot like a brotherly kiss, and I ran around the car and plopped in the seat. We roared away. As we drove we plotted more plans. We would like to have been able to toss caution to the wind, shoot the home turf a finger, or whatever is appropriate when you really want to say 'fuck all of you we're out of here,' but we were good kids. We had been raised well. We wanted our responsibilities taken care of and we wanted to get out of the area without burning bridges. After all, there were lots more friends here than family. I had lots of family while Willow was taking all but Nancy and the rest of the Bradleys.

Willow interrupted my thought at the right time. "let's take care of Mama because she is on the way. We then have to settle you down by stopping off in your fields to see how Chuck and Bill are doing, then tonight we have to meet with your family."

"We have two cars and we only need one or so it seems," I spoke without knowledge of what to ask or what to suggest, "so what do you think we need to do?"

"I know you love this one and so do I," Willow said, "so let's present the question to Mama and see if she wants the Mercury, then we can keep yours and you can put the red paint job on it that you have been wanting."

"Then if she doesn't want yours?" I asked.

"We drive one up to New Jersey, fly back for graduation and drive the other one up, and we will be a two-car family," Willow proudly acknowledged.

"Or, I could give the Studebaker to Frank," I suggested.

"Why would give up your pride and joy, just at the wink of an eye?" Willow inquired in disbelief.

"You, Willow. Among all that I have past, present and future, you are the only thing that matters to me, I promise you. Nothing else matters to me but you, Willow."

"I keep thinking there are no more reasons to love you, then you keep giving me more," she told me quite seriously.

"We will need a pick-up at the vineyard and Frank would love to have the Studebaker. Should we do that little deed," I recommended, "could I get you to give him the keys? It would be more of a way to tell Frank and my family that we are ..., well tell them that we are a family but you are a part of my family, too."

"How would you feel," Willow suggested, "if we give him the Studebaker anyway, even if Mama takes the Mercury, then we could get us a pickup in New Jersey?"

"Beautiful idea, beautiful girl with all the best ideas." Suddenly, I realized, "I never drove this car but once, anyway, so the attachment should not be that great."

"Okay, so now we are down to one car or none," Willow said, "so what is next?"

"Georgia," was the one-word response.

"We have to have a witness," Willow responded. We can get Nancy to go with us Saturday, and she is already 18, then leave for New Jersey immediately or wait for Sunday. Or, maybe we can sweet-talk Louise Landry into going with us tomorrow."

"I agree it needs to be done before we go to New Jersey and how we do it is in the plans, so let's talk to Mama Preston first.

She was home. Willow parked the car, we walked in together. She had heard about the two boys jumping us at the school and what the school had done for both of us to take care of getting me rehabilitated. She has heard nothing of the others, so we told her the full story.

"Three times before noon those people attacked you," she said in amazement.

"Yes Ma'am," I responded myself, "and we have decided to go away so they don't have anybody to attack."

Willow told her of the Georgia plans. She felt it was appropriate that she tell Annalee because of the mother-daughter relationship. "We want to do this now because we are going to do it anyway and this way we don't have to compromise any of our values." Willow stopped just long enough to take aim and told her mother pointedly, "we are almost to the point of the compromise every day and I might have crossed over already were it not for the strength of his love for me and knowing what my values are."

"I am speechless for the moment," Annalee admitted, ""so please continue."

"He called me a horny little bastard," Willow laughed and we all laughed until Willow interrupted and admitted the truth, "he never said that Mama,. I made it all up for a good laugh and we did get one."

"I thought about it," I said, "I wasn't so certain I hadn't let it slip out."

"Willow should have said she read your mind," Annalee continued with our joking session.

"Oh, really seriously, Annalee," I told her, "this girl is magic when it comes to reading my mind and anticipating my actions, especially during those gosh-awful altercations, it was like she was reading my body movements and knew when and where she would have to be to throw her punch or kick. Oh, she was amazing, She really is the most amazing human being that I have ever run across, and I am starting to really like her."

MY WILLOW

"I suspected as much," Willow jokingly admitted. "Next thing you know, Mama, he will be trying to take advantage of me, so you help me keep and eye on him and you can help me to make sure that he does."

"I walked toward her and put both arms around her and whispered in her ear, "I love you Willow, which is why you will never need that help, I promise you."

Okay, so now that all the joking is out of the way," Willow took control, "can we make serious plans?" Willow turned to her mother, "we want to leave as soon as we can, so when will you be ready?"

"As soon as I can retrieve my personals from the compound," her mother agreed, "and that is Saturday morning."

"I could take you there tomorrow," Willow offered.

"I can't get in until Saturday," Annalee said, "because everybody is in that conference in Nashville."

"Our plans, Mom," Willow outlined, "are to go to New Jersey immediately, then return for graduation. Pack what you have to have and we can send a moving truck or take care of moving when we come back for graduation. Now, for your personals at the compound, can you get them Saturday morning and we can return here and leave immediately for new Jersey?"

"I hate to have to bust up a good thing going between Mama and daughter but we do have Georgia," I pointed out.

"Georgia is on the way to New Jersey and we have a perfect witness right here." She patted her mother on the head.

"Hey I wish I were not so dumb and I could come up with good ideas," I said.

"But I love you," Willow assured me. "I love dumb men that I can dominate, push around, and control."

Willow moved immediately to the next question. "Mama, I know you don't like to drive here, but what about New Jersey, and do you want the Mercury?"

"No," Annalee was quick and emphatic, "the maid can take me shopping there as she always did before."

"Then the plan is set girls," I rushed them, "we need birth information and a couple of other identification papers for the two of you and we have to get the same for me when we get to my house, my love."

Willow and I gave Mama Preston a hug and headed to Newton's Bluff.

Chuck and Bill were still planting. I figured they would start at the nearest field and work their way toward the back of the property, thus should be about to what Chuck had named "Hell's Half Acre."

While we are driving, I'll tell you a story about Hell's Half Acre. "Daddy would come home early some days and I would see that his truck was home and take it to the fields knowing he had driven the tractor out. I found him one evening after a basketball game that I had attended and he was tilling Hell's half Acre. I could let him sleep and Bring the truck back at breakfast time, then I could sleep in the day time. We did this type of routine often.

"Hell's Half Acre was difficult to till. It was 12 acres in size but it had several levels. It was totally enclosed with trees with two outlets , one each direction, as if in or out, at a corner of the field. In the middle was what was described as the village toilet for what was formerly a native Creek village that took out about an acre. It was merely a hole in the ground with lots of trees and foliage around it. I dropped the truck off to my father and took over the tractor when he had gotten to what appeared about half done with the acreage. Daddy said, "finish this one and come on home. No need to plow all night and the tractor is due an oil change."

"To reduce our chances of erosion, I plowed portions, then backed it in, which is a procedure whereby you reverse till at the center to fold the soil back toward the middle where you had tilled away to the center originally. Anyway, about two or three in the morning, I was finishing up the portion that was at the higher elevation, when I looked down toward the corner where I was to exit in 15 minutes or so when I was finished.

"There a bit of a distance and I could not see clearly, but there was a huge pair of eyes aimed directly at me. I stopped the tractor in a position whereby I could see more clearly. There had been a train wreck about a year and a half ago and the only large animal that had never been caught was a fully grown female lion. Nobody had any idea where she had gone but we had not seen her since the previous summer when she wrecked a friends turkey pen to get to her supper.

"I couldn't see her that well but I knew that was her and I knew for an absolute fact that I couldn't get out of that field without having to pass right by her. I decided that if I kept plowing she might just go away. After all, she had been very successful at avoiding people all this time. I worked until I finished my work, making maybe a dozen loops, each loop assessing the details of the animal sufficiently to know that there was no mistake, it was a lion and she had settled herself comfortably in the dusty road right where I needed to pass to get home, acting like she was positioning herself to pounce on me when I tried to go home.

"The lug wrench for the John Deere is about 20 inches long so I retrieved it. I thought about it as the only weapon I might have. I also knew that you never are to ever drop a plow in a completed field but I could drop it at the toilet area and not so severely break the rule. The toilet area was so close to the lion that she might be able to reach me before I could get the plow disconnected and get back upon the tractor and prepare myself to make a run for it. I decided to drop the plow in the middle of the field and just come back and get it if I could survive the ordeal that I was right in the middle of convincing myself that I couldn't survive.

"I calculated what I knew about the speed of the tractor. Let's see, first second and third gears are 1, 2 and 3 mph respectively, fourth and fifth gears were 1.5 mph each more and sixth gear was 3 mph more, giving me 9.0 mph. I figured a lion could do maybe 20 mph. I had no chance, but she was not going to leave me. I sat on the tractor with the lights illuminating the eyes of the beast and somehow worked up the bravery to climb down off the tractor and release the coupling.

"I disconnected and climbed back up in record time, hit the throttle with the left hand and prepared to ram the hand clutch with the left, when she jump up from her comfort in the dusty road and aimed those headlight eyes at me. I figured the acceleration of that massive two-cylinder "popping Johnny," so she is called, startled the animal from her comfort.

"She didn't charge me, but began to walk toward me at what I was fully convinced was the normal pace for a full-grown female African lion, a slightly hungry one I must have surmised. I was frustrated. Yes, I was scared, but I had figured everything and had calculated myself zero chances to survive. I thought about it as I stared at both eyes in my headlights as she approached me. I couldn't see driving the tractor and letting the beast rip my back open.

"No, I will fight," I convinced myself. "I will wait and I will fight," I told myself as I gripped my only weapon, a green 20-inch lug wrench, maybe worthless against a hungry lion, but "By god, I will die fighting." There was another problem, however, that I realized that might need mentioning. I was having problems seeing how to fight with all those tears flowing down my face . . ."

I interrupted myself, "pardon me my Willow, but I love you too much to say the word, yet it is the exact one I used. The back of her hand on my cheek was approval enough.

"I laid my head on the steering wheel, closed my eyes and waited to die. After plenty of time had expired and she didn't swipe me off the tractor, I accepted the realization that I was still alive and raised my head to see that she was a big old yellow dog. I left the plow in the middle of the field anyway, pushed the clutch and drove home.

"No wonder you fight like a beast," Willow stated, "you have faced death and reconciled yourself to it once, and my darling boy, I have been totally dumbfounded, as has almost everybody else, that you have handled these injuries that you are encumbered with right now and not once have you expressed any feeling of self sympathy, just anger."

"Okay Dr. Preston, go past the turn-off and I will show you how to go in the back of the farm, then I need a psychological analysis as to why I am so totally enthralled with your beauty, charm, grace . . . , well, and that cute little butt of yours."

"Because I help you fight like a beast," she first analyzed, then added, "and my butt is so cute when I do it."

It was funny but I was playing with her and trying hard to keep a straight face.

"Because I love you so completely, I express my love for you and I am always looking for ways to show that I love you, and . . . , lemme see here, and I have a cute butt."

"That's it girl, now make a quick left into that grove of pine trees there and I will make mad passionate love to you."

"I started my period yesterday."

"Then go on through the trees and past the field on the right and you will see a fence. Stop and I will have to show you how to open that cranky old gate."

We stood in front of the car, embraced, laughed kissed and ignored the gate.

According to Willow, "it could be that our lips match so very well." I added, "and because you have a cute little butt."

We took care of the gate and laughed a lot, then drove on in to Hell's Half Acre. There was Chuck and Bill, just as I figured. Bill was driving, so we waved at him and hung out at the trailer with Chuck. He showed Willow how to pull the string from the bags and how to make the huge string ball that we always made every year at planting time. We told Chuck about our ordeal for the day at school then the two at Sparkman's store.

Chuck asked in surprise, "you kicked Shorty's ass again, Willow?"

"I am delighted to say that this one was a thorough ass kicking, but Bud had to nail him first," Willow admitted, "with a kick in the throat that I must learn how to administer because it shuts down your opponents ability to speak."

"Three kick-ass sessions in a half day and not a scratch on either one of you," Chuck said, "and it is almost unbelievable. You two are such a matched pair."

"Really, Chuck," I spoke seriously, "this is almost uncanny, the match-up that we two are, in almost every way that can be imagined, our feelings, our interests and our training and it seems that we are thinking most of the time from the same head. It's like if I want to do something it is never something that she is not willing to pursue and the vice versa is true. We want to please each other and be in on whatever the other one wants to do."

"I found him and I am not letting him go," Willow told him.

"And, I am not letting her go, either," I said, "which is why we came by. Our jobs start in the Delaware Bay area whenever we can get there. The school has allowed us to skip classes the last two weeks so we hope to be able to go there for those two weeks and get a jump start. The vineyards are in pathetic shape and I need to see what I can do to get them cleaned and prepared to harvest this season and to do a proper pruning for next season."

"You have a good reputation because of how good you did for that lady here last year," Chuck said.

You know I appreciate you guys taking off and coming home to do my planting here," I sincerely told my friend, "but those 100-pound bags of fertilizer could get the best of you in short order, do you need Willow?"

Chuck said, "I'm not laughing at your dumb jokes, for one she could do it and another you would beat us to death if she got even a little blister. "That's what I told Benny down at the store, "if one of those fat-asses put a scratch on my Willow, I would have murdered both of them."

"We made believers out of them, Chuck," I said, "and I think this should cause the people to understand that their days of bullying people are over."

"Willow is ignoring us," Chuck pointed out, "look, she has five bags open and a nice start on a string ball."

"Can I come out and help tomorrow so I can complete my string ball? Please," Willow begged me."

"No! Chuck will be looking at your butt and I will get jealous."

Chuck said, "now that is the first part I noticed, so you are right." Willow gave him a hug and they both laughed at me.

"You know, Chuck," I said, "I'm thinking about being out of here Saturday morning, going to my new job, so what do you two think about what it will do for the farm?"

"We can get done here tomorrow, we get the corn in next week, and the wheat is already looking good, so we got time to get our stub-outs done in Tennessee and the rest of that is one day at a time. We can all handle it 'til we start the wheat combine and we may have to send somebody to get you."

"Maybe I'll bring Willow back to run the combine."

"That makes it all good, then, so you two have a good trip to Delaware Bay, and we will handle the rest."

We waved a goodbye to Bill and gave Chuck a verbal one and headed for the house. "It's about time for Daddy to get home and we have had another of those hugely busy days, but we have accomplished a lot," I assessed. "I need to get my birth and whatever other records Mama has so we can be certain to have everything together. And Daddy needs the full story from us, direct, and we have to make certain that he is good with my leaving the way I am, right in the middle of planting."

"Knowing how he rallied Chuck and Bill and the way all of the rest of the farm schedule is arranged, I think your Daddy is already reconciled to the fact that you are leaving."

"He wanted me to go to college anyway, so I am certain that he arranged for Chuck and Bill to allow that. I think the most important thing for me right now, Willow, is that I want to feel your warm and wonderful fingers on my left shoulder with that balmy stuff you use, but your fingers caressing me is what does me so much good."

"So there is more to me than just a cute butt?"

"There's so much more than just a cute butt, however, when I talk about your butt being so cute, you talk about beating me up. I get all worked up, you know, thinking about you putting your hands on me when you beat me up."

"I have to do everything, is that the way it will always be, me doing everything to you?"

"No, but now we are not legally bound to each other so I have to worry about your honor, your commitment to yourself, your promise of purity, and all that social stuff, but after we get you all legalized, I am going to stroke that bottom with both hands with both lips . . . , yeah, I think I'll do that first, I mean take every stitch off you, throw you face down and stroke and caress that bottom with both hands, gently and sweetly until I feel you start to move and to breath heavily, then I will kiss each cheek with lots of warm tongue and kiss you more until you are moaning with desire, then I'll run out and climb up a tree and watch you hunt for an axe.

"It's funny you didn't ask about those men."

"What men?"

"I'm bringing two lumber jacks to bed with me. You didn't see me looking from side to side as horny as a mountain goat. I was trying to find a pine thicket so we could blow off that commitment and purity bullshit, then you had to mention climbing a tree and my body went cold. I'm having my lumber jacks cut down the tree so I can beat you up."

"Oh, lordy mercy, anyway. We're joking around and getting all worked up and don't forget . . . , I was serious. My period started yesterday. What are we going to do?"

"Please note that I am not laughing. Willow, the love of my life, to whom I am dedicated to love and honor, eternally. We have one day in our schedule through Georgia. We do it that one day and the consequences are what they are. I love you enough."

"And, I love you enough," Willow assured me, "it does make us want to kick some teeth out of Shorty Terrell."

"Yep, kicking some Terrell teeth is a good idea but he didn't schedule the period." I hoped I would get a smile, but didn't."

"He forced the rest of the schedule."

"That is true, but we need to knuckle down and let life flow by as it may. We can be patient as we have been. I love you and will keep loving you, no matter what."

"I love you, but you are getting pushed around at every turn and even I am letting you down on the most important day of our lives."

"The most important day of our lives is this day, then another day. That way we get to have two."

"I am coming around to help you out of the car and putting a monster kiss on you."

CHAPTER FOURTEEN

Doing This for Each Other

All else that has to be done, and the long step toward a new life together without the conflict that was feared to be faced among these people and finally the realization of living in our own dream and not one encumbered with the dreams of others.

"I HAVE HOPED I could be with you when you wake tomorrow," I told my Willow, "that way we wouldn't have a break in our lifetime together and I could be with you every day from now and forever." Seeing those eyes every morning and feeling those lips on mine is about the only thing I could imagine could make it worth all that we have had to go through to get from birth to the final day of the long years. Willow held my hand so sweetly and put it against her cheek, the ultimate expression of love with Willow.

"I have an idea," Willow whispered. "I will get you to sleep tonight, then go to my house and sleep. Don't say it, Please! I love you more than anything and want to be with you every minute, but they won't let me take you into that compound. Honestly, they may not let me in. Mama may have to drive herself in and get her stuff, and it is our records of birth, all the files that we must have. We will be back as soon as we can get back."

"You have agonized over that decision, I am more than aware, but I am a big boy," I told my precious Willow. "I know that there will be some times when we have to be separated, but the lifestyle that we have planned is just about all I would accept because we will be together, and I will force myself to endure the separation tonight so that it makes all the things fit together to make the rest of it happen for us."

"Get your lazy bottom out and let me know about the left arm."

"Shall I try it around the girl of my dreams for the big test?" I asked. She walked into my arms and held me. My entire life was in my arms at the time. I held her awhile but I knew it couldn't be for so long as our bodies seemed to want to be there touching. "You promised I would drive today, angel, and I think I can. The left is sore because of my indiscretion yesterday but I can use it with pain and I can endure the pain. There is no pain when I hold you, at least not so much that I can't lie about it, but I think I can steady the steering wheel while I shift with the right hand."

"Your father has gone to town to take some money out of the bank for you. He says it is mostly yours anyway, and I told him you had plenty of money waiting in New Jersey, but he wouldn't listen about like it would break his heart not to be able to do a duty of some sort. I told him we didn't even check on what was coming into my bank. You were supposed to have another $10,000 there. My thoughts did turn to consider that Grandmother may not have sent it because we changed plans to go there much earlier."

"I have enough travel funds in my account," I assured Willow. "You likely have some in your account and your mother likely has money. Oh well, Daddy is the good guy and he wants to do something. We can always put it back."

"We have an agenda. It says here that Bud eats, Willow loves Bud; Bud showers, Willow loves Bud; Bud dresses, Willow loves Bud . . ." I did the shower first and Willow helped to dress me, shirt and shoes anyway.

Daddy made it back with $500. I looked at him and said, "this is enough to keep this family fed and clothed for close to three months, and you know I never check my account below $300. We will be back in two weeks. Willow and I each got a relocation bonus so the money comes back to you. We will use it if needed for car trouble, whatever.

We made a sandwich with my breakfast and went to Decatur. The bank was across the street from the clinic where Willow picked up her instructions including a prescription for stuff for the cuts and abrasions that were still needing more time. Plus, we had a list of the gauze and bandages that would be needed and a bunch of instructions. Willow was excited to have the chance to take over for all the duties. The goodbyes at the clinic were on the edge of heartbreaking, a little more than one might usually think for the last trip to the doctor's office. We had bonded well. Willow and I even promised to stop by on the trip back for graduation. A couple of weeks with Willow and the old left could be in good shape, no doubt.

We went to Willow's house and helped her mother pack and to get Willow packed. Nobody wanted to take much so the packing was easy. All of Willow's, as well as her mother's, belongings were packed in the event we decided to drive back for graduation rather than fly. We had talked about buying a pickup for work and

MY WILLOW 165

decided we may load it all and return it with us after graduation or call a moving company. Whatever the choice, boxes were packed, labeled and stacked.

Willow and I had lunch with Dan, Nancy and some of the others at school, told them the generalities of our plans. Nancy knew exactly where we would be. Dan knew as well. They had Summer plans with us in New Jersey. The rest were told that my job was in the Delaware Bay area, close to where Willow would be with her family in New Jersey. We told them that we would get to spend some time together and we would have details for them at graduation.

We met a friend of mine in Hartselle who had gotten married in Georgia. He told us exactly where to go and what was needed. We did not know what to do with the rest of the day, maybe three or four hours, because we had worked so efficiently.

"There's not time to go to the island, if that is okay with you," I suggested to Willow. "I know I promised but that would scare me anyway with our adversaries having the equipment necessary for our harassment. "I have wanted to show you Johnson's Landing, the place where my Cherokee family all lost their lives except for Mama's great grandfather, the father of my mentor and best friend Ol' Charlie Wolf."

To be sure everything was packed for the road, we drove to my house. I chose to leave as much as I could for my brother. We could buy new when they got to New Jersey. Our lifestyle was going to be different and we were not so certain that what we were wearing here would necessarily be what we would even want to wear there. Furthermore, starting a new life simply demanded new clothing.

Willow decided that it was such a good idea, her clothing could be given to friends at school, or she could encourage them to donate her clothing one of the big sharing events that the churches were famous for conducting. She could have Nancy do it, "like I want everybody to have something of mine to remember me by," Willow said, "then when that runs out donate the rest to a drive,"

"Hey there, one and only, I can help drive to New Jersey since your car has automatic," I suggested. "Mine with that handle in the floor . . . well, in the center console, is a different story, but I would like to try it. You want to go to Johnson's Landing? Or, we could go on a final walk along our favorite path?"

"Johnson's Landing!" Willow handed me the Studebaker key and I headed for the driver's side, excited, of course. "Oops, I need to hold the door for my girl," I said. I seated Willow, then let myself in, sat in the seat and pulled my feet inside, just as my precious one had taught me. I hit the shifter to the right and pulled it back, released the clutch and backed out into the road. With the left hand in my lap, I hooked the steering wheel with the thumb, shifted up and accelerated away, with an expert shift to second, then up to third and back down to fourth and we were on our way. I could drive. Yea! I could feel the pride and it had been bothering me that I was so totally dependent upon Willow yet that had kept us together so tightly, and that was certainly a good thing.

Willow was excited for me because she knew of my passion for driving. This was my first time since the arm was damaged and it was still not the most comfortable thing to do but I could do it "if I didn't have my Willow who liked to take care of me and be my slave while she pretended she was going to control me later on," I joked, "even though I could not imagine that wonderful girl being anything other than a perfect partner."

I realized that there had been a subject that we had missed or avoided that should be important to a couple setting out on a life-long adventure as one entity, children. We had not talked about children. Wow, we had talked about the sex act, even masturbation and the intimacies, but the subject of children had not been offered up to us for discussion. I decided to break the question the fun way. "Willow, you know I love you no matter what may come between us, but what if you get pregnant while we do what I plan for us to do at Johnson's Landing?"

"First I would think it would be cruel," Willow said, "of my sex partner to put me through the pain and humiliation of sex while in only the second day of my period and secondly I have never heard of anybody getting pregnant during their period."

"Oh, you mean it's not caused by kissing a lot?"

"No, but actually, that can lead up to it if you lose control and get further into it," she explained to her goofy partner.

"You mean there is more?" I pretended to be even more ignorant.

"Yeah, there's more, and I guess I'll have to show you what that is someday."

"Are you going to show me how to get pregnant?"

"What I will do is show you what to do to get pregnant but we won't do the whole routine, like swelling up and having a baby."

"You don't want to have a baby?"

"Not until later on."

"How much later?"

"After we graduate from college."

"Then how many?"

"Twenty, maybe," she responded but turned around in the seat to get full view of my response.

'Aaaargh! Twenty? Can we negotiate?"

"How about what I meant is that we do what it takes about twenty times just to get one baby?" She laughed at me because she turned my joke back on me. "No, seriously, silly person, I have always hoped for about three. Maybe a couple of girls and a boy. What do you think?"

"Maybe a couple of girls and a boy was exactly what I was thinking but then you mentioned doing that fun thing about twenty times and I started to really liking the number 20."

"Methinks you have been lying to me that you don't know what to do," my Willow teased.

MY WILLOW

167

"I read a book about it." we laughed at our silly exchange but arrived at the Landing and got out of the car. "All it is since the river was dammed up is rocks and trees but before that it was an active place for people to land and board river boats and for commercial loading and unloading."

'Sit with me here by this tree and let me hold you and I will tell you about some of my family history. I went on to explain that before they built the dams and flooded the valley the river at times here was a raging torrent. As you look up river, it is very narrow until it gets to here, then it widens. This means that the water that came through the narrow part spreads to fill the wide area and is therefore shallow and raged around the corner as it turns North here then turns immediately West at Triana that you can see directly down river.

Exactly a hundred years prior to the TVA flooding the valley, the Cherokee who were my mother's family that had taken the name of Johnson, petitioned the Andrew Jackson government for permission to build a raft, deciding their only chance of survival was to get away from the death camps. Their intent was to float down river all the way to the Ohio River, then down to the Mississippi River where they would cross and make their way by whatever means they could muster to the promised land of Oklahoma. Likely with the lack of experience, they were not able to negotiate this turn and the raft slammed against the rocks wall here, broke into pieces and killed or drowned all on board except for a young 16-year-old Charlie Johnson.

"There is quite a lot more of Charlie Johnson that might be worth hearing, but he was nursed back to health by a tribe of Creeks of the great Chief Cotaco, their village being about five miles down river at Cotaco creek and another village at Talucah, a few hundred yards west of here, named for the wife of Cotaco. Tribal members found Charlie clinging to the rocks, took him to their village and nursed him to health. Upon maturity, which was in the eighteenth year according to tribal law, Charlie married into the tribe and had two daughters, supposedly the fairest of all the maidens in these parts, so the story is told.

"Both Creek and Cherokee were agrarian by nature, so Charlie took on a sharecropping deal with a white land owner, since Natives couldn't own land in Andrew Jackson's world. When the Civil War broke out, Charlie was forced to fight for the South in place of his land owner. It is said that Charlie returned home a hero having killed 141 Yankees single handedly. He brought home the knife, his only CSA issued weapon, the standard issue weapon for night fighters. What he left was not here, however, no crop, no wife and no two daughters, nothing.

"The new government awarded Charlie Johnson 360 acres and he started all over to build the showpiece farm for the area. In the meantime, he married and fathered a son that he called Charles. Young Charlie was 15 when his father passed on. Young Charlie took the farm and continued to build and expand to make it into the jewel of the Tennessee River Valley. He married and had two sons of his own,

Charles Henry and John Herbert, the latter known in these parts as Ol' Hub, my maternal grandfather.

"The TVA came into the valley and built dams, flooded the valley and ran the people off their land. Well, all except my mother's grandfather. As a former member of the wolf tribe in native North Carolina, Charlie Johnson in his defiance became known affectionately as Charlie Wolf and that did distinguish him from his son Charlie Johnson. Then for 16 years the TVA, the FBI, and it is said an Army unit, tried to run Charlie off the land.

"Ol' Hub had built a small cabin on a hill, the high point of his father's farm, near a small cave. It was high enough that Charlie Wolf was not drowned so the government apparently tired of messing with Charlie and just left him alone. That didn't set well either, supposedly, or according to the legend. Charlie built a bonfire on that island and kept it going for many years. Actually the fire still burns, making it close to 18 years. The fire didn't intimidate enough, I guess so Charlie got himself a pair of mating wolves.

"The call of the mating wolves was enough to scare the bravest of us. That's how I found him. Three of us stole a boat a couple of years ago and went to the island. I found out that he wasn't the crazy old Indian recluse that he gained his reputation as being through the legend of the stories that were told, but a brilliant, well educated old man of leisure who played some fun games with people. My father and friends had kept him fed and entertained, one item being all my books. He and I were friends long before we met because of my books that my father loaned him. He knew more about me than maybe even my parents," I told my audience of one as I completed my story.

"I loved the story, Willow told me. "I know you had to skim over it to get 118 years into a few minutes but I want to know so much about this man, and the story teller. I am so very sorry we can't get out to see him. I so want to meet him."

"We will make it a point to go to the island when we come back for graduation, okay?"

"We have a pact," Willow looked up at me with all of her charm, "and I know you well enough that I know you will never break a pact."

I couldn't miss the chance, "You know me well, you say?"

"I know you well," and she was firm about it.

"Well I know I don't have to tell you this but I have good taste in women," I told her, "so I ask what makes you think I will make a good husband?"

"I get the idea that you and I would fail miserably at trying to establish a relationship with any other person because we have failed at it for three years already. And, if that is not a good enough answer, I know I love you too much and you love me too much. It will happen that we will make a helluva pair, unbelievably devoted with no concerns whatsoever for doing what would cause us not to be the most exceptional mate.

"Do you think things might change for us later on?"

MY WILLOW   169

"No! We feel that we are a part of each other. It is not just bullshit garbage talk between two teenagers. We even think alike."

"Would you be mad at me if I held your bottom with my left hand?"

"No, I told you it would be okay but why do you think you have to ask?

"Respect. But, it is getting close to sundown, we have a big day tomorrow, and we don't need to be out here after dark.

Willow stood and reached her hand for mine. As I rose she put her body against mine and held me. I held her. I felt each other's body move and neither could resist the feeling we had for each other. I was so aroused and I was against her, not exactly in the right place but close enough and I knew about the period and what she had to wear. We kept holding each other and I felt her bottom move as if she wanted me to caress it. I held her so firmly, then held her bottom with both hands. She found mine and we moved together and helped each other.

"I love you so much! And, No, I am not ashamed this time, because I understand the love we have for each other and there is no questioning it and there is no need to concern ourselves for being what we were before the union that we have effected. No preacher or Justice of the Peace can bind us so well as we are bound in our own hearts for each other. I love you so completely and I am so unfair to you making you wait and I don't even want to wait. We don't need to wait, I guess we have to wait. I wonder what happens when you are wearing a tampon." She laughed a bit.

"I wonder what happens if you have sex the first time in your period. What the hell, there is blood anyway, is it painful breaking the hymen when you are already in the painful part of the period?"

"Honey, I don't know any answers to the questions but I am a willing partner and I love you enough that I can stop if it becomes too painful or unbearable in any other way. Are you horny now?"

"Not so much but one hand on my bottom and it is like I am jumping your bones."

"Take my hand and let's walk. We do our best work walking. I don't know what it is about walking. I love walking, looking at the flowers, the grass, even the weeds are beautiful if you take them from around or among a pristine universe, maybe we create it for the purpose of excluding some beautiful things. I remember my grandfather used to walk with me. He never walked with a cane – that's for old people he would say – but he always had his Barlow. 'Barlow handle, Barlow blade, best old Barlow ever made.'"

"Papa would take his Barlow that he always had honed to the sharpest condition," I showed Willow my Case knife just to keep my story on the correct or intended path, primarily just to keep a story going since the whole idea was to divert her attention, "and he would whittle a branch from a tree. As he trimmed and clipped the excesses from the limb or twig, he would point out beauty spots on the excesses and note that there was nothing wrong with what he trimmed off, but that it was not needed for the purpose for which he intended to use his educational instrument. 'the leaves', he would say, 'are for the deer or goats to consume, the twigs were for compost and keeping the soil loose and productive while the shavings are for the soil like the twigs,' as he trimmed with his Barlow to create a work of art from the clipping from the tree. Papa would tell us that the piece that was cut off was to be made as creative as possible as a tribute to Mother Nature for her work in making it for us in the first place and putting into her best creation, the tree. Except for you, I think I agree with Papa," I added.

"Then there is the Raymond Loewy designed Studebaker Starliner Coupe," Willow mentioned, "where does it stand among the best creations?"

"Raymond Loewy was among Mother Nature's finest creations," I responded.

"Papa never had a religion, I don't guess. He would tell us that it was very difficult to wax poetic without a god but he overworked Mother Nature to make up for the loss that he experienced. Papa always talked about Mother Nature should have been paid at least-time-and-a-half, double time on Sunday, for her work. I was almost a teenager when I learned what Papa meant by that statement.

"Why can't we meet papa?"

"After World War II so much of the family migrated back to Germany," I told her. "You know, Papa grew up in the wine country of Germany. I learned so much from his small vineyard over in the Rockhouse area of Limestone Creek but the adults wouldn't let us learn about how he and Dave Swoopes made wine from his grapes and from the blackberries and the plums that they would pick in the Summer."

"Did he go back to the wine country?"

"They live in Frankfort now, a lot further East of Weisbaden, which is the center for the German wine country, but they want to come home, to the USA. You know, I haven't talked much about it, but so many of our problems with melding in the society over the years of our youth was stimulated by the fact that my father is German. World War II was in our years of age four to eight and those are hard years to hear reference to yourself as a 'goddamned toe-headed Kraut' and be able to take any pride in being what you are. I pretend that I was likely a teenager when I learned that 'goddamned Kraut' was an insult. I love you so much Willow that I feel so very guilty when I use these words, and I am so sorry," I apologized.

"You have to use the words to tell me and I want you to tell me." She squeezed my arm and looked up at me with those blue eyes and smiled, "plus you always tell me you love me when you say those bad words." She gave me a kiss, too, and that made everything good, maybe even better.

"You know back there where Chuck, Bill and Addie live now, we rebuilt that old house for my grandmother who is half Cherokee, half Scot. Daddy says 'half Scotch, part Bourbon,' for a laugh. My grandmother is the defiant member of the family, who is Cherokee, dresses Cherokee, lives Cherokee and would speak

MY WILLOW | 171

Cherokee if she knew how. Grandmother Johnson stimulated the weak minded to coin a term especially for us, 'Kraut Breeds.'"

"I am understanding more your social defiance and your willingness to throw yourself, body and soul into a fight," Willow told me, "but it must be the Scot in you that lets you take it all from the weak-minded before allowing the Cherokee to explode upon them and the German to give you the will to do harm in the battle."

"There you go again," Dr. Preston, "analyzing me."

"Maybe I should be a psychologist when I grow up," Willow said.

"Maybe you should never grow up, you're so perfect as you are."

I spotted a branch on a tree off the road. I had to have it to get myself back to the position in the talk or walk from which I got pushed away. I stepped off the road, pulled out the Case knife and clipped the limb from the tree. As I trimmed twigs and leaves, I threw them into the brush and weeds beside the road. I noticed Willow watching and she began to pick up the clippings and whatever fell, and in a most demonstrative manner and a huge confident smile deposited the little leavings into the grass, the weeds or woods, anywhere but the road. I saw what she was doing and waited until the limb was all done and presented it to her.

"What am I to do with this?" my love inquired of me, "and I must admit that Mother Nature would be pleased that you have been creative with her creation."

"It is an educational instrument as Papa would tell us, used to point and the draw in the sand and the dust of the road," as I demonstrated, pointing to a hickory tree a pine a cedar and so on, then making a loop in the road with the point with an arrow at one end.

"I understand, now," Willow said, "the loop says that we are to turn around and go back toward the car."

"Are you okay to go back to the car?

"You know we have been doing this to each other for five days now and it really works," Willow informed me, "and I think that I have the most wonderful person that I could have in a lifetime because you are so capable and you do it whether or not there is an innate willingness. You do it for me."

"Whatever I did, yes," I admitted, "I did it for you, but all I did was to tell you some bullshit and cut you a limb off a tree, and I trimmed the limb a little so you could ridicule me for putting the leaves back into their place of natural state because I was trained as a small child to do so and never realized it was habitual, and you laughed at me for it."

"I laughed because I was so very proud of you for doing what I didn't understand but knew you would explain."

"You know a lot of our silly little things in life are maybe silly on a small scale but so very sensible on a larger scale," I informed my Willow, just about the best student I ever had, "which is why I think I have decided that I want to be a teacher when I grow up. You can be a psychologist and tell me I am crazy for wanting to work for peanuts when grapes will make us wealthy beyond our wildest dreams."

"I could teach psychology," Willow said. "That way, I would be able to tell us that we are so crazy about each other that nothing else matters."

"Is that why we are standing here in the middle of Johnson's Landing Road with our arms around each other just like we have been for quite a while now?"

"I think so but I am not allowed to make a diagnosis until I get my PhD."

"Do you have to have a PhD to tell us how we can find our car?"

"No! See this arrow here? We follow the direction of it . . ." Willow traced the loop and turned ourselves around in the road with lots of tiny little steps and some giggles while we were still holding each other, then pointed in the direction that the arrow pointed. She then asked, "do we really have to turn loose of each other to go to the car?"

"I wish we could call the car like we do a dog," I said. I loosened my hold on her just a wee bit to get the reaction. She released me. "I just loosened my hold on you and you released me, what gives?" She grabbed me again and held on tight. "Okay, I'll count to three and we let go together."

Okay, count."

"One . . . ! After a while she asked, "do you not remember what comes next?"

"I remember," I said sadly, "I just don't want to say it."

"Two," Willow was pretending it was a painful thing for her to do.

"Three. Wow, we are silly," I made the final number and we released each other and walked back toward the car, holding hands, of course."

"The sun is setting," Willow noted as we walked back. "We have had a wonderful day and you demonstrated to me that you love me more than feeding those natural instincts."

"We were both on the verge of doing what we really need to go ahead and do, but here is not the place. We have no facilities, to note the bucket seats, and a back seat the size of half a two-by-four, no blankets to go to the woods, then we can't go to my house, we can't go to your house and we can't rent a motel room at 17. So, what do we do? We take a cool-down lap.

"We've been doing that all week. Do you think I didn't know?"

"I love you, Willow, what could we do?

"What we keep doing. We have a lifetime ahead of us and I am confident that I will go through it with you caring more for what I feel than for what you do, and I am going to try my best to deserve you. Before you say anything, when I said what I said a while ago about the period and the hymen and that, I knew I had you and your strength. Maybe not just as I was saying it, but I knew. I knew that I could swing out into that zone that I had avoided and that you would swing me back."

"Honey, all I am trying to do right now to live up to a standard that is deserving of you."

"You know, you and I have frittered around and missed supper so now we have to go out to eat," Willow announced, "but we both need to change."

MY WILLOW

"Or, we could go to one of those drive-ins in Decatur. Nobody can see our spots," I suggested. We did. We found the closest one, grabbed food and headed back home. The idea was to get my left shoulder massaged, knock me onto my butt with that pain pill or sleeping pill or whatever that I was just about desperate for anyway and get me to sleep, so I would not whine like a bleating nanny goat because I was separated from my precious Willow for the first time in five full days, except for those five-minute showers that seemed as if they went on for an eternity.

Though I knew our being separated could be withstood without a lot of duress but we played the game to express our affections for each other. We knew there would be disappointment when each awoke. I knew my Willow would probably not sleep well. The last thing I remembered telling her was, "If you get lonely, remember that you can never go anywhere without me, that I am with you, in your heart. "Nor can you, I am in your heart," sweet Willow whispered and kissed me, long and warm. I must have gone to sleep with her lips on mine.

CHAPTER FIFTEEN

Feel It in My Mind

Any time to wait for my Willow is a lot of time, but to have to turn everything inside out and face tomorrow on short notice with no plans and nobody to help to point in the right direction is a task that I could never hope to ever again undertake.

IT WAS SATURDAY, the big day! I had slept well but was having trouble reconciling myself to the difficulty that I was having with the knowledge that Willow was not with me. I knew I could take it. "I am a big boy now," I told myself. "I wasted some extra time in the shower and getting my pants on. It was a bit tough getting the sock on with one hand but I wanted to try and did succeed. I told Mama I could have done it better if she had not laughed at me so hard and picked on me because I couldn't get along without Willow."

"You don't know how true that is Mama," I told her in sincere honesty. "After five days with that little girl, we can be certain that I will have to, but I don't want to spend a minute without her. I am thinking she is my whole life, and I know she has embraced the reality of me as much as I have of her but I have a bit of wonder if she maybe has latched onto me so securely because of the recent loss of her father."

"Maybe, but she latched on," Mama emphatically stated. "Take that for what it is worth and never know or care why. That is the most real devotion that you will ever experience so long as you shall be taking deep breaths while telling yourself to shut up and be thankful that you have Willow."

Little 13-year-old, almost grown up in her own mind, Linda had spent enough time around Willow to know how to massage the shoulder with the balm. She wouldn't do it. Refused! Frank was quite good at it, because he cared, was the likely assumption that I arrived at. Frank even helped to get me into a t-shirt. I could get the outer shirt on but had to call him back in to button it.

"We all missed Willow at breakfast." I picked at everybody about the fact that I suspected that they would be missing Willow more than me when I was gone. Daddy said he would for sure because she looked so much prettier than me. Frank said he was just about ready to make his move on her. I told him that she had a present for him and that I might just not let her give it to him if he didn't keep his hands off my girl.

Linda said she was mad at me for taking away her best friend. I promised they could still be best friends and that Willow and I would fly her to Philadelphia so she could spend her Christmas holiday with her friend, then wondered for awhile how I could get out of the promise but was self assured that I had some time to work on it. Charlie and Garey said they were going to hitch-hike up and spend next Summer drinking wine. "Maybe some straight grape juice," I informed them.

Daddy had the half day of Saturday work. Frank and I talked a bit. I was really going to miss this young man, a little brother but not so much of a little as he was a brother and about the best friend a person could hope to come up on. Frank had been my sidekick over the years. "Hey Frank," I called with a trick up my sleeve, "lately I have been when Willow would drive me," as I extended to him the keys for the Studebaker, "stopping to grab a Dr. Pepper first thing. How about you run down to Sparkman's store and grab us one with this dollar. Tell Benny, Willow and I will be stopping by in a couple of hours."

My motive was to get him to drive the car, because I didn't think Frank had ever done so, unless maybe Daddy took him out in it on the first day that it was running. I had seen him in it a couple of times, clutching and shifting the four-speed shifter on the console and getting acclimated to the shift pattern. Frank liked to demonstrate a little slap-pull maneuver to bring it to reverse. They had not yet seen many four-speed shifters and reverse was considered to be awkward to some drivers, where on a three-speed column shift, reverse was straight up from low gear.

Upon his return, Frank flashed the big smile that he was famous for and pretended he was to pass on by and go for a longer ride. I yelled out "Dr. Pepper," and Frank turned into the back yard and stopped at the well pump. He was going to wash it.

Likely I had seen the beer drinkers do it, Frank thrust the bottle toward his brother who grasped it and Frank popped the top. The rascal had a hidden bottle opener. He thrust the keys toward me. "You hang onto those," I told him, "and take care of it for me for a couple of weeks. You know Willow and I are coming back for graduation?"

MY WILLOW | 177

'Yeah, you told us, and man I can really use it for the newspaper route."

"Holy shit, Frank!" I screamed. "That's Nancy! Something is wrong!" I turned toward her as the little rose-colored Chevrolet almost jumped into the back drive and saw no joy in the faces of the two Nancy Bradleys in the car. I ran toward the car, though my desire was to run off the edge of the world. I knew certainly something was badly wrong. I knew too much was badly wrong.

Nurse Nan moved slowly but Nancy bound from the car and threw her arms around me and told me what I knew she was to say, "Willow was killed. Head-on by a drunk, both of them, Willow and her mother."

I collapsed to the ground, Nancy went with me. I could feel the arms of Nurse Nan around both of us. "I have to go with her. I have to go with her. I have to go with her . . . ," I cried and continued to cry out. "I have to go with her," I yelled. I remember the needle going into my arm, looked up to see Dr. Haggerty and his pretty wife. I didn't remember anything more for awhile. "They said I was secured to the gurney so I could make the ride to the hospital."

I remembered Angela. "They strapped me to the goddamned thing, Angela, to keep me from killing myself and I am going to Willow. There is no place for me anywhere but with Willow. And there is no need to try to keep me from it, I swore to her, I am going to go to Willow."

My nurse looked at me for a moment then turned. "Angela, please don't leave for another of those fucking sedatives. There's no need to waste them. Please Angela, let me loose and let me go to her."

She left me, but my friend Nancy was there. I knew she would let me go. I looked into her eyes and begged. "Take me loose Nancy, please. Willow knew that my life and her life were the same and I can't leave mine here without hers being mixed and stirred right in with mine. Please! It's not a life. I don't have a life without Willow. I don't want a life without Willow," I continued to plead with Nancy

"You have a life. You have a life with Willow," Nancy said.

Nancy wiped her tears and my tears and kept repeating the routine and tried to laugh at both of us a little because, as she said, "one person can't wipe these two faces fast enough."

She sat for awhile wiping our tears and bringing me down a bit. My emotional state was a wreck. That was the ultimate understatement. Nancy told me, "I have to find a place where I can talk to you about Willow."

"Let me have a little time. I don't need time for it to sink in. It sunk in when I saw your car today, or was that today?"

"It was today," Nancy assured me. "Maybe three hours ago."

"Why won't anybody let me die, Nancy?"

"Because Willow didn't want you to die. She wants you to live for the both of you. Willow told me with her last breath that she loved you more than life. She said that the last thing that you had said to her was that you were in her heart and she was in yours."

"I know I told her that. I told her that when we were alive because we were alive."

"She said that she was dying with you in her heart. She wanted me to plead with you to live with her in your heart. She wanted the two of you to be together for eternity and this is the only way. Can you do it for Willow?"

"I can do anything for Willow. I don't understand fully. I just know that the easy way would be to go with her. She just laid out for me the most difficult task I can imagine, living without her touching me. It was so very important for Willow to be able to touch me. But I can do it for Willow." I knew I could. I had said it so many times and I had proven that I could do anything for Willow. I knew that Willow was my life. I just knew also that the thought or the realization of that same thought had to have time to get itself acclimated to my brain and the condition of my brain at the time was not such that it was allowing anything to get in and establish itself.

"She knew before she died that she was with you. She will know now that she is with you. Willow told me that where ever you may go she will be with you. Willow died with the happiness of knowing that she had the greatest love a person could ever have. She knew that you would never let her down in life or in death."

"Go walk with me Nancy. That's what Willow and I did. Everywhere we walked and we talked and we touched. I can feel her touch. Can you get them to take me loose?"

"You are not tied or strapped or tethered in any manner," Nancy assured me.

"Then who released me?" I inquired.

"Nobody released you. You haven't been secured to that thing since we brought you in here. While you were in the ambulance you were secured to keep you from falling while the ambulance was moving, but the straps were removed when they rolled you in here. You scared Angela. She was stunned when you ordered her to release you and she came to get me."

"Willow? Could it be that I merely thought I was secured to that damned thing? Can we go now, Nancy?"

"Sure, Dr. Haggerty wanted to bring you in so he could be with you and make certain that he was with you when you recovered. Were you conscious when you told him, "I will talk to nobody but Nancy Bradley about Willow?"

"No, but I remember that was what I wanted to say and couldn't seem to get conscious enough. to say it," I responded, feeling strange about having actually done what I was thinking yet not knowing that I had done it.

"Both Dr. Haggerty and Aunt Nan felt that I would be the only one to whom you could relate and still discuss her," Nancy confided.

"I know she never took time away from me to call you when she was caring for me but when I would go to sleep, she told you everything, so I know that you know her feelings when nobody else could but me. I liked hearing her tell you how much she loved me, but I didn't like the eavesdropping part of it. I didn't ever hear

MY WILLOW

179

anything that it was wrong for me to hear. It was about us and it was true. I would have been happy to tell you the same thing. I wish I had a friend that I could tell."

"Well, I had one. I had you. I didn't know it. What do you think would have happened for Willow and me if I hadn't gotten hurt?"

"We had a plan from the day after the ill-fated kiss in back of the stage. We had decided that I was to get you alone somewhere somehow, and pound it into your brain that she was in love with you and that I knew you were in love with her and there was nothing that you two were gaining by being the way you were."

"I couldn't imagine how anybody could kiss somebody the way she did me and I felt the love coming right out of me into her and right out of her into me, and I still had no idea what could be done about it. I know she told you, Nancy, but I tried every way I could to crank up a romance or something with someone and never got past hanging out in school together. As long as I saw Willow in School, that was getting me through, but school was ending and I was desperate to go for broke with her. I would have walked right up to her and said, "Willow, I am in love with you, so what are you going to do about it?""

Nancy asked, "What are you going to do now?"

"I want to get away for a few days. I can't go back to that place. The place I called home, but it is the place that was Heaven for me when I had my Willow. I can't bring myself to allow my family to see me and not see my Willow. I don't think I can go to the Bluff or to Johnson's Landing, the place where we spent the last day together, but I will try someday.

My life is back to considering the Methodist scholarship. I have choices of four campuses in four states."

"There's one thing, and it is tough to ask, but she clutched a pillow and a small tree limb that was whittled beautifully. Now she told me about her Willow pillow but the . . ."

"Educational instrument," I explained, "a pointer that I whittled for her to mark in the sand and dust in the road and to point out things and places of interest. Damn, I love my Willow! Can you tell me what is to happen with her remains."

"With no arrangements on record and no legal guardian, They have to be offered for returned to the Penobscot Reservation where she was born."

There was just no stopping the tears. They were just allowed to flow. "Be sure her pillow and her pointer, her educational instrument, go with her."

"We did that already."

"Thank you! I love you for that. Little things were so important to her. If you could make arrangements to have my car brought to me. I can't bear to go home to get it. Frank has keys. Willow was going to give him the car today. Now I have to take it. Tell my parents what we talked about. Tell them I will come back when I can talk about Willow. I hurts too badly now. She meant so much to all of us. I was not even close to the only one who loved her in my family. I can't stand seeing their tears and I know they can't stand mine."

"We have made the loop back to the clinic," Nancy pointed out. "We can pass by or I can take you somewhere. Can you stay at my house tonight? My parents will be okay with it. "I will talk to Frank and see if Dan can go with me to get your car."

"Frank will worry. Convince him that I will be okay. I want to hide, that's all. I want to learn how to accept that I have Willow inside while I want her holding me and I can't have that. Tell him I will come back. I don't know when, but when I come back, I'll bring him the Studebaker, as a gift. Tell him it will get a new paint job, red."

My car was there the next morning. I told Nancy that I was staking claim on her as my best friend, "I know I have Dan," I told her, "but I probably owe you my life, Nancy, and that is a priority for best friend status."

I came back two weeks later for graduation as Willow and I had planned. I was awarded the Alabama State Star Farmer Award, the Agricultural Accomplishment Award, and the I Dare You Award. I accepted the Citizen Recognition Award for Willow with most of the comments regarding Willow's accomplishments centered on how well she took control of my health and rehabilitation and how she lost her life on the way to take care of me.

I gave Willow's certificate to Nancy Bradley for safe keeping and for having something with Nancy that the two of us could share. Frank, Linda and my parents attended the graduation. They never mentioned Willow. They all believed there were no reasons to shed the tears at that time.

I wanted to drive past the home place one more time. I knew that I was going away on this day and would likely never return to this place, but I knew for certain that I would not return until classes started for the Summer Session at that Methodist school in Kentucky. I knew I would not see Ol' Charlie Wolf at the reunion in Triana. It was like I knew that everybody would understand because I was not the same as before. Maybe a little of the same was there, but Willow and I were so much a part of each other, and that one part was gone. That part couldn't be brought back and held. This was one of those times when I wanted so badly to hold her. These times always brought the tears, they would have to be endured. There would be so many times like these.

I passed on by the home place. The last place Willow and I were together with a chance to hold each other was Johnson's Landing. That was where we carved her pointer, educational instrument. I needed to see if I could face up to the reality of not being able to hold her. I drove to it. I was okay. I sat by the tree where we last held each other so tightly.

Nobody knows how long I was there. A man touched me on the shoulder. "You were crying and calling out for Willow," the man said, "over and over again, and I thought I would help you find her." I didn't remember the man ever telling me his name, just that he was a man from Hartselle. I was gaining control by talking.

I told the man about Willow, mostly how we were so much in love, then how the drunk driver took her from me.

"Willow didn't die completely." The man told me this and I did listen. Again to my surprise, I found that it was soothing to me just to hear about Willow. Though I could accept the feeling, I wanted so badly to touch her, to hold her. I couldn't. It didn't occur to me that the man had no way to know much at all about the things that he was telling me.

"She is with you now. The two of you pledged to each other every day, you told me that, giving your hearts to each other every day and sometimes more than once a day. Listen to me. I can see it, feel it in my mind, and you can too, if you will. I know you feel it there and you can know what it is that you are feeling, and it is not the pain that you can't bear, but she has given you something that not many have had the opportunity to have. Willow has given her life to you so that you might compound any joy that you find in your own," the man stated to me.

"It is Willow's heart and her spirit within you that is pressing hard on you to cause you to understand. She will stay with you and you will understand. She will come to you at times in your life," the man continued to tell me.

I told the man that Willow had started on our second day to work with the right arm and to make it work well enough that I could hold her with it. Then on the third day, she worked with the left arm to make it work out some of the pain so I could put both arms around her. I was able to do so on his own on the fourth day, Thursday, then hurt it again. Friday I held her. We held each other and we had so much difficulty letting go of each other. I never saw her after that evening together.

"She will always be in your life because you have her in your heart," the man said.

"Our plans for a life together were so complete," I began telling the man. I looked around and there was no man. I didn't see a vehicle that the man might have driven to the landing. Did I imagine he was here like I imagined that I was strapped to the Gurney that day and couldn't move until I promised that I would live for Willow. Is Willow with me more ways than I could know?

"I think I'll go out to the island and tell Ol' Charlie that I will be taking off for about a month," I spoke aloud and to nobody but maybe Willow was really with me. With some comfort that Willow was there with me, I continued, "I think I will tell him that Willow never got to meet him and she wanted to so badly and I was hurt so badly I couldn't get out there, and he never got to meet Willow; Willow never got to see the island; Willow never got to learn to drive the little Ford Tractor; Willow never learned to grow grapes." I thought for a minute and said, "maybe Charlie can tell me how to live this way with Willow in my heart."

Maybe Willow wanted the other Terrell boys about as much as I did but I made a promise and had to do what I did. In my condition, I couldn't accept going on with life without doing what Willow and I had promised. I didn't even tell my grandfather about Willow, but he knew something was wrong and offered me his "house of ill recluse," he called it, a place he built where he could go sober up from his binges, "when the wife won't let me into the house," he told me. It was just up the road, back in the woods, just over the line in Tennessee, about 20 mile from Huntsville.

Willow had been gone close to three weeks. The last two boys in their plans had laughed at Mr. Sparkman when he told how Willow walked over bad-assed Uncle Shorty, so I had heard. The job had to be finished. I knew there was no need following them but I knew that Thursday was a big night for movies in Decatur at the Princess Theater. I found Fats Terrell's pickup in the parking lot out around the corner, siphoned the gas out and waited for the movie to end. They made it to about three miles from home before running out of gas and started to walk. I stopped and flashed my lights. I showed them that I had a gas can so they came running back to see that it was their own can. I left my lights on so they could identify their worst nightmare.

It seems the grandfather had called Mama. He knew something was wrong. Mama told him about Willow and how I was hiding from anybody who could talk about her. Mama called her father back the next day after the last two Terrell brothers had "been hurt really badly." Grandpa went to the shack and told me about what had happened, arriving about the time the Sheriff's deputy drove up.

The deputy told me and my grandfather that he got the idea that the deputy down in Morgan County, Alabama just wanted "somebody to help him fill out his damned report but I drove out anyway. Can you tell me anything?"

Grandpa Johnson told him, "Nah, the boy was here. I'd have seen him if he'd left."

"Grandpa goes to sleep early," I told him, but the deputy was satisfied.

I drove back to Alabama a few days later, stopped in at the Deputy Becker's office. "I will contact you," I told him, "when I get to Kentucky and have an address, or if I change my mind and end up in Minnesota or Texas, so you can let me know if I need to come back to testify." As I dismissed myself and Becker I walked toward the parking lot, I asked, "how badly did I hurt those two last Thursday night."

Becker laughed, "rather badly since you were sacked out and sleeping like a baby up in Tennessee."

"My trips back through here will be rare ones inasmuch as I will not even visit my family in this neck of the woods," I told the officer, "so I will let you and Sheriff Brown have the Terrells and they can have Newton's Bluff, and they can have the girl that left those two in the ditch last Thursday, or the rest of the girls who are taking care of the work that Willow and I can't do ourselves."

"Another girl got those two?" Becker laughed again, "now I see why they lied about it being you, but I know who did it now."

"Nancy was in Tuscaloosa," I assured the deputy, "I heard it was a friend of hers." I waited for a few seconds for the confusion on the Deputies face to be allowed to fade somewhat, then added, "Willow and I are leaving a network of friends here and when the martial arts gets to be ineffective, there is always the County Sheriff's Department."

"We're here," Becker offered, "and you can be certain that the Sheriff and everybody here will miss you and Willow."

"By the way, Deputy Becker," I requested, "go by and see how Phillip and his brother are doing and see if they will tell you that I did that to them." Realizing that the deputy had not gotten a report, I continued. "Two girls picked them up at the drive-in hangout last Friday night and brought them to me at Cotaco Landing." Becker stood silently but smiled, so I told him the story. "I left the kid in fair condition to drive Phillip home where he will be laid up for awhile, but he will not tell you that I did that to him, because the girls promised to exact revenge upon him for Willow if he did."

Deputy Becker thanked me with a huge smile. There might have been a sense of relief in the officer as he saw that I got into my Studebaker and drove away.

I hired a boat to take me down river to the island, to wait 30 minutes and to take me back to Cotaco landing. I told Charlie about Willow and my injuries that maybe I would be back for the Johnson Family reunion in Triana on the Fourth of July." I wouldn't tell him where I was going to be because I had not the slightest idea. "Maybe I will camp out with Ol' Hub for the night, maybe two, then again maybe I'll check out the campus in St. Paul, maybe Dallas.

CPSIA information can be obtained
at www.ICGtesting.com
Printed in the USA
JSHW012347081222
34571JS00003B/16